T0385100

HOW POWERFUL WE ARE

Behind the scenes with one of Australia's leading activists

Sally Rugg

hachette
AUSTRALIA

Published in Australia and New Zealand in 2019
by Hachette Australia
(an imprint of Hachette Australia Pty Limited)
Level 17, 207 Kent Street, Sydney NSW 2000
www.hachette.com.au

10 9 8 7 6 5 4 3 2 1

A catalogue record for this
book is available from the
NATIONAL
LIBRARY   National Library of Australia
OF AUSTRALIA

ISBN: 978 0 7336 4222 7 (hardback)

Cover design by Ngaio Parr
Author photo courtesy of Rebecca Hitch
Text design by Bookhouse, Sydney
Typeset in 10.9/15 pt Sabon LT Pro by Bookhouse, Sydney
Printed and bound in Australia by McPherson's Printing Group

To the 1s, and to Tyrone Unsworth

Contents

Introduction

Two nights before Australia changed the law to allow same-sex couples to marry, I had an argument at a party. Well, calling it a party is probably being generous. I was upstairs in Parliament House, in a corridor that had been transformed into a Christmas drinks hosted by a hodgepodge of cross-bench MPs. The ones who aren't with a major political party and whose offices all share a wing of Parliament House. The party buzzed with chatter as politicians of all persuasions and their staff mingled with lobbyists, reporters and activists. Party guests spilled from the MPs' offices and into the shared hallway, leaning against walls and squeezing past each other to greet new arrivals. The atmosphere was merry; after all, it was almost Christmas.

A table of finger food stood untouched but for a growing collection of popped beer tops and champagne corks. My friend Nadine, a Greens staffer, excitedly pointed out the plate of red sausages and cheese cubes generously supplied by the federal member for Kennedy and exclaimed, 'Look, it's the Katter platter!'

Christmas parties are fun, and those within Parliament House are something to behold, but I wasn't in parliament that week for the free drinks and small talk. I was there to see a bill passed and a law changed.

It was a change so simple, with overwhelming public support and real-life significance that had been stalled and rejected for too long. It would symbolise who we are as a nation: what we stand for, what we celebrate and who we treat as first-class citizens. After decades of campaigning from thousands of activists,

How Powerful We Are

including five years of my own hard work, I was in parliament to witness the passage of an amendment to Australia's Marriage Act that would mean that someone like me could marry someone I love.

I slipped into the office of Greens MP Adam Bandt to grab a beer and bumped into the deeply conservative Minister Kevin Andrews. A budding viral sensation, Andrews had garnered international notoriety through his suggestion on *Sky News* that the love of LGBTIQ couples wasn't worthy of marriage because he understands it to be the same as the fondness between himself and his cycling buddies. Amusingly, former Prime Minister Tony Abbott, a rabid opponent of same-sex marriage, happens to be one of Andrews' 'cycling buddies'. I do assume that my hot, queer love is significantly different from the relationship between Kevin Andrews and Tony Abbott, but far be it from me to be a gatekeeper.

I chatted politely to Andrews when a man I didn't recognise joined us. Before long I was left with the older gentleman. For some reason I assumed he was the father of the young member for Brisbane, Trevor Evans, and thought it sweet that the gay MP had brought his dad in for the big marriage equality week. The gentleman continued to talk to me about marriage equality to avoid an uncomfortable silence.

'Now, I know you lot were opposed to the postal survey, but now that we've come out the other end of it, surely you can see the good it's done and that it was the right thing to do,' he said, conversationally.

'Oh, absolutely not,' I replied to his surprise. 'The postal survey was a disgrace and shouldn't have happened under any circumstance.'

The man was taken aback. My disagreement with his vague platitude was likely not the pleasantry he expected from Christmas-party chitchat.

'What about the weight it's given the decision?' the man countered. 'It means it's decisive, and it's brought everyone along with the change.'

As I began to explain that marriage equality had enjoyed majority public support for over a decade and that holding a national survey actually undermined the authority of parliament and the weight of every other decision we pay them to make, I noticed the man was wearing a small green pin in his jacket. Oh, crap. He was an MP.

At that moment, I should have retreated. I was there representing my employer, GetUp, and needed to be polite and respectful. Did I though?

'People may have anecdotally enjoyed participating in the vote, but how is that worth the harrowing ordeal we unnecessarily thrust upon the LGBTIQ community?' I challenged. I studied his face as he brushed off the trauma of my friends as 'complete rubbish', and thought to myself, *Who on earth is this man?* I thought I knew every MP by face and division, but it was like I'd never seen this person before in my life.

'It's not rubbish,' I interjected, frustrated at his refusal to believe the postal survey was anything but a gift from the government for which I should be grateful. 'People died during the survey.'

'People *died*?' he spluttered, a fleck of spit hitting my cheap suit jacket.

'That's right,' I told him. 'We lost people to suicide, people who didn't have to die.'

'Don't be ridiculous! What utter nonsense!' the man was incensed. '"People died" . . . how dare you say something as ridiculous as that.'

'People did die,' I insisted, indignantly. Any effort to be polite or measured had gone out the window and I could feel my heart pounding with anger. I did not know who this man was, but he was wrong, and I couldn't let it go.

'Normal people don't just kill themselves within six weeks!' the man exclaimed.

'That's the point!' I shouted. 'These people were already vulnerable!'

Several heads turned towards us. Across the room my friend Nadine covered her mouth to suppress a laugh.

The thing is, it's completely understandable that this MP had lost his patience with me, a random GetUp campaigner who he was simply trying to make polite conversation with. And normally I wouldn't have lost my temper at him either, but I, like most other activists in the LGBTIQ community, had been ground down to the end of my emotional tether. I was exhausted. I was furious. I was dizzy from holding myself and my loved ones together to get to that point.

'This is outrageous. People would have died in *my* electorate with the Whyalla debacle; people were losing their jobs – the whole town was at risk! You can't just list every person who's suicided and say it was the fault of whatever it was the government did at the time that impacted their life.'

He'd dropped a clue to his identity. Whyalla was the town that was supposedly going to be 'wiped off the map' by the Gillard government's mining and carbon taxes, and the man was presumably referring to the job losses associated with the downturn in mining. Whyalla ... South Australia ... he'd have to be the Liberal member for Grey!

'This is different, Rowan,' I tutted, remembering his name. Rowan Ramsey: not a marriage equality supporter. 'The postal survey was completely unnecessary and, arguably, most other government policies aren't. The government was willing to put lives at risk just for its own political gain, it was disgraceful.'

If my time as a campaigner has taught me anything, it's that you can't convince everyone of everything, and that's okay. You must find the people you can persuade and focus your energy there.

But in those final moments of the battle for equal marriage rights I'd already seen history begin to be re-written. I'd watched the years of work from activists and the LGBTIQ community be paved over so that the government could perform a victory lap. I was witnessing in real time a shameful period of politics and politicking suddenly heralded as functional, fair governance that had delivered equality for my community.

In that moment, my response was to shout at a member of parliament at a Christmas party. Now, it's why I write this book.

The stories we tell of how change is made matter. If we are led to believe that the powerful granted rights to the marginalised because the powerful had a sudden change of heart, we strip ourselves of the knowledge needed for the next fight. If we can't see the work that's gone in to making change and if we allow the end to be glossed over with a rose-coloured finish, it will always justify the means. And the means by which we operate as a society should always be held to account.

Even if you're not an activist (yet), at a time when the news is written for clicks and elections are fought with three-word slogans, it's crucial to preserve some record of events that isn't 'fake news' or political spin.

In part, this book is my attempt to counter the re-writing of how Australia achieved one of the most significant social changes in a generation. The activism it took was too brilliant to be chalked up as timely inevitability or political generosity.

In these pages I'll teach you some of the things I learnt on this campaign: how to develop a strategy, how to frame your messages, how to get your campaign in the media, how to build community power. And I'll share with you the much harder lessons I learnt: the consequences of campaign decisions; how to weather criticism and harassment from every angle; and how, in mass campaign movements, nothing is black and white.

My story spans from the depths of Australia's most sophisticated campaigning outfit to LGBTIQ communities across Australia, from behind closed doors in parliament to the homes of couples fighting for reform to their dying days. It pushes back against the placards held high at the 2018 Mardi Gras that bellowed, 'The Liberal party delivered marriage equality!'

The Liberal party did not deliver marriage equality. Parliament, save for some heroes within its walls, did not deliver marriage equality. We achieved the reform not because of our political representatives, bound by their factions and their own self-interest, but in defiant spite of their shameful heel-dragging and obfuscation.

Australia did not achieve marriage equality because we voted Yes. The postal survey was a shameful, callous political manoeuvre that cost lives, broke families, saw communities divide themselves in two and gave a national platform to an underbelly of homophobia and transphobia.

Marriage equality was achieved in Australia after decades of work from ordinary people who organised strategically, digitally and collectively to leverage their power in numbers to force parliament to deliver. And it was spectacular. Groundbreaking. Historic.

If you have come to this book looking for a comprehensive campaign history, you'll be disappointed. This is not a campaign diary. If you are an activist seeking recognition for your work, you likely won't find it here.

It's completely impossible to capture the entire marriage equality campaign in a book. We would need a whole library, full of stories. We would archive newspaper clippings, meeting minutes and joint statements. There would be anthologies of photography, shelves of analysis and a section dedicated to the lived experiences of all the people impacted and involved.

This book is not that.

But if you'd like to hear an experience of how the LGBTIQ community and the people who love them created the largest social movement of a generation, you've come to the right place. If you want to talk about how power works, how politics is broken and how decisions are made in this country, you're going to love it here. If you want to learn the basics of how to run a sophisticated, digitally-enabled campaign and hear an incredible story of how ordinary people changed their world, stick around.

If you've come for an inside story complete with scandal, triumph and tears, settle yourself in. If you're here for the time I spontaneously got both my nipples pierced during the intense stress at the crux of the postal survey, well, strap in/on.

I write this book to bear witness and to share lessons, but also because using storytelling as a tool for change is in my blood.

Every inch of LGBTIQ progress has been fought for, and won, on a foundation of my community's personal stories. We tell stories to connect, to resist, and in the hope that those listening might see their own humanity reflected in ours.

Here's mine.

1

Not Marriage

The sun was beginning to set over Sydney's Oxford Street, covering Taylor Square with warm, fading spring light. Outside the old Darlinghurst Courthouse, hundreds of people made a restless, jostling crowd. Held high above the congregation were homemade signs and rainbow flags; exhalations of cigarette smoke were blown politely towards the sky. David Bowie sang about heroes from a battery-powered stereo someone had put in a shopping trolley as the noisy mob heaved against police officers forming a barrier to the road.

The chanting began, 'Out of the bars and into the streets! Out of the bars and into the streets!' Those gathered, young and old, gay and straight, were there to march. In celebration, in protest and in resistance.

As the sun disappeared, finally the police let us spill onto the road. Cheering, with tears streaming down our glittered faces, we ran, skipped and danced. Shoulder to shoulder and hand in hand, we were a sea of costumes, colours and concealed liquor. We flung ourselves into the arms of friends, kissing each other's lips and holding each other tight. Shirts were stripped off and fists punched the air as we chanted, 'Yes! Yes! Yes!'

It was 15 November 2017, and a survey of the Australian voting population had delivered a decisive majority supporting equal marriage rights for LGBTIQ couples. The national survey was the torturous climax in the government's utter pantomime of unwillingness and inability to legislate a reform so basic, so popular and so long overdue.

When the Yes result was announced earlier that day, the feeling most LGBTIQ Australians felt was staggering relief. Not only had we avoided a loss, we had survived. It was over, we made it. Any gratitude for the Yes victory was bittersweet, muddled with anger at the process and the wash-up of tight anxiety we'd carried for months. But by this evening, this confusing mix of feelings had turned into celebration and defiant pride.

As I whooped and cackled my way down the street, a police officer approached me to confiscate the longneck of beer I was chugging, conspicuously disguised by a brown paper bag. As he swaggered over and told me to tip it out, gesturing aggressively at the bottle, my friends protested, 'Ohhh, let her have it! She's worked so hard for this!'

'Come on, mate. Don't be like this,' I wheedled, and as he tutted and walked away, I called out, 'Thank you!'

When I told my friend Peter de Waal that a cop let me keep my beer he was incredulous. 'Extraordinary,' he chuckled, 'it's certainly a stark comparison!'

Peter is exactly 50 years my senior. In 1978, he and his friends held a march on the very street we were walking that night, Oxford Street, calling for the liberation of LGBTIQ people. The 78ers, as they're fondly known, were protesting police brutality and the discrimination they faced as LGBTIQ Australians, but they decided the tone would be like a street party parade. Inspired by activist friends in the United States, they called it a Mardi Gras.

Back then, police deliberately hunted LGBTIQ people. Cops would disrupt private gatherings of gay men to beat them up before arresting them, and it was within their remit. Homosexuality was a crime, and the legal punishments included up to fourteen years in prison, a court-ordered lobotomy, or being forced into 'conversion therapy', a process now classified by the United Nations as akin to torture. In 1970s Australia, LGBTIQ people were sacked from their jobs if they were outed to their employer, vocally condemned by the church, the parliament and the media, and risked complete ostracisation from society. The first discovery and diagnosis of HIV/AIDS was still a few years away.

Hundreds of people marched Oxford Street that cold June night in 1978. They had a permit, but the cops still weren't happy about it; at the bottom of Oxford Street the crowd were intercepted by a swarm of police officers who refused to let them enter Hyde Park, despite the activists' permission to march. After a scuffle, the parade decided to head towards the El Alamein fountain at the heart of Kings Cross, chanting, 'Stop police attacks on gays, women and blacks!'

What followed is described as a riot.

Close to midnight, the now-diminished crowd walked to the end of Darlinghurst Road where the police descended, brutally beating the activists with fists and batons. Witnesses say police targeted young women by violently grabbing their hair and their breasts before putting them in handcuffs. Garbage bins, shoes and bottles were thrown back and forth as the police waged their assault. Fifty-three people were arrested and taken to the cells of the Darlinghurst police station. Police officers continued to beat some of the incarcerated protesters; their cries of pain and distress could be heard from outside the building into the night.

Forty years later, many spent fighting for his right to marry his partner, Bon, Peter walked with me and the rest of our elated rainbow mob through Darlinghurst to celebrate Australia saying Yes to marriage equality.

Marching down Oxford Street that night felt like a dream to Peter; like he was re-living the first Mardi Gras back in 1978. When he was about two-thirds of the way down the street, he turned to look back and saw people were still spilling out of Taylor Square. Up until then, Peter had no idea just how many people were marching with him. That moment on this night, 15 November 2017, Peter describes as the most wonderful, exhilarating moment of all his activism.

We were thousands now, swirling down the street with our flags and our cheers. People staying high in the Oxford Street hotels came to their balconies to wave, and we waved back at them. We sang 'Freedom' by George Michael at the top of our lungs, and we meant it when we promised not to let each other down, nor to ever give up.

At the intersection of Oxford and Crown streets, my friends and I stopped to lie down on the road. Feet stomped around us as we looked up into the dusk sky. I wanted to feel Oxford Street under my body. I closed my eyes and felt my heart pound into the tarmac, the warmth of the recently departed sun softly radiating from the concrete to my skin.

As I lay with my friends Rok and Axel, I was overcome with a deep sense of lineage. Peter de Waal and the activists from 1978 had paved this road for us, and I felt a burning pride to walk in their footsteps. Because I too had marched demanding equality, again and again and again, along this very road. Some of our marriage equality rallies saw thousands of people swarm that street, completely stopping traffic as we chalked rainbows at the Taylor Square intersection. Sometimes just a few dozen people would show up, as pedestrians looked on at our feeble demonstration with kind pity. I'd paraded down this road for Mardi Gras, taken queer teenagers on history walks of our community's treasured landmarks and jay-walked across it late at night between gay bars. This street was our home. We got up from the road and began the call and response, 'Whose streets? Our streets!' and we bounded on, swigging our secret beers.

In that moment we didn't care that the campaign for marriage equality was far from over, and we still needed to push legislation through a hostile, conservative parliament. We weren't thinking about how many people voted Yes, what the wording of the new law would mean or what the prime minister had to say for himself. We marched down Oxford Street, reclaiming our space, our bodies and pride in our identities. Walking with our community, battered and bruised, we picked up each other's pieces and we were unbroken.

•

Here's a confession: when I first started campaigning for marriage equality, I didn't really support it. I thought the concept of marriage was weird and naff and dated, and that instead of pushing for gay marriage rights maybe heterosexual people should also stop doing it, seeing as one in two marriages ended in divorce. I didn't want to get married, and I certainly didn't think it was something we LGBTIQ people should aspire to emulate, or want to participate in. I would loudly tell anyone who'd listen that the energy put into campaigning for marriage equality should instead be spent addressing the harrowing struggles of young people with LGBTIQ identities, or the disadvantage LGBTIQ people face in accessing healthcare, housing, employment and social inclusion. At the time, I didn't see the connection.

I joined the campaign for marriage equality when I got a job at an organisation called GetUp. GetUp was launched in 2005, while I was still in high school, by Jeremy Heimans, David Madden and Amanda Tattersall. The organisation was formed in response to John Howard's Liberal party winning a majority of seats in both houses of parliament: the House of Representatives (to form government) and also in the Senate. The Senate is normally made up of a diverse range of representatives from different states and political parties, so it usually works as an upper house that reviews laws the government makes in the lower house, but when the Liberal party took control of both, it meant they could just make whatever laws they wanted in the House of Reps, and then wave them through the Senate without scrutiny. For example, it was under this configuration of parliament and John Howard's government that the Northern Territory Intervention – a $587 million suite of laws that saw the government send the military, tanks and all, into remote Indigenous communities to enforce punitive, racist laws against Aboriginal people – was rubber-stamped within a single day in 2007.

There was an urgent need to create a way for ordinary people to engage in and influence the laws that the government was making, because government can't be trusted to hold themselves to account. GetUp's mission was, and remains, to make democracy more participatory by using the internet to coordinate collective citizen action. The idea was that ordinary people should be able to influence decisions being made by the government on the issues they care about, outside of an election, and the internet allowed people to organise at scale so they could leverage their power in numbers.

Back in 2005, a petition that you could sign over the internet was *very cool*. Using an email list and a website to tell people what politicians were trying to do – whether it was trying to stealthily cut funds to the ABC or send us to war in Iraq – and then mobilising those people to contact their politicians, share information on their new social media pages, rally in the streets or crowdfund to put ads on TV was groundbreaking.

GetUp began campaigning for marriage equality the year after it launched. In 2007, GetUp members raised money to poll the general public on their support for marriage equality, and found majority support for the first time ever. During the early years, GetUp co-organised some of the biggest mass rallies for marriage equality to date, lobbied the Labor party to repeal 58 pieces of discriminatory legislation and went viral with their now famous marriage equality video called It's Time.

When I started at GetUp, it was still quite small and though there were other LGBTIQ staff there, I was the only queer person in a campaigning role. The national director at the time, Sam McLean, asked me to take the lead on the marriage equality campaign, and I pushed back. 'You're only asking me because I'm a lesbian!' I'd protested, as if there was some sort of homophobia at play.

'Well, yes?' McLean had replied, bemused. 'Don't you think a gay person should lead this campaign?'

He had a point. So I took over from a straight colleague on the promise that I could *also* work on what I deemed to be more important LGBTIQ issues.

By the end of that year, I found myself in the courtyard of Old Parliament House in Canberra at one of the first same-sex weddings to happen in Australia when, via a bureaucratic glitch, marriage equality was accidentally legalised in the Australian Capital Territory (ACT) for five days in 2013. Whoopsies!

To understand how same-sex marriage was briefly legalised for five days, four years before it became law, we need to revisit John Howard's both-houses-of-parliament government. (I do apologise.)

In 2003, my friend Jac Tomlins and her partner, Sarah, married in Canada, legally. When they returned to Australia, Jac and Sarah began speaking to lawyers about whether their overseas marriage would be recognised in Australia. The law at the time clearly specified the types of unions that *couldn't* be classed as a marriage, like if one of the couple was still married to someone else or if both members of the couple were from the same immediate family. The list went on: there must be an authorised celebrant, both parties must be over eighteen years old or have special permission, there must be no cases of fraud or mistaken identity, both members of the couple must be able to fully consent without coercion. To Jac and Sarah's delight, there wasn't actually anything in the law specifically precluding same-sex couples.

Heartened, Jac and Sarah launched a case with the Victorian Family Court. They hoped a win in court would have significant implications for the wider LGBTIQ community and could even pave the way for the legalisation of marriage equality in Australia. But when Jac spoke to her lawyer, Kris Walker, about her hopes to win the case based on the wording of the Act, Kris replied, 'Under the current legislation, maybe. But they can always just change the law.'

'You're kidding!' Jac said. 'Surely they're not going to change a federal law because Sarah and I are running a case in the Victorian Family Court?'

That is, of course, exactly what they did. Howard had control of both houses of parliament, and so his government could do whatever they wanted.

In 2004, in direct response to Jac and Sarah's marriage, as well as another Canadian marriage of Australian couple Jason and Adrian Tuazon-McCheyne, the Howard government pushed a bill through parliament to explicitly define marriage as a union between 'one man and one woman'. In addition to the new defin-ition, the amendment also added sub clause 88EA, stating:

Some unions are not marriages. A union solemnised in a foreign country between a man and a man or a woman and a woman must not be recognised as a marriage in Australia.

When put to the upper house of parliament, senators from the Greens and the Democrats voted against the bill, with Greens leader Senator Bob Brown labelling it 'hate legislation'. Their opposition wasn't enough. Though some within the Labor party broke party lines to speak out against the amendment – Tanya Plibersek, Anthony Albanese and Senator Penny Wong to name a few – the Labor party, led by Mark Latham, voted as a block to support the amendment, leaning on the fact that public support for the reform was less than 50 per cent. The bill passed, and the Act was amended.

LGBTIQ couples already couldn't get married in Australia, but because this amendment was made specifically to ward off any challenge from LGBTIQ people who had been married overseas those words were more than a reinforcement of the status quo. Those words marked a calculated, discriminatory exclusion of LGBTIQ people from a civil institution.

Amending the Marriage Act to exclude same-sex couples, in the twenty-first century no less, was a deliberate tactic from the state to deny a group of citizens rights. At its heart, it was just horridly mean.

Another part of the Marriage Act says the law must be read aloud by the celebrant at the ceremony for the union to be legal. So, for the fourteen years that followed Howard's amendment, no marriage was legal unless vows were declared beside the words:

Marriage is the union of one man and one woman to the exclusion of all others, voluntarily entered into for life.

As a queer person you don't hear the words 'one man and one woman to the exclusion of all others' and think about resisting hypothetical future infidelities. You don't hear 'to the exclusion of all other lovers', you hear, 'to the exclusion of *you*'. Every wedding was a reminder that not only did marriage law not include us, it was written to explicitly exclude us.

For fourteen years, every time I heard those words they were like cold water to the face. Standing among close friends, caught up in the romance of a wedding ceremony, they would shock me back to reality with an ice-cold jolt. Everyone else there hears the words too, and all of a sudden it feels like they're all watching you. It doesn't matter that you're there with friends, your partner, or even if you're in the damn bridal party; suddenly you're an imposter. You're a child dressed-up in a grown-up's clothing. Those words remind you, and everyone else, that this privilege is not for you because you're not the same as the people around you. Your love doesn't qualify. They puncture the ceremony, echoing 'not you, not you, not you'.

For five days in 2013, it was different. I was going to a wedding, and the happy couple were two men.

I'd met one of the grooms, Ivan Hinton-Teoh, only a few times at that point. Ivan was a marriage equality activist and worked with Australian Marriage Equality (AME), a key organisation in the campaign. I didn't know his soon-to-be-husband Chris, but already felt fond of their relationship, as I had watched Ivan propose to Chris live on television a few weeks earlier. They seemed sweet and very much in love. The following years would see Ivan and I work closely together, including travelling the country to speak at marriage equality rallies.

It's a little odd being at the wedding of someone who's a recent acquaintance, but I was technically there to work. I certainly wasn't out of place with my videographer; the courtyard was full of journalists and camera crews who were all there to capture the historic occasion. Rows of plastic chairs were covered in white fabric and a chandelier hung from a large gazebo. The guests mingled in the sunshine, sunglasses on and hands to their foreheads, as we waited for the grooms to appear.

I spotted Senator Sarah Hanson-Young from the Greens and Senator Louise Pratt from Labor, both of whom had been campaigning with Ivan for marriage equality for many years. We wore suits and cocktail dresses, and we fanned ourselves with the folded order of service booklets as we said to each other, 'I can't believe it!', 'What a turn of events!' and, 'Is there any possibility they'll stay legal?'

Soon enough, word travelled that the grooms had arrived, so we shuffled into our seats. To my genuine surprise, my eyes sprung with tears as Chris and Ivan began to walk down the aisle, each flanked by both their parents. Judy Garland's gentle voice filled the courtyard telling us of a place she'd heard of in a lullaby. As the grooms passed me, arm in arm with their parents, I saw every face in the crowd light up with joy, one after the other like dominos. I'd never seen a wedding like it; it wasn't just acceptance, it was pride.

Chris and Ivan took each other's hands and said their vows. They promised to love and to hold, in sickness and in health, for as long as they both shall live. And, for the first time in almost a decade, the joy of the ceremony wasn't spoiled by the celebrant saying those awful words we'd heard at every wedding since 2004.

After longing for it, and fighting for it for so long, Chris and Ivan were a union of 'two people voluntarily entered into for life'. As I watched these two people, so deeply in love with each other, promise to spend the rest of their lives loving and honouring each other, I didn't feel assimilated into something I thought was weird and naff and dated. If anything, it felt subversive. It felt like progress. As I watched the celebrant pronounce Chris and Ivan 'husband and husband', I felt as though the space where I was standing belonged to me. It was mine, and this marriage was theirs. I wasn't even a real guest of Chris and Ivan's, but for the first time during a wedding ceremony I felt seen, and included, for who I am and for the love I have to give.

Rodney Croome, veteran marriage equality activist and then director of AME, told my videographer and I, 'Today is so important. For the couples who have married, and their families. But it's also really important to the nation as a whole, because today we are a more equal society. A fairer society. And a society that values love more than it did yesterday.'

At the reception, Chris and Ivan danced with each other, and then their parents. Two little grooms sat atop the rainbow wedding cake shared among guests in the function room of the iconic Telstra Tower. As the sun went down, rainbow fireworks spattered the Canberra sky.

Judy Garland told us that day that dreams really do come true, but they didn't in 2013. Ivan and Chris were among 31 same-sex couples who tied the knot in the ACT that historic December weekend. The very same day the ACT parliament passed same-sex marriage laws for their territory, the Liberal government launched a High Court challenge to have them repealed. After five days, every one of those marriages was voided and annulled.

The way our constitution works means that states and territories can only make laws in their parliaments that don't clash or interfere with federal laws. It's sensible, otherwise citizens could be obeying the law while simultaneously breaking the law, creating a big mess.

With this in mind, when the Howard government amended the federal Marriage Act with the delightful words 'one man and one woman', campaigners saw a potential opening for states and territories to pass separate state legislation for same-sex couples that, in theory, could run parallel to the federal law but grant LGBTIQ couples the same protections. A state law that could allow for 'one man and one man' and 'one woman and one woman' to marry, we argued, didn't clash with the federal 'one man and one woman' definition. For many years, marriage equality campaigners lobbied state and territory governments to legislate the reform locally. GetUp partnered with AME to put the issue on the agenda at state elections, we fundraised to put ads on TV, ran petitions and even sent New South Wales (NSW) state politicians cupcakes, pleading with them to think of our love too.

State marriage equality legislation was rejected by the Tasmanian parliament in 2012, and then by NSW and South Australia in 2013, with a committee in the NSW state parliament correctly assuming it would be immediately challenged in the High Court. The ACT government knew their law would likely face a court challenge too, but tried very hard to get around the clash with the federal law. The bill literally spelled out that the ACT law was for 'all marriages between 2 adults of the same sex that are *not marriages with the meaning of the [federal] Marriage Act*'. It was a nice try.

On 12 December 2013, five days after Chris and Ivan's wedding, the High Court unanimously ruled that the ACT law was indeed unconstitutional. The court's ruling noted:

The federal Parliament has not made a law permitting same sex marriage. But the absence of a provision permitting same sex marriage does not mean that the Territory legislature may make such a provision. It does not mean that a Territory law permitting same sex marriage can operate concurrently with the federal law.

People who opposed marriage equality delighted in the ruling from the High Court and the annulment of these precious weddings. Responding to the verdict, Lyle Shelton of the shamelessly anti-LGBTIQ pressure group the Australian Christian Lobby (ACL) told the ABC that marriage equality activists had 'pretty much exhausted all avenues through the democracy and the courts and I think it's time to move on.'

Contrary to Shelton's generous advice, we did not move on. And, actually, the ruling was a gift to the national marriage equality campaign. Knowing 31 marriages had just been voided was terrible, but there was one small, clear silver lining: when the High Court ruled the ACT's marriage law couldn't stick, it confirmed to campaigners the only way to achieve marriage equality was in our federal parliament, with a legislative change to the federal Marriage Act. We couldn't go through the courts, like they'd done in Germany. It wasn't going to work going state by state, like they did in Canada. A referendum, like Ireland would go on to do, wasn't an option for us because marriage wasn't part of the constitution. The laws that were passed and then repealed in the ACT clarified exactly what our pathway to victory would be and refocussed our fight.

It wouldn't be easy: by then, Australia's prime minister was Tony Abbott, who once called equal marriage rights 'simply the fashion of the moment'. Some MPs and senators supported marriage equality, but the majority didn't, which meant that even if the government was planning to introduce same-sex marriage legislation to parliament (which they most certainly were not) we were a long way off getting the numbers we needed in both houses to pass a law. A growing majority of the general public supported marriage equality, but in 2013 when Australia had just elected their most conservative prime minister in living memory, parliament's inaction on the reform held no electoral cost to either major party. It wasn't an issue that voters cared about enough for most politicians to bother with.

The fight ahead for marriage equality activists was huge, but we knew exactly what we needed to do. At least, we thought we did.

•

I met about a dozen newly married couples that weekend in Canberra. They beamed with excitement when I asked how they met, what the day meant to them or to see their rings. Some couples wore rainbow details on their suits or dresses to show how proud they were of being LGBTIQ. One couple said their vows at the stroke of midnight, in the first seconds that the ACT law came into effect, so they didn't have to wait a moment longer than they had already been forced to.

I'm embarrassed to admit that being at that wedding on that day, 7 December 2013, was when it became urgently clear to me that marriage equality really wasn't about me and my politics. This was about real LGBTIQ people, many of whom had fought for decades for the rights and freedoms I took for granted as a queer woman. Who was I to tell a group of 78ers that they were on their own because I thought marriage was patriarchal? It wasn't even really about marriage, either, despite it being the centrepiece of the reform. This was about the government telling LGBTIQ people that they couldn't do something that everybody else could, simply because of who they were. This was a symbol of inequality that inspired other discrimination in every corner of

LGBTIQ people's lives. This was a lesson taught to children, all of them, about who was worth less than someone else.

It took me experiencing a wedding that I didn't feel automatically excluded from to realise what my community and I were being denied. This weird and dated thing should be ours too, if we wanted it. Civil marriage didn't belong to heterosexuals. Rights don't belong to the majority, theirs to share at their discretion. Rights are for everyone.

Judy Garland sang to us and I agreed with her; why, then, can't I?

One of my earliest memories is from when I was about four years old. I'm playing with a toy in my family's house in White Gum Valley, just outside Fremantle. Beside me is a bookshelf my mum built, filled with May Gibbs and Mem Fox and Dick Roughsey, all tattered from the second-hand shop. Brahms fills the house, which is part building site, as my mum lays the red bricks she's 'reclaimed' onto the open-dirt ground that's our kitchen floor. She's also 'reclaimed' a wooden lamppost that stands in the middle of our self-made house, bearing the weight of the roof and measuring our growing heights. My sister Bessie, who if I was four would have been three, wanted to play with the yellow truck I had, but I refused to give it to her. No matter her pleas, increasing in desperation, I wouldn't let her have it. 'No, no, no,' I insisted. Bessie worked herself into hysterical tears, begging for a turn with the toy and, feeling guilty, eventually I gave it to her. My mum swooped in, took the toy back from Bessie and put it firmly back in my hands.

'You've made your sister cry,' she scolded me. 'If you were going to give it to her all along, you should have given it to her at the start. If you're not going to give her the toy, you need to stick to that. Don't make your sister cry, if you're going to change your mind.'

Her words are crystal clear in my memory, and they've fundamentally shaped who I am. I'm reluctant to argue with the people I love if, ultimately, the argument isn't important. I don't want to fight for no reason. But when I do fight for something – when something really matters – I won't let it go. That little exchange when I was a tiny child took residence deep inside of me and made me determined beyond discouragement, committed to fighting for what I believed in, and decisive in what warranted my commitment and what did not.

I'd been working on the marriage equality campaign for the best part of a year before I attended Chris and Ivan's wedding in 2013, but I left Canberra that day with a deep sense of determination. I became obsessed. Making Australia change its Marriage Act became my North Star, and I couldn't take my eyes off it.

I didn't know that on that exact day, 7 December, four years later, I'd be singing from the House of Representatives gallery celebrating marriage equality becoming law.

2

An Impatient 62%

Activism is about changing things that those in power don't want changed. Activism doesn't have to be adversarial, but it does need to make power bend and relent. It does need to displace privilege, even if that privilege is just the unchallenged ability to make decisions for other people. It needs to be the external force in Newton's laws of physics that changes the course of something that would have otherwise continued on forever.

The law is a powerful thing. The law is something that tends to not want to change. Or rather, the powerful people for whom the law is made don't want it to change. It's not easy for ordinary people to change a law.

Let's briefly revisit high school civics lessons – I'll be Miss Honey. Australia's political system is a representative democracy. What that means is that neighbourhoods of people are grouped together into electorates, and electorates nominate a person to take note of all their concerns, understand the area's priorities and then represent their interests in parliament, where laws are made.

There are 150 of these nominated people across Australia, called Members of Parliament (MPs) who sit together in the House of Representatives and, largely, are responsible for making our country's laws. As well as MPs who represent us at a local, neighbourhood level, we also elect senators to represent us as an entire state or territory in parliament; there are 76 of these in total. So, each of us technically has one MP and anywhere between two and twelve senators, depending on the population of the state or territory we live in.

As we touched on, the most common way for a law to be made or changed is when legislation, also called a bill, is introduced into the House of Representatives, debated, and passed (or not). If passed through the House, the bill then goes to the Senate, where it's reviewed, debated and passed (or not).

Because the MPs and senators who are debating and passing these laws are elected by the people it is their responsibility to do as the majority of their constituents would wish. To do the opposite of what their electorate desires would, in effect, mean risking their jobs, because the literal role of our elected officials is to fairly represent our views.

I am, of course, absolutely kidding. This is not remotely how our democracy works in Australia. This is a comedy book now, surprise!

If every politician genuinely made laws that the people of their electorates wanted, I just really doubt that politicians would keep taking money from our pay packets and giving it to giant corporations, like Rupert Murdoch's News Corp, in the form of a tax subsidy, you know? Or maybe suffering, terminally ill people might have the choice to legally end their own lives, a right that more than 70 per cent of Australians support, if Christian churches didn't hold disproportionate power over parliament.

There are many factors that bust up our democracy. First, I'm going to talk about political factions. The 150 MPs and 76 senators who represent us in parliament nearly all belong to a political party (unless they're an independent, like the Member for Clark Andrew Wilkie). The two major political parties are the Liberal party and the Labor party; with stable minor parties, the Nationals and the Greens; and then there are an array of changing micro-parties who, if they're lucky, can pick up a Senate seat or two.

As you can imagine, MPs and senators are loyal to their political party, which has an agenda and a set of values and, you'd hope, a strategy on implementing both. That's your MP's team and, *you'd hope*, you know what team your MP is on when you vote for them at the election. But it's not as simple as that, because within the big political party teams, there are smaller teams. These are political factions.

Sometimes political factions within the same party differ on small things, like who their favourite former prime minister is. Sometimes, the difference of views between factions in the same party is huge, like whether global warming is real or not. Or whether same-sex marriage is good or bad.

Imagine the TV show *Survivor*: the beautiful scruffy people form alliances with each other, finding strength in numbers to advance themselves and each other in the game. If you're not in an alliance, you're vulnerable and exposed, but if you are, then you have the backing of the pack.

Political factions are a bit like this. They even have funny names like the moderate Liberal faction the Black Hand and the centre-right faction of Labor called Labor Unity. Unlike *Survivor*, they have far more rules, far more strength and, if you cross them, far worse consequences. For instance, if you want to be the person that a political party nominates as a candidate for an electorate at an election, and that electorate has 100 registered members of your party and 70 of those people belong to a particular faction, then those 70 people are going to hold a lot of sway on who your party chooses. If you're intent on trying to get the spot to run for election as an MP, you might promise those 70 members that if you're elected then you'll listen to them more than the other 30 party members from the electorate (and indeed, the rest of the people you're representing). If you get elected, your position then might depend on doing what your faction says, because they supported your nomination as candidate.

When things are good, your faction is the best. You're a group of people making change from within the party, and you have the power in numbers to convince the larger party to adopt certain reforms or change laws the way you think is best. But if you cross the leaders of your faction, you're toast. It's not just that you're on your own, you're taking up space that could belong to someone loyal to the faction.

Not all MPs are part of factions, but many are – they're proud to be, and loyal to them. What this means is that sometimes you think you're voting for an MP who is on the team you want to support, and this may be the case, but the next level of detail is that your MP might actually be part of a faction within the party that is actively trying to change the party's position on something.

The Labor party are transparent about their factions and publicly list the politicians in each of them and the values and beliefs that faction advocates for within the larger Labor party. You can even join one, if you like.

Labor MP Terri Butler explained to me, 'The Labor party is a very big organisation. You have to find ways to organise in that, as you do in any big organisation.'

But if you ask a politician from the Liberal party, the Greens or the Nationals what faction they're in, chances are they'll laugh and tell you they aren't in one, or that factions aren't really a thing. Politicians don't like to talk about factions. However, they exist, and the stranglehold political factions have on our democracy is part of the reason why our MPs and senators didn't legislate marriage equality for all those years that it felt like they should have.

Detailing factional power plays within political parties might feel like an unnecessary level of detail, but I assure you that getting a sense of how these factions operate is crucial to understanding what marriage equality campaigners, and indeed the entire country, were up against when trying to change the law.

Let's go back to 2012. Carly Rae Jepsen had just gifted us all 'Call Me Maybe'. Sally Pearson won the gold medal for the 100-metre hurdles at the London Olympics. We all shared that viral video about catching an Ugandan warlord. Gay man Benjamin Norris won *Big Brother* season 9. Julia Gillard was Australia's first female prime minister, duly elected, and delivered a scorching speech about Tony Abbott's misogyny. The ACT were still a year off legalising same-sex marriage for five days. In my opinion, we should have legislated for marriage equality right there in 2012.

Even though Julia Gillard had only just scraped in to power at the 2010 election, the election of her government was a nod to progress. Under her stewardship, the Labor government introduced laws to tax the super-profits that mining companies were making from the land we stole from Aboriginal Australians and would fund a National Disability Insurance Scheme. Her government focussed on future-facing priorities like needs-based education funding and the National Broadband Network. Even Gillard's 2010 campaign slogan was centred on progress: 'Moving Australia forward'. Gillard herself was a 'progressive' choice of leader: an unmarried, childless, atheist, feminist woman.

Gillard's government had plenty of opportunities to pass marriage equality. Four same-sex marriage bills were put to parliament in 2012 alone, two were brought to vote and all of them failed to pass. Prime Minister Gillard allowed Labor MPs and senators a free vote (or conscience vote) on these bills, which meant that each MP could choose the way they wanted to vote rather than being told they had to vote a certain way, like the Labor party was told in 2004 to vote for John Howard's 'one man one woman' wording under Mark Latham.

Many Labor politicians voted against these 2012 marriage equality bills, including Julia Gillard and her deputy Wayne Swan. One of the bills that the Labor government voted down actually came from Labor politician Stephen Jones, the local member for the seat of Whitlam. After the failed vote, with 98 MPs voting against the bill, Jones remarked, 'We've won the debate in the Australian community – over 62 per cent of Australians believe that we should make laws to allow for marriage equality. Unfortunately, we haven't won the debate in the Australian Parliament.'

Do keep that number in your mind, now. Sixty-two per cent public support in 2012.

So why didn't progressive, feminist Prime Minister Julia Gillard vote to legalise marriage equality in 2012? You guessed it: factions. In 2012, Gillard's government was particularly swayed by the powerful Shop, Distributive and Allied Employees' Association (the 'Shoppies' union or SDA) and its then-secretary Joe de Bruyn, who former Labor Prime Minister Gough Whitlam described as 'a Dutchman who hates dykes'. It's fair to say we don't like him much either. De Bruyn was vehemently opposed to LGBTIQ rights, including marriage equality. Because he was the head of the SDA, a powerful union that made up much of the right faction of the Labor party, his opinion on these things bore weight.

Louise Pratt, who was first elected as a Labor senator to federal parliament in 2007, and who was instrumental in advancing marriage equality within the Labor party, explained how the SDA had huge influence on legislation for decades. 'Still in the mid-2000s the SDA used those conservative values to wield an enormous amount of power in the Labor party,' she told me when we met in her office in early 2018. 'Julia Gillard's never been on the record about this, but I can only imagine her leadership was conditional on not making progress on these things and it was those numbers in the party that controlled that.'

'No one believed her view that she opposed it. No one,' Phil Coorey from the *Australian Financial Review* told me. 'Everyone knew it was because she was trying to keep the right [of the Labor party] happy.'

And so, in 2012, we had a prime minister upholding discrimination against LGBTIQ people because their job security depended not on the will of the people who elected them, but on the will of factional power-brokers. The power of Labor's right faction and the SDA meant that not only Julia Gillard was forced to oppose marriage equality, but nearly every MP and senator who belonged to that faction within parliament did too.

'Progressive' Labor government aside, we should have achieved marriage equality in 2012 because that year saw some absolutely brilliant activism that really deserved a bloody win. There were demonstrations, petitions, advertising campaigns, online videos of people telling their stories and 3000 red roses delivered to parliamentarians on Valentine's Day begging them to recognise all love as equal.

One of my favourite campaign tactics to this day was far cheekier than all of the above combined. Each year, parliament's Midwinter Ball – an off-the-record party for politicians and the press gallery, which begins with the equivalent of red-carpet photos in the marble foyer and finishes with many people cheating on their spouses – holds a charity auction. In 2012, one of the prizes was lunch with Prime Minister Gillard. So, GetUp members crowdfunded more than $30,000 in one day from thousands of small donations to win the first prize. We gave the opportunity of an audience with the prime minister to lesbian couple Sandy and Lou and their two sons, so they could look Julia Gillard in the eyes and ask her why their family wasn't good enough to be recognised under the law. The stunt, which was co-run with AME, led the evening news bulletins and created a setting in which Gillard looked mean and silly in her refusal to personally support the reform, which was the angle we wanted. The dinner may not have changed her mind, but the media stunt focussed the public eye on her failure to lead on the issue, thereby increasing public pressure on her to do so.

This was also the year Cory Bernardi resigned as parliamentary secretary after linking same-sex marriage to sex with animals. Senator Bernardi's unoriginal bigotry came hot on the heels of Jim Wallace, then-leader of the anti-LGBTIQ group the ACL describing homosexuality as being as bad for your health as smoking. It was a year of highs and lows.

There was still far more work to do. And first, we had to get through the 2013 election.

•

When Donald Trump became president of the USA in 2016, shock reverberated across the globe. People had laughed off his candidacy, partly because it was absurd and partly because to take it seriously would force us to acknowledge how deeply fucked the world was. When he won, much of the world went into a tailspin. How could have the polls have been so wrong? How could the pundits and campaigners alike have misjudged this so badly? I watched in horror as the results came through on a television in Surry Hills, surrounded by agog Australian activists. The entire affair became so distressing I ended up wandering out into the rain, buying a packet of cigarettes and weeping. Later that night I got drunk and made out with my friend Nayuka Gorrie as we furiously tried to distract ourselves from the impending global political apocalypse. Another instance of highs and lows.

After Trump was elected, the Australian left panicked. The United States had lurched to the far right and the left predicted Australia would soon follow. To me, it felt strange to chalk it up as a cautionary tale because I felt like Australia had already lurched to the far right three years earlier with the election of Tony Abbott, the most conservative, right-wing prime minister Australia had seen in generations.

Politics nerds knew that Tony Abbott was set to win the 2013 election. The *Daily Telegraph* had announced from its front page 'Australia Needs Tony' and the Labor government couldn't even decide which leader to take to the election. Few were surprised when the Liberal–National Coalition won government and Tony Abbott, who once bit into a raw onion for absolutely no reason, became our prime minister.

There are, of course, differences between Tony Abbott and Donald Trump. Abbott was a dyed-in-the-wool politician, rather than a political outsider like Trump. Abbott adhered to political norms and codes of communication, and wouldn't be caught tweeting in capital letters some borderline gibberish about North Korea at 3am. But Abbott was elected on a platform of xenophobia and immigration panic, climate change denial and trickle-down economics, just like Donald Trump. His time in parliament before becoming prime minister gave insight into his hostile attitudes towards women, marginalised communities and science. He campaigned in three-word slogans that articulated not what he was for, but what he was against. Stop the boats. Axe the tax. Ditch the witch. The night Tony Abbott was elected, I also cried out of fear for the country's future, but I didn't drunkenly smooch any of my friends, so it was objectively a less-good night.

Tony Abbott once said that homosexual people make him feel 'a bit threatened'. Most people thought that comment was homophobic and nasty, but I actually think it's fairly understand-able. Most of the LGBTIQ community aren't big fans of Abbott and his ilk, and many of us were plotting his electoral defeat from the moment he took the top job. He was wise to feel his electoral power threatened by us, and I can imagine if he were to accidentally arrive at a queer bar, he'd be gruffly removed by some butch lesbians, the drag queen on the door reminding him, 'And STAY OUT!'

Abbott, who also trained to become a priest for a hot minute there, was staunchly against same-sex marriage, but that didn't mean that the campaign rested. When, in 2013, the High Court ruled in response to the ACT's five-day gay wedding bonanza that same-sex marriage legislation must pass in federal parliament only, and never individual states or territories, the marriage equality campaign knew we couldn't miss a beat. The public support was there, but there were not enough supportive MPs in parliament.

Let's take a moment to talk about someone else who was elected to the Australian parliament at the 2013 election. His name is David Leyonhjelm. Leyonhjelm is a libertarian, which is either someone who prefers to be controlled by enormous tax-avoiding super-corporations rather than a government that people have elected and can hold to account, or someone who hasn't completed their thought yet. He likes guns. He's known to use public tragedies such as the Martin Place siege or the Bourke Street Mall attack as opportunities to advocate for the relaxation of Australia's gun regulation. Leyonhjelm also likes political parties, having joined the Labor party, then the Liberal party, then the Shooters party and then the Liberal Democrats party, with whom he was elected to the federal Senate.

Senator Leyonhjelm and I subscribe to wildly different political philosophies and would disagree on many things. In fact, we frequently do disagree with each other on Twitter, because that is apparently how democracy works in this, the new millennium. However, he and I did and do agree that the government shouldn't be able to stop someone getting married because they're LGBTIQ, and so in 2014 Leyonhjelm introduced a private member's bill for same-sex marriage. And because the man is a gun-toting, tax-denying, free-market-loving right-wing senator rather than the consistent LGBTIQ allies the Greens, his push for marriage equality was politically interesting.

When Leyonhjelm announced he would put the bill to the Senate, a group of GetUp members and I delivered an enormous novelty ring box – complete with a giant gold wedding ring – to Tony Abbott's electorate office with champagne, balloons, a petition and a proposal: 'Will you allow a free vote on marriage equality?' The Liberal party were bound by Abbott to all vote no on same-sex marriage legislation, but a free vote would have seen many Liberal MPs support a bill. When I ordered this novelty ring box from a prop specialist in Marrickville, I thought it was going to be about the size of five pizza boxes stacked on top of each other. When I arrived to collect it, I found a thing the size of a small elephant. Whoopsies! So, I hired a truck and drove it out to Manly, calling every television station in Sydney to make sure that news cameras would be there to capture his rejection of our marriage proposal.

Leyonhjelm's aptly titled 'Freedom to Marry' bill wasn't intended or expected to pass. At this point in time, November

2014, it was the fifteenth marriage equality bill that had been introduced to parliament. By the time we changed the law, a cool 23 bills for marriage equality had been put to federal parliament, fourteen of which were sponsored or co-sponsored by the Greens as private members' bills (which means the bill hasn't come from the government).

Leyonhjelm's private member's bill would be ignored by the government of the day, just like all the rest. Putting up legislation that's destined for failure might sound like a pointless exercise, but the tactic is common in parliament.

'It's rare that a private member's bill will get supported by the old parties and certainly by the government,' Leader of the Australian Greens Richard Di Natale explained to me. 'It's a tool that can be used to advance the debate and discussion. It provides a space in the parliament for MPs to give a speech on a topic that they care about.'

The tactic provides a little more context for the 23 pieces of legislation for marriage equality introduced to parliament between 2004 and 2017, perhaps.

'It also forces other parties to go on the record and each time we do it you have supposedly progressive MPs on both sides voting against legislation like this,' Di Natale continued. 'It makes it harder for them and puts pressure on them to internally change the position of their own parties.'

•

I know that a moment ago I said that we should have achieved marriage equality in 2012 because Julia Gillard's Labor government should have just got it done but, failing that, parliament *really* should have achieved marriage equality in 2015. The madness and the momentum of that year moved marriage equality to the tips of our fingers, before it was snatched from our grasp.

2015 ruled. The year began with an exciting snowballing of politicians in the Labor party suddenly announcing that they had changed their minds and now supported marriage equality! Wayne Swan, Tony Burke, Chris Bowen, Anna Burke, Ed Husic . . . one after another, they each had an epiphany, opened their hearts and minds and bravely declared their new-found love for equality. The entire nation celebrated with abandon!

Okay, that's not *quite* true. Only those obsessively following the minutiae of political play (hello) were excited by this sudden slew of Labor MPs announcing their formal support of marriage equality. And, really, their announcement wasn't sudden at all; it was the result of many years of work, from outside and within the party. Securing Labor's support for a change in the law was the focus of most external campaigning from activist groups and lobbyists for over a decade. The Labor party's journey to supporting marriage equality was also externally influenced by the Australian Greens, who since their formation had been vocally supportive of LGBTIQ rights and marriage equality and who were increasingly winning the vote of people who had previously voted Labor but who were frustrated with the party's opposition to marriage equality.

It was also no coincidence that old mate Joe de Bruyn, the factional heavyweight with a huge say in how the party was run, had just stepped down as president of the SDA. Within months of his departure the mega-union moved to drop their opposition to same-sex marriage, but it took only weeks for the Labor politicians I mentioned above, all members of Labor's right faction, to finally voice their support. It's chilling that one man's attitude towards LGBTIQ people can have such an influence over political parties and thus the laws of the entire country.

So, a slew of Labor politicians announced their support. It wasn't actually a huge surprise on closer examination, and it didn't exactly create a buzzing social appetite for marriage equality, but it was very good all the same! A note: I can't promise that I won't again overstate how exciting a relatively small shift in political power dynamics is, but perhaps as this book continues our excitement for such things will converge.

Something else extremely exciting happened in 2015. Thanks to the hard work of thousands of people working with organisations like AME, GetUp, Equal Love and Parents and Friends of Lesbians And Gays (PFLAG) who had been lobbying their local members to support marriage equality, a conservative count of the numbers suggested that *if* a marriage equality bill was put to parliament *and* Tony Abbott allowed the Liberal party a free vote on the legislation, rather than forcing them all to vote against it, then we *probably* had enough votes in both houses of parliament to pass the law. This was a tentative and secret development because there were many MPs, such as the then-Liberal member for Lindsay, Fiona Scott, who had privately expressed support for marriage equality, but remained undeclared on the public record. But it was extraordinarily exciting all the same.

David Leyonhjelm's 2014 'Freedom to Marry' bill was well and truly gone, and in its wake came a series of good pieces of legislation. One stood out above all others because, for the first time ever, it was a cross-party bill. Two Liberal MPs, Warren Entsch and Teresa Gambaro, wrote a bill for marriage equality that was seconded by Labor's Terri Butler, and co-sponsored by Adam Bandt from the Greens and Independent MPs Cathy McGowan and Andrew Wilkie.

By 2015, the political pieces were technically in place: the High Court had ruled that marriage equality must be legislated by the federal parliament, there was very likely the numbers in parliament if this gorgeous cross-party bill for marriage equality was brought to a free vote, and, as we have repeatedly established, the public support was there. But the complicated state of political affairs, as much as I could nerd out over them for hours, could barely compete with the profound significance and social impact of Ireland winning a referendum to allow marriage equality.

When the news broke that the Yes side had won and that Ireland would allow marriage equality, the Irish cheers echoed loudly down under. Their victory streamed in from across the world to our social media feeds and nightly news bulletins. Crying couples flung themselves into each other's arms on the streets, crowds roared with joy while waving rainbow flags in the air. We watched children and their same-sex parents embrace, finally knowing their families were equal. I'll always remember the footage from the announcement. A gruff, middle-aged Irishman choking back tears, saying that for the first time in his life, at 57 years old, he didn't feel like a second-class citizen in his own country. A young Irish woman held by her girlfriend, tears running down their faces, explaining to the camera that, 'It means the world. I'm not less than anyone else.'

Catholic, conservative Ireland, from where so many Australian families hail, had beat us to it! Bloody Ireland had gone and done the thing laid-back, gay-friendly Australia couldn't. The joy for Ireland was tangible, palpable, enviable.

Although it was months, it felt like only moments later that marriage equality was legalised across every state of the United States in an historic ruling from their Supreme Court in June 2015. The ruling was touted as the most important civil rights decision in a generation and was reached after gay man Jim Obergefell sued the state of Ohio for denying him the right to have his name listed on his late husband's death certificate. Five votes to four, the US Supreme Court ruled that the right to marriage equality was enshrined under the equal protection clause of the 14th amendment. President Obama declared the ruling a victory for America, saying, 'This decision affirms what millions of Americans already believe in their hearts: when all Americans are treated as equal, we are all more free.' Once again, images of people weeping with joy in the streets and celebrating in their communities poured into Australia.

Ireland and the United States achieving marriage equality were triggers for a surge in public support for a change in the law, but as the years prior confirmed, pubic support alone wasn't enough. We needed to strengthen our theory of change.

Every campaign should be underpinned by a theory of change. It captures the precise cause and effect that your campaign is trying to achieve, and describes how the external force will change the course of existing power. This is how you can tell if a campaign is real or not, for example, 'sign the petition to end global warming' does not show a theory of change. How would the act of signing one petition help to stop global warming? There is no realistic cause and effect within that idea. Theories of change are developed thinking about the concepts of 'if' and 'then':

IF enough shareholders pressure the company's board, THEN the bank will withdraw its funding from the mining project.

IF we can raise $15,000, THEN we can put ads all over *Sky News*, which politicians keep on in their offices.

IF an LGBTIQ couple in every electorate meets with their MP this month, THEN politicians will return to parliament with our stories in mind.

To push our politicians to act we needed to keep transforming the 62 per cent of public support into political pressure, and so, with the goal of changing the law to allow LGBTIQ people to marry, our theory of change was: IF we publicise an impatient 62 per cent, and show hard evidence of the political cost to individual government MPs and the Liberal party as a whole should they continue to delay the reform, THEN the government would hold a free vote in parliament on marriage equality legislation.

Let's start with the first part. How do you publicise an impatient 62 per cent? You put demonstrations of that loud majority where everyone can see it: in the media.

We started by holding eight marriage equality rallies, organised by GetUp and AME together, in eight capital cities over the eight consecutive weekends of the parliamentary winter break. The timing was deliberate; instead of a national day of action with events in every capital city all at once, we drip-fed images of huge, diverse crowds marching the streets with smiles on their faces and signs declaring, 'Love is love!' and 'Free vote now!' over two months to the media in the lead-up to parliament's return in August.

Rallies for marriage equality had been a fixture of most capital cities by then, primarily organised by local grassroots organisations like Equal Love in Melbourne and Brisbane, Community Action Against Homophobia (CAAH) in Sydney and collections of LGBTIQ activists passionately, tirelessly working on a volunteer basis. The very first rally for marriage equality in Australia was in 2004, protesting John Howard's 'one man one woman' amendment, organised by CAAH in Sydney. From there, slowly but surely, the rallies grew. More people came, higher profile speakers joined, the media began to take interest in an issue that kept popping up on the streets and didn't seem to be going away.

Years later, the leader of the Labor party Bill Shorten confirmed to me that 'the pride marches were significant in raising my awareness of the mainstream nature of marriage equality. It wasn't just an issue for a few people; it was actually a view about all of us.'

By 2015, building upon the work of grassroots activists, marriage equality rallies were enormous. I travelled to every one of them, speaking with AME's Ivan Hinton-Teoh and Rodney Croome. First-hand, I saw the country heave with demand for reform in a way not seen since the huge campaign push of 2011–2012 under Prime Minister Gillard. At each of these rallies in the parliamentary break of 2015, I led the crowd in the catchy chant, 'What do we want? Free vote! When do we want it? August!'

As well as rallies, GetUp demonstrated an impatient 62 per cent by driving phone calls and emails to MPs from their constituents and delivering huge petitions. And to give hard evidence of the electoral cost, we picked ten MPs from the Liberal, Labor and National parties who were yet to declare their support and applied massive political pressure to each of them as individual MPs in their own electorates; crunching data and conducting local polling to show just how many people in their electorate would not vote for them again unless they supported marriage equality.

Political factions are influential, but nothing is more influential to an MP and their faction than what the majority of their electorate wants on an issue if it's actually going to change their vote.

Before we knew it, our plan was working. On 11 August 2015, Prime Minister Tony Abbott was forced to call a crisis meeting to figure out what the hell the government was going to do with the 62 per cent of impatient Australians who were loudly shouting about how much they wanted the law to be fair for everyone and that they wouldn't vote for the Liberal party again unless they made it so.

The meeting went on and on, hour after hour. Calling on MPs and senators from around the country to return early from their winter break for an emergency meeting about marriage equality was unheard of, and a party room meeting running this long was extraordinary. At GetUp, I waited with bated breath, meticulously preparing responses to the two possible scenarios: Tony Abbott would allow every MP to vote in accordance with the wishes of their electorates, or he would not. There'd be a free vote, or there would not. Those were the only two options, right? Right?

Six hours later, Tony Abbott emerged and announced that the government would not allow a free vote on the cross-party legislation for marriage equality. Instead, the government would hold something called a 'plebiscite'.

3

The Bastard Plebiscite

I'm at a terrace house in Glebe, Sydney, in an old kitchen sitting at a small table. There's a clear plastic covering pulled tight across the wood, protecting it from damage. Behind me is a brick wall adorned with a collection of china plates patterned in blue, each commemorating a new year. There might be 50 of them.

It's only three in the afternoon but Peter de Waal is fetching me a glass of red wine. We've egged each other on a little with a cheeky exchange of, 'Oh, well if *you're* having one, I won't say no!'

We decide to sit outside because it's a beautiful day. As I make my way through the side door, Peter turns on the water features, which make a gurgling, gushing sound. The courtyard, shaded from the sun by high trees and the two-storey house, feels like it could be anywhere in the world. I spot a packet of cigarettes up on a window ledge and, ever the trying-to-quit smoker, ask Peter if I could bum one from him.

'Oh, they're Bon's actually,' he tells me, reaching for the pack. 'That's where he always kept them, and he was only halfway through this packet when he died. I know it's a bit silly, but I just like to keep them there. They remind me of him.'

I immediately begin to reassure Peter that it's okay, I don't actually need a cigarette. I'm extremely reluctant to disturb this precious relic of someone passed, especially for something as crude as a nicotine craving. Peter passes the pack to me.

'No, it's okay. I would like you to have one.'

I take one of Bon's cigarettes, the tobacco dried out and faded from sitting untouched on that windowsill for nine months. I light the tip and take a deep drag, feeling the smoke reach every inch of my lungs. This cigarette was far heavier duty than my rollies, and it made my head spin, but more dizzying was the sudden, overwhelming feeling of closeness to Bon. It was as if he were right there with us in that shaded courtyard, his packet of cigarettes right where he left them when he left this world.

'Bon was much quieter than I am,' Peter muses to me, as I smoke. 'He was very generous, he was very kind. He had an unspoken vision of what our lives and what our community could be like. He had a strong sense of what's right and what's wrong.'

Peter tells me how Bon, whose full name was Peter Bonsall-Boone, had wanted to be a priest and trained at Moore College in Perth. In the 1950s, before starting his training, Bon received two convictions for having sex with a man. It's easy to forget, in the wake of an historic reform like marriage equality, that sex between men was only fully legalised across Australia in 1997, when Tasmania was forced by the federal government to decriminalise homosexuality. When the bishop in charge of Moore College found out about Bon's criminal record, he confronted him.

'The bishop demanded, "Why have you not told us about these convictions?" to which Bon replied, "Well, my lord, you never asked me!"' Peter chuckles as he tells this anecdote, absolutely not for the first time.

The bishop sent Bon on a spiritual retreat to pray, study the bible and think through what he wanted in his life. After a week, the bishop came to see him to ask what insight he'd gained through reflection and prayer. Bon told him, 'My lord, I want to live with the man I love.'

'The bishop told him, "Then there's no room for you here!"'

Bon was forever hurt by this expulsion, feeling that the religion he so loved had rejected him. He went on to get a job as a secretary at an Anglican church, but kept his sexuality hidden.

Fifteen years later, in 1972, Bon and Peter made history by sharing the first same-sex kiss on Australian television in the ABC documentary series *Chequerboard*. The kiss was fleeting, like something you'd give your grandmother, but it was enough for the Anglican church where Bon worked to fire him.

With his gay rights organisation, Campaign Against Moral Persecution Inc, flourishing, and relentless rejection from the faith he held so dear, Bon knew where his gentle heart and generous soul were needed most. So, he and Peter set up the first gay and lesbian helpline in Australia called Phone-A-Friend, taking calls from LGBTIQ people wanting to come out or simply needing someone to talk to. The hotline operated out of their house – the same house where we were sitting in the courtyard, smoking a cigarette 45 years later – and went on to become the Gay and Lesbian Counselling Service of NSW, which still runs to this day.

Peter and Bon were together for 50 years, and they desperately wanted to get married. When, in 2017, they realised that Bon was very ill and didn't have long to live, they wrote to Prime Minister Malcolm Turnbull begging him to put marriage equality legislation to parliament before it was too late.

'He could do something about this to make our wish come true. To be married before Bon passed away,' Peter said.

They posted the letter to Prime Minister Turnbull's office, and faxed it over too, just for good measure. On their behalf, Greens Senator Janet Rice, a dedicated voice for LGBTIQ rights in parliament, hand-delivered a copy of the letter to Turnbull's office in Parliament House, giving it directly to a member of his staff. Malcolm Turnbull ignored the letters, and they never got a reply.

Bon passed away on 19 May 2017. As if to never let the injustice he faced be forgotten, his death certificate will forever show the words: 'Never married'.

The day Bon died, I spoke to Peter on the phone. He was grief-stricken, and he was furious. He felt that he and Bon were robbed of their rights by politicians who didn't care for anything other than their re-election to power. Peter wanted the world to know what the Australian government had done to them. He sent me some photos, taken by William Brougham, of Bon's body, resting at last, surrounded by flowers and draped with the pink triangle flag, and asked that I get them into the newspaper. I contacted journalist Michael Koziol and sent him the photos as an exclusive and set up an interview between him and Peter. The next morning the photo of Peter cradling Bon's dead body was on the front page of the *Sydney Morning Herald*, so everyone could see what the government was doing to our community.

I was devastated for Peter and unable to comprehend what it would be like to lose the person you love, let alone your partner of 50 years. Beyond my sorrow for Peter, I felt like I'd been hit by a bus. I felt crushed by failure and fury. This wasn't how Peter and Bon's story was meant to end, especially not after everything they did for our community. People across the country took to social media, writing of their harrowing grief and pointed anger. Bon's death was a blow to us all and a reminder of every person who had died before him as a second-class citizen, not worthy in the eyes of the law of the same rights as their neighbour. That front page of the *Sydney Morning Herald* read, 'Lifelong Gay Activist Dies Waiting for Permission to Marry'.

Peter and Bon didn't just wait for permission to get married, they fought for it for 50 years. They pioneered the LGBTIQ rights movement in Australia and supported countless people in the community. They marched in the first Mardi Gras in 1978 and spoke at marriage equality rallies right up until the very end.

I asked Peter what I'd been wanting to ask him since Bon died.

'You knew that Bon's time was running out and that doing the plebiscite could be the fastest way to change the law,' I ventured, carefully. 'It would have happened in February that year,' I continued. 'It would have meant that you and Bon could have married. Why did you campaign so hard against a plebiscite, to make sure it didn't happen?'

Peter paused, raising his glass to his lips. I wondered if I shouldn't have asked this so directly, if I was rubbing salt in a wound.

'Having been involved in our community's struggle for equality, we'd learnt some lessons,' Peter began, softly. 'People would say disgusting things about us, untruthful things. Our community got badly done, we got really hurt. We realised that by having a plebiscite, the same would happen. We wanted to prevent that from happening, because we knew it would hurt our community.'

As Peter explained this to me, a new sadness came across his face. It was like I'd momentarily lost him in his memories. 'I particularly felt for the rainbow families,' he continued, 'For the children to get damaged by these campaigns was, to me, the most horrific thing to happen. The children are our next generation, not necessarily as gays and lesbians, just as community members.'

I stared at Peter, his fine white hair standing straight and his hands trembling as he held his wine. I thought about his determination and sacrifice, and how he and Bon had served the LGBTIQ community so selflessly until their final moment together.

'If we could prevent that hurt from happening,' he shrugged his shoulders, 'that's what we tried to do.'

•

Here's another confession: when Tony Abbott announced the government would hold a plebiscite on marriage equality, I had to google what the word meant. The dictionary told me it was a direct vote of all the members of an electorate on an important public question, but it still wasn't entirely clear to me, or most others, how that vote would happen or what its results would trigger.

See, in Australia we don't do plebiscites. We do the thing we talked about earlier where we elect representatives who make and change laws as part of our representative democracy. A feature of representative democracy, I should spell out here, is that individual people don't have an individual say on individual policy initiatives. That process is called 'direct democracy'. There are plenty of reasons we don't have national votes to change or create laws, including that it would be extremely expensive and impractical to organise everyone to go the ballot box multiple times a day. Can you imagine the work that would have to go into studying each proposed law, weighing up whether it's good or bad and how you'd cast your vote, all the while being campaigned at and lobbied to make a decision one way or the other? It'd be like a full-time job! That's one of the reasons we pay politicians lots of money to do it as a full-time job for us. Of course, those politicians could do a much better job at representing our wishes, such is the premise of this book, but the answer is not for each of us to do their job for them.

Another significant reason we don't do plebiscites is that plebiscites aren't procedurally necessary. In fact, they are pro-foundly unnecessary, particularly in the era of fairly reliable public polling. If a country wishes to change their constitution – like they had to in Ireland because their Marriage Act was part of their constitution – they have no choice but to hold a referendum. The difference between a referendum and a plebiscite is that a referendum is necessary to change the constitution and a plebiscite is an expensive opinion poll that has no bearing on anything whatsoever. For example, Australia had a plebiscite in 1977 to gauge opinion on whether we should change the national anthem. I know that I am unusually into marriage equality, but I would argue that it objectively carries greater real-world weight as a crucial civil rights decision than deciding to move on from 'God Save the Queen'.

Just like political factions are a nitty-gritty political detail particularly relevant to this story (even more so as we go on!) it's important to understand how completely alien plebiscites are to our democratic process to fully appreciate how much of a shit-show Australia's journey to marriage equality was. Plebiscites in Australia are almost unheard of, so why should a law about my community be put to an unnecessary popular vote when politicians have voted in parliament on literally everything else? They managed to abolish the death penalty, send the country to war, recklessly dismantle the policies implemented to save us from catastrophic climate breakdown – how was it reasonable or fair to single out LGBTIQ Australians and subject them to this horrible exercise? The process was, in and of itself, completely discriminatory towards the LGBTIQ community.

Prime Minister Tony Abbott did not actually want to legislate marriage equality. He didn't and doesn't think same-sex relationships are equal to opposite-sex relationships. He thinks our love is at best a close friendship, just like he has with his cycling buddy Kevin Andrews, and at worse, a sin that could land us in hell. Don't get me wrong; Tony Abbott didn't really want to hold a plebiscite either, but the political reality for his government was that of a restless public who were no longer willing to let their LGBTIQ friends and family members be treated unfairly. Poll after poll showed that in order to save its own skin, the Abbott government would have to deal with marriage equality.

Our campaign had worked in that we'd driven the government to crisis point: we thought that would mean they had no choice but to hold a free vote in parliament to pass marriage equality legislation. What we hadn't expected was that Tony Abbott would play us all. In proposing this shiny new thing called a 'plebiscite' that sounded like a way forwards, (and that would maybe even be a little bit fun?) he'd effectively neutralised the impatient 62 per cent who were threatening the tenure of his government but in a way that *wouldn't actually deliver marriage equality*.

I want to be really clear here: the plebiscite was not a pathway to marriage equality. It was a delay tactic. Its sole function was to protect and prolong the stability of the Coalition government, who were divided on the reform, by delaying the parliamentary free vote the government should have held that day by another six to twelve months. It was kicking the change to the law down the road a bit and, in doing so, kicking the LGBTIQ community in the throat.

I couldn't stop thinking about a couple I'd met at a marriage equality rally in Tasmania just the week before, Karen and Treen. They had their wedding dresses hanging in their wardrobes, all set to go as soon as the government granted them permission. They'd excitedly told me how they planned to marry in the local wildlife sanctuary they loved to visit together.

Not forcing the government's hand to pass marriage equality with a free vote felt like a huge campaign loss, and with it came my first real experience of activist guilt, as if the expectation of every couple and their family across the country was on my shoulders. I imagined the disappointment of hundreds of thousands of GetUp members who I'd told, 'We can do this.' People

I'd convinced to write to their MPs, to march in the streets, to donate for an advertising campaign, to chip in for my salary, all with the promise that together we could make power bend and relent. My activist guilt told me that I'd let each one of them down – I should have worked harder, smarter, faster.

Activist guilt is common. It's why so many activists burn out, physically exhausted and emotionally drained. I think it's because to be an activist, you must be deeply affected by injustice and feel an overwhelming responsibility to help fix it. It's not easy to just switch those things off, even when you know that those feelings aren't useful to anyone, like when you're meant to be recharging your batteries. It doesn't matter how hard you work, how little you rest and how much of yourself you give, if you have the makings of an activist you will get activist guilt.

Being hit with a plebiscite when our goal was parliament just passing a bill felt like I, Sally Rugg, hadn't done enough even though there was no way I could've possibly worked harder. My best friend Rebecca Shaw says that 'our entire friendship just consisted of me pleading with you to stop working so hard, because I was concerned you might literally die of exhaustion'. Rebecca would drop food and medicine to my house when I was bed-ridden with chest infections, which was every six weeks for years on end. She would lovingly shout at me, 'You're insane! Stop!' In a way, she is the true hero of this story.

Activist guilt is also underpinned by ego, even if it's not conscious. My activist guilt at failing to get Tony Abbott to allow marriage equality legislation to pass was particularly silly because I was absolutely not solely responsible for changing the Australian Marriage Act, and even though I was working very, very hard my contribution to the overall cause was proportionately minuscule. My work wasn't irreplaceable, either. Someone else would have plugged the gap I would have left if I decided to call it quits. But I couldn't help it. This activist guilt and sense of failure and shame stayed with me from that night in August onwards, taking residence in the pit of my stomach and the walls of my chest, staying with me for years.

•

The morning after the idea of a plebiscite was announced in 2015, marriage equality campaigners were either running around parliament house between lobbying meetings or chained to their phones urgently formulating a response across state lines.

That morning, less than 24 hours after the shock announcement, the leader of the Greens, Senator Richard Di Natale, announced that the Greens would reluctantly support the plebiscite and introduce an amendment to existing plebiscite legislation seeking to make the result binding. Did I mention that this plebiscite thing wasn't binding? As in, even if the majority of the country voted for marriage equality, MPs and senators didn't have to actually change the law.

For those playing along with the campaign for the following two years, this might sound surprising; after all, the Greens went on to vocally oppose the plebiscite a few months later. But it took some time.

'It was a bad idea. [The decision to support the plebiscite] was under particular circumstances and we very quickly decided that no, it was a bad idea,' Greens Senator Janet Rice explained to me when we spoke about it in early 2018. 'At that stage, people hadn't really thought much about the damage that would come from the plebiscite,' she said. But even though I'd only just learnt what a plebiscite was, I certainly had.

Before the Greens made that announcement in support of the plebiscite, Senator Richard Di Natale, his chief of staff Cate

Faehrmann and Director of AME Rodney Croome called me to say that within the hour the Greens would announce their support for a plebiscite. Pacing around my office, I pleaded with them not to. Over speakerphone, I warned them of the dangers of a national vote, citing how Irish campaigners were already speaking out about the distress caused by their referendum. Offering strategic advice, I urged them to consider that the public were furious that Tony Abbott had again stopped a parliamentary free vote on marriage equality, so immediately supporting his plebiscite meant that the Greens wouldn't be able to capitalise on that outrage by positioning themselves as allied with the majority of people. I asked them what message we were sending to the government as marriage equality advocates and allies if we don't hold them to account for what they do with marriage equality and instead accept their avoidance of a free vote? The phone call was terse and heated.

When I interviewed Richard Di Natale for this book in early 2018, I asked him about this conversation and he said that while he could recall Rodney Croome being there that morning, he didn't remember the phone call with me. I asked him if he had any reflections on the Greens' decision.

'I mean, we didn't support a plebiscite,' he told me. 'It was one of those difficult decisions about not supporting something, but if it passes . . . what should be the terms of that legislation? I think we made the call at the time based on what we knew.'

The Greens went on to be the first political party to formally oppose the plebiscite and spent months vocally advocating against it, citing harm to the community and the unfairness of the unusual process. Without their votes, plebiscite-enabling legislation would have passed and without their leadership on explaining why the plebiscite was unfair and harmful, the public narrative would have been very different. Political parties get it wrong sometimes, and it would appear that, similar to other parties who weren't straight out of the gate with their position on this plebiscite thing, they spent time listening to the LGBTIQ community's concerns about the process, changed their minds and dropped their plan in favour of standing with our community. That's what this whole campaign relied on, really. People in power actually listening to our community.

•

Can you imagine opening the door to a room filled with strangers, wanting to get inside, but first you have to stand there while they argue with each other about whether you're good enough to be allowed in? They don't know you, but they talk about you like they do. They make sweeping statements about your disposition, your lifestyle, your values, your ability to parent. They make assumptions about your interests, your childhood, your sex life. They theorise what terrible thing must have happened to you to make you this way. They unashamedly announce that you make them feel uncomfortable, or that they don't want you near children, because these are things they've heard so many people say before that it doesn't even feel like a particularly rude thing to say anymore. They say you are deserving of hell. Other people are arguing back, saying that you're a lovely person and great with kids and your lifestyle is totally normal, but in a way that makes it worse because you don't want anyone to be talking about you. You don't want there to be a discussion at all, and you don't want people to have an opinion on your worthiness, you just want to get on with your life.

Now imagine that the people talking about you are celebrities, politicians and radio presenters and that room is your right to be treated equally under the law. And you can't just leave the room because every street you walk down is plastered with messages for and against you, and your social media feeds are strewn with people's thoughts on you, now that they've been told they must shout their opinion. Imagine it's not a silly hypothetical, but that this debate has very real consequences for your life.

Most of the LGBTIQ community knew the plebiscite would be horrific the moment it was announced (after we googled what it meant) because we know what it's like to be singled out, to be excluded, to be hunted. We remember standing in front of the classroom and being jeered at. We remember having cigarettes flicked at us in the streets or rumours spread about us online. We know the jolt of terror when someone screams a slur out of a passing car or hisses it across the dinner table. We know what it's like for a queer character to appear on the television and have your family members wince. We know what it's like to be afraid the next hate crime will be us; we know what it's like to never feel safe at the cliffs at Bondi. We know what it's like to be questioned in taxis, in doctor's surgeries, at the front desk of airports, hotels, restaurants and support services.

But the fear of enduring a public debate about our community runs deeper than our personal experiences and the experiences of our friends. We inherit this fear from our history, handed down through the generations of queer family. The memories of our collective trauma run in our blood. Our community is still made up of people who were beaten by police for marching in the street in 1978 and the years prior. Together, we remember the boys who were murdered in Sydney in a wave of homophobic violence known as 'poofter bashing' and how those murderers were never charged. We know of women who were 'correctively raped' by their husbands. We remember thousands of our gay brothers who we lost to the HIV/AIDS epidemic that ravaged our community, where our cries for help were met with punishment, stigma and ostracism. We remember our lesbian sisters having their children taken away from them. We remember our transgender siblings of years past who lived in hiding and are no longer with us because so many simply couldn't imagine a world where they could be who they are and be safe.

We remember the jail sentences. We remember the internments. We remember the pink triangles and the gas chambers.

I'm what you would call 'straight-passing', which means that unless I'm actually holding hands with a woman or seen kissing a woman then chances are I would be assumed to be heterosexual. This in and of itself is bad enough, but many other people have written books about compulsory, assumed heterosexuality so we won't go into that today. Being 'straight-passing' keeps me safe a lot of the time but can be infuriating when strangers assume I'm lying or declare with surprise that I 'don't look like a lesbian'. This is ridiculous. I am what a lesbian looks like, because I'm a lesbian and this is how I look.

Despite being 'straight-passing' and being privileged in other ways, such as being white, able-bodied and thin, I've still experienced my fair share of harassment and discrimination. My ex-girlfriend and I were refused a rental house, after being approved by the agent, because the landlord didn't want 'people like us' to live there. I've been denied sexual healthcare and cervical screening from two doctors who insisted I didn't need it. I've been kicked out of taxis twice for holding the hand of partners and once for briefly kissing the woman I was riding with in the backseat. While walking down the street I've been called a dyke, a faggot, a lesbian bitch. I've had rubbish thrown at me, been pushed towards oncoming traffic and had my arm grabbed from the waist of a girl I was walking with and flung away from her by an old man. I've been threatened by lecherous, drunk men in bars too many times to count because I've been there with a woman.

My experiences of harassment, discrimination and potential violence are nothing compared to what my friends who are transgender face. My dear friend Tammy, who is among the funniest and most thoughtful women you'll ever meet, explains that as someone who's 'visibly trans' she's been attacked for simply walking down the street. She's been spat on, verbally abused and physically assaulted in the neighbourhood we shared, Sydney's LGBTIQ haven of Newtown.

'I don't catch public transport at night or walk alone after dark. I have to screen the people I choose to sleep with for any signs of potential violence,' she tells me.

If you are a cisgender woman reading the precautions that Tammy takes and thinking 'I do that too', I want you to consider the significantly higher rates of violence transgender women face. It's difficult to accurately record incidents of violence against transgender people in Australia. In states such as NSW, for a person to legally change their gender on their official documents, they must have had gender reassignment surgery (a prohibitively expensive, major operation that some transgender people don't want to have) and have their sex amended on their birth certificate. However, surveys show that transgender Australians experience violence and harassment at higher levels than any other group of people. An Ipsos survey from 2018 found that three in five Australians deliberately misgender transgender people, that is deliberately use 'he' for a transgender woman, 'she' for a transgender man or use either 'he'/'she' for non-binary people who use the pronoun 'they'. The research spanned 27 countries and Australia was the country second most likely to deliberately misgender a trans person. The only reason someone would deliberately misgender a trans person is to wilfully hurt them, and three in five Australians admit to doing it, which is a good indication of the level of disrespect and degradation towards trans people that lays the foundation for violence.

Anyone who understands the violence and disadvantage that transgender people already face in Australia could appreciate that a national vote on LGBTIQ rights would undoubtedly scratch at the underbelly of the three in five Australians' prejudice and put transgender people at even greater risk.

Maybe it was because of our personal experiences, maybe it was our collective unconscious trauma, but the LGBTIQ community in its majority knew that some of us wouldn't come out of a national vote alive, that the plebiscite would be incredibly harmful. The largest survey ever conducted of the community commissioned by PFLAG and just.equal in 2016 confirmed that 85 per cent of us didn't want the plebiscite to go ahead. The thing had to be stopped, even if it meant a delay in marriage equality.

•

I don't believe in karma, but I'm certainly not above schadenfreude. As such, you can rest assured that I took great pleasure four weeks after the plebiscite announcement watching Tony Abbott be unceremoniously dumped as prime minister and leader of the Liberal party. His legacy in the top job will be that he swept to power in the wake of Labor's Rudd/Gillard/Rudd leadership mess and just absolutely shit the bed. Whether it was trying to introduce a co-payment to Medicare; his archaic and sexist views on women; his planned cuts to education, hospitals and the ABC; his refusal to do what 62 per cent of Australians were begging him to do and pass marriage equality, Tony Abbott was so deeply unpopular that his own government decided to kick him out. In his first term.

Phil Coorey, the political editor at the *Australian Financial Review*, told me that people underestimate how much marriage equality led to Tony Abbott's loss of the Liberal leadership and Australian prime ministership. 'He had that big screaming match in the party room in August 2015 – he tried to shut it down and he came out of there absolutely ashen faced. He did a press conference at 10pm at night saying, "We'll have a plebiscite".'

Tony Abbott was opposed to a plebiscite going into that Liberal party meeting. Coorey tells me that in private Abbott was saying that he wanted the issue to stay subterranean. Abbott completely underestimated the level of support for marriage equality in his own Liberal party – no doubt because of the massive campaign that activists had been running showing these MPs the electoral cost of their inaction.

Coorey told me, 'that was when they decided they were going to roll him as leader. That's when it really began, and two months later he was gone.'

In Tony Abbott's place, the Liberal party installed a man by the name of Malcolm Turnbull. You know Malc, the cool guy on *Q&A* with the leather jacket who effortlessly toggles between charisma and snobbery. The guy who calls journalists to bellow at them for a quarter of an hour about some minor detail in an article only to take a breath and say, 'Anyhow, how are the kids?' The guy who had been previously deposed as leader of the Liberal party for trying to introduce laws to address climate breakdown.

Malcolm Turnbull is far less right-wing than Tony Abbott. He doesn't think that global warming is a conspiracy for a start and, crucially, he was both a strident supporter of marriage equality and deeply opposed to the idea of a plebiscite. None of that mattered, though, because it turns out there might be no greater example of a leader's self-serving kowtowing to political factions at the direct expense of the Australian people than how Malcolm Turnbull became prime minister.

In factional politics, remember, it can matter less what an individual politician thinks (or what their electorate tells them) than what a small group of king-makers (or queen-makers) think. Like the Labor party, the Liberal party is also split into factions that run along ideological lines. The most powerful of the Liberal factions at this point in our story is the hard right faction of conservatives. The hard right are full of everyone's favourite anti-LGBTIQ politicians such as Eric Abetz, Peter Dutton and – you guessed it – Tony Abbott. It's rumoured they call themselves the 'Taliban'.

To become the prime minister of Australia, Malcolm Turnbull needed a majority of MPs and senators within the Liberal party room to vote for him in a leadership spill against Tony Abbott. To make up the numbers, Turnbull needed to secure the support of the members of Tony Abbott's own faction. The hard right 'Taliban' members were extremely opposed to marriage equality (and all LGBTIQ equality measures) and along with the Liberal's smaller Coalition party, the Nationals, who don't directly vote on the Liberal leader but are known to threaten mutiny if they don't get what they want, they suspected that if Malcolm Turnbull became prime minister then he would abandon Abbott's plebiscite plan and just pass marriage equality through parliament straight away. Turnbull was, after all, vocally opposed to the idea of a plebiscite.

The hard right faction refused to vote for Malcolm Turnbull in a leadership spill against their man Abbott (who was desperately unpopular and looking like he couldn't win the next election) unless Turnbull promised he wouldn't do this; and the Nationals refused to remain in coalition with the Liberal party unless Malcolm Turnbull signed an agreement saying that he wouldn't hold a parliamentary free vote on marriage equality, but would instead force the entire country to a useless, cruel plebiscite, because that's what the members of the Liberal party who opposed marriage equality wanted. In short, Malcolm Turnbull sold us out. He sold Peter and Bon out. He sold out the country for his own ambition.

It's seems a bit complicated, because it was. By this point – late 2015 – there were many people within the Liberal and National parties who supported marriage equality and knew that they would have to find a way to deal with it before the next election, lest they face the impatient 62 per cent. Hence their rolling of Tony Abbott. But they weren't willing to just do it themselves as a government because of the power wielded by a small group of ideologues in the far right of the party. The plebiscite provided cover for their inaction. To the Coalition, the plebiscite was all about looking like they were addressing the issue, but actually just delaying a vote in parliament.

I don't really give a shit about the opinions of people like Eric Abetz or Tony Abbott – but there is something quite hurtful about an elected member of federal parliament being willing to hang their entire career on their belief that you are not worthy of rights. To think that my existence is so reviled that elected leaders of our nation would be willing to lose their job, lose their mates' jobs and their party's governance of the country – presumably something a politician has been working towards for decades of their life – simply to ensure I remain discriminated against.

I steady myself in the knowledge that if a government was ready to implode because it was internally ill-equipped to address discrimination against people within their electorates, it deserves to.

•

When the government didn't legalise marriage equality in 2015 despite the cacophony of calls from their constituents, this was a failure of representative democracy. When the Liberal party introduced the idea of a plebiscite in place of a parliamentary free vote, it was a sign that our democratic processes had all but broken down. It was emblematic of the fact that old, rich, white men with views completely out of step with the Australian public were holding the country ransom with their disproportionate factional power.

Then again, this is how the system has always worked. You only have to look at Australia's politicians to see that our political parties and parliaments privilege white men over anyone else, and it's not a coincidence. White men aren't better at being politicians than anyone else, but while women were told to stay home and raise babies, the dudes ganged up to build the system and not let anyone else in for hundreds of years. While white men were running the country, people of colour weren't allowed to migrate and Aboriginal people weren't even allowed to vote. This same system now runs on foundations of sexism, racism, nepotism, colonialism and genocide. It's ruthlessly power-hungry. It fosters factions, favours donors and will gladly sacrifice the weak for the survival of those at the top. There are many ideas on how to fix a broken political system. One is that we tear it all down and start again. We storm the federal parliament, fire the lot of them and completely overhaul the political and economic system. We make sure no person is without shelter, healthcare and sustenance, and that no person owns more than one million dollars because you cannot ethically own one million dollars. We abolish prisons, scale back the police and decriminalise non-violent offences. Instead of digging up the land and commodifying our natural environment, we give it back to its traditional custodians. We halt climate breakdown. We radically reimagine work and community, moving towards a socialist utopia.

There's probably a lot of value in that plan, but that wasn't our plan to legislate marriage equality, and it also wasn't our plan to stop the plebiscite. Our new plan had more of an immediate urgency to it. Instead of tearing down or rejecting the system, our plan was to reclaim it. Instead of systems of power only working for the powerful, we would work together to make them work for us. We'd use the courts. We'd use the parliament. We'd use the internal processes of political parties and the formal legislative tricks and procedures that apply to every other law written. We'd take the system as our own, and use it to get what we want. We'd wrangle back control of our country from the pocket of rich, old men and take back our power as people, because the future doesn't belong to politicians – it belongs to us. Incestuous groups of old, rich men may have built the system, but we know how to work it too.

The LGBTIQ community in its majority were clear that they did not want the plebiscite to go ahead, so as 2015 ticked over to 2016, a group of campaigning organisations and activist groups set out to stop it. They included, but by no means were limited to, Rainbow Families, PFLAG, Equal Love, CAAH, the state-based Gay and Lesbian Rights Lobbies, DIY Rainbow, Rainbow Rights WA, Equal Voices, Equal Marriage Rights Australia and, after a weird few weeks of trying to make sure we were on the same page, long-time campaign partners GetUp and AME. As a rough and ready coalition, our plan started with basic legislative process. The Liberal–National Coalition had the majority of votes in the House of Representatives, so a bill for a plebiscite would pass through that house no matter what we did. And so, our goal was to convince enough of the Senate to block the legislation that would create a plebiscite.

To pass legislation in the Senate, you need 39 votes. To block legislation, you need 38. Here was what we were working with: after their brief period of supporting a plebiscite, the Greens changed their mind and began vocally opposing it, which gave us six votes. Independent Senator Derryn Hinch also thought the plebiscite was a horrible idea, as did the three senators who at the time made up the Nick Xenophon Team. That was ten all up. I'm no mathematician but it seemed quite a way off 39. If we wanted to stop the plebiscite from happening, we needed to convince the Labor party senators. And it was going to be tough.

At first, Australia loved the idea of a plebiscite, with 88 per cent of people thinking it was a good idea (though I imagine they probably would have loved a free parliamentary vote and the immediate legalising of marriage equality even more). It made sense: 62 per cent of people really wanted marriage equality for all Australians, politicians weren't getting it done and so the general public really took to the idea of *forcing* them to do it. It sounded like a great plan!

It was not a great plan. Not just because a plebiscite was a bastardisation of our representative democracy or because it was inherently discriminatory towards the LGBTIQ community. It wasn't even a terrible plan based solely on the fact that it was expected to cost about $150 million and, being non-binding, would have no actual effect on any passage of legislation. The main reason it was a terrible, terrifying idea was because of the harm a hysterical public debate on whether LGBTIQ people were worthy of equal treatment under the law would cause to the community and their families. The LGBTIQ community knew this, we just needed to explain it to everyone else who didn't immediately see it from our point of view (which is totally understandable).

The Labor party were keenly aware of how popular a plebiscite was with the public, and people who voted Labor really liked how supportive of marriage equality the Labor party had become. Labor Opposition Leader Bill Shorten went to the 2016 election saying that if Labor were elected, marriage equality would be the very first thing his government did, which was a powerful promise and even more powerful political wedge against the Liberal party. For Labor to be the ones who blocked the plebiscite when the majority of people were in favour of it and after they had become so strongly supportive of marriage equality could confuse their voters and be electorally damaging for them. The Labor party weren't going to block the plebiscite until the general public also understood the LGBTIQ community's fear.

Luckily, we'd been here before. Activists and community members alike had become deftly skilled at changing the public's mind. The main complication was that 'every one should be able to marry the person they love' was a far simpler idea to explain than what we were about to try to convince the nation of: Yes, we want marriage equality. Yes, it's very urgent. No, we absolutely can't do it with a plebiscite. No, trust us, it's a really bad idea. Yes, we understand not doing a plebiscite might mean we'd have to wait another few years for marriage equality. Yes, we would rather wait than endure a plebiscite. No, we shouldn't actually have to wait at all because a plebiscite isn't a real pathway to reform, it's just a delay tactic. Yes, we could do it right now in parliament and no, we're not going to stop pushing for a parliamentary vote even though the government and the press keep telling us the plebiscite is the only option. Got it? Great.

The message was complicated, completely counter-intuitive to everything we'd been saying for the previous three years and required enormous amounts of empathy for LGBTIQ people, so to communicate it, we simplified the message into soundbites that could be easily understood and repeated. We gently explained again and again, in the media, in campaign videos, in letters to MPs and senators: the plebiscite was unnecessary, expensive and harmful. Soon the drumbeat of 'unnecessary, expensive, harmful' echoed across the country, repeated by journalists, politicians, influencers and throughout the timelines of social media platforms.

In the middle of 2016, the peak group campaigning for marriage equality – AME – fell apart. In a shock to the activist sector, veteran marriage campaigner Rodney Croome stepped down as the national director, writing in the *Guardian* that he could not accept the government's ultimatum of a plebiscite and that he was unable to reconcile his position with the AME board. There is conjecture as to whether this was a resignation or a removal of Croome following pressure from new Liberal-party aligned financial backers of AME who wanted the plebiscite to go ahead.

AME created a new sister organisation called Australians For Equality (A4E) which would prepare to fight a national Yes campaign under a different logo to avoid confusion (it did not really avoid confusion) and imported Irish marriage equality referendum campaigner Tiernan Brady to be its national director. Liberal MP Tim Wilson had met Tiernan Brady in Ireland when the government was preparing for a plebiscite and recommended to the AME/A4E boards that he come to Australia and lead our Yes campaign too.

So, Tiernan Brady was running pro-plebiscite A4E, Alex Greenwich remained the chair of vaguely positioned AME and Rodney Croome had started a new anti-plebiscite group just.equal with former AME campaigner Ivan Hinton-Teoh. It was all pretty complicated, and led to suspicion from parts of the LGBTIQ activist community about whose interests AME and A4E were actually working for – the community or the Liberal party?

Then, in late 2016, AME and A4E 'merged' (seeing as they shared the same staff, offices and campaign resources they were pretty merged already, if you ask me) and made a new organisation that would become the main vehicle for the Yes campaign, the Equality Campaign. The Equality Campaign's co-chairs were Alex Greenwich and Anna Brown, with Tiernan Brady as the executive director.

While this was happening the remaining organisations fought tooth and nail to try to stop the plebiscite from going ahead. We used the same tactics as we'd done for years prior – social media campaigns, videos, media tactics like exclusive polling and personal stories, rallies, community meetings, organising people to contact their MPs and senators, fundraising to put ads in the newspaper and on television – and we repeated the same words: unnecessary, expensive and harmful. All of these tactics were useful for explaining to the general public why the LGBTIQ community opposed a plebiscite, but when it came to convincing the Labor party to block plebiscite legislation in the Senate, in the end there was nothing more powerful than a bunch of kids.

Children would be the most harmed by a plebiscite on marriage equality, and children were the ones who, in the end, stopped the plebiscite from happening. Kids of queer parents and kids who themselves were gender diverse or queer led the charge joyously, selflessly and enthusiastically.

Jo was one of the many parents who met with the Labor party in 2016, alongside heads of LGBTIQ community services. 'We had a big round table at Drummond Street with Bill Shorten about why we didn't want the plebiscite,' Jo explained. 'I felt like they really listened and they understood why it must not go ahead.'

The three children of Jac Tomlins and Sarah Nichols – whose Canadian marriage triggered John Howard's 2004 amendment to the Marriage Act explicitly excluding same-sex couples – were among the kids leading the fight. In the final weeks before the government moved to pass plebiscite legislation, they joined a group of families who travelled to federal parliament.

'The experience of taking the kids to see politicians in Canberra was, honestly, quite remarkable and it will stay with me – and them – forever,' Jac told me. 'The kids were sensational – thoughtful, confident and articulate – and even though some of them were nervous, they overcame that because they knew they were there to do a job: to represent all the kids of rainbow families. I saw quiet courage everywhere and I can't tell you how many times I had to hold back tears.'

I don't have kids, but I did attend a big meeting with Rainbow Families in federal parliament, as an ally to the organisation and rainbow kids everywhere. I remember sitting with these children and their parents with the members of the Labor party – Bill Shorten, Tanya Plibersek, Penny Wong, Mark Dreyfus and Terri Butler – as they begged that they be spared the pain of a plebiscite. The Labor party listened, and heard these families loud and clear.

Within twelve months of Tony Abbott announcing a plebiscite to huge public enthusiasm, a Galaxy poll found that public support for a plebiscite had dropped to just 25 per cent. That's utterly extraordinary. I can't think of any other policy that experienced such a watershed shift in public support in such a short period of time, and that's a testament to how hard the LGBTIQ campaigning sector and grassroots activists had worked. With public support in their favour and a commitment to protect the children they'd met with, Labor announced they would vote against legislation in the Senate, making up the numbers needed to block the bill.

We'd done it. We'd stopped the plebiscite. We didn't sit down and shut up, like the government had expected us to. We didn't care if we were scorned or laughed at. We didn't take no for an answer. We fought for our kids. We fought for each other. We fought for Peter and Bon, who shouldn't have had to choose between hurting vulnerable people and marrying each other after 50 years of waiting. I watched when the bill was voted down in the Senate and will always remember Senator Penny Wong's decisive nod when the speaker confirmed the bill's defeat. The Greens senators hugged and cheered and embraced Labor colleagues in the chamber. I felt like I might be able to sleep through the night once more, activist guilt assuaged, safe in the knowledge that the LGBTIQ community had protected ourselves and our children from the public debate.

•

If you had told me in 2016 that I would explain the magnitude and complexity of the campaign to stop the plebiscite in a few pages, I probably would have thrown my drink in your face. I am absolutely not a violent person, but I was an emotional wreck and would have loathed your suggestion that I could reduce everyone's hard work into a few paragraphs. But what we can take from this period of time isn't our stunning execution of campaign tactics, the sector's collaboration and teamwork, or our pride in that we kept going even though loud and powerful voices kept telling us we should give up. What will stay with me forever is that the Australian people in their majority were able to appreciate that even though a big gay vote initially sounded like a good idea, they listened when LGBTIQ communities explained that it would actually be really awful and then they *changed their mind*. Support for the plebiscite dropped more than 60 percentile points because ordinary people understood that the process would hurt us, and *they didn't want to hurt us.*

It wasn't as loud or as sparkly, but to me, the emotional maturity and solidarity shown by the Australian public during the 2016 campaign to stop the plebiscite was far more meaningful than the overwhelming majority voting Yes in the survey the following year. It demonstrated a collective empathy and a willingness to engage with complex ideas, and a changing political landscape. It proved to me that Australians can and will go out of their way to stand up for the downtrodden and speak up for injustice, if only we can get them to listen.

I hold on to this when I think about settler Australia finally signing a treaty with Aboriginal and Torres Strait Islander people, providing a legal, binding framework that recognises the sovereignty, history and attempted destruction of their land, cultures and communities. Australia is the only Commonwealth national government that hasn't signed a treaty with the First Nations people whose land they occupy; state, territory and federal governments have made vague sounds about agreements, but these whittle into 'documents of reconciliation' or 'constitutional recognition', or simply wither away in the light of day. First Nations have never ceded sovereignty to their lands and their waters, which remains unfinished business for all Australians. There have been many calls for a treaty, so why has it taken almost 250 years since invasion? I think it's because without an impatient 62 per cent or demonstrated electoral cost to the government of the day, there aren't enough people pushing.

The LGBTIQ community have been there. As have Aboriginal and Torres Strait Islander communities, many times, but in the marriage equality campaign, LGBTIQ folks had a crucial advantage. We had widespread allyship from straight and cisgender people who went out of their way to back us up. We couldn't have achieved marriage equality alone – we simply didn't have the people power.

I speak as a white settler, who is constantly developing as an ally of Aboriginal and Torres Strait Islander justice work. Being an ally isn't a qualification you'll one day be granted and then never have to think about; it's something we settlers have to deliberately work on, consciously undoing our own socialisation within white privilege and choosing to join with the people pushing and challenging the power that we ourselves were born into. Being an ally is listening, learning and supporting, with an understanding that I probably will make mistakes, but when I do that, I hold myself accountable and commit to being better next time.

The fight for justice, sovereignty and self-determination for First Nations people doesn't need more expertise. Aboriginal and Torres Strait Islander people already make up the very best community organisers, advocates, academics and digital campaigners in this country. They are leaders, experienced and emerging. They know their plan, they know exactly how to achieve their goals. What these communities need is allyship and hard resources: our time, our voices and our money.

Statistically speaking, there's likely an LGBTIQ person in each extended family, workplace and sports team. We are certainly in every school and every neighbourhood. Every time an LGBTIQ person comes out to their friends and family, more people understand LGBTIQ justice. I wonder if LGBTIQ people have considerably more active allies than Aboriginal and Torres Strait Islander people because us queers tend to be dotted out all over the place, like decentralised sleeper cells ready to make the people around us feel connection to and compassion for us, and to advocate for our rights. Though there is probably some truth to this, I think what's more likely is that to be a true ally of Aboriginal and Torres Strait Islander people, white Australia needs to confront and take responsibility for our racist, genocidal colonial history. We need to face up to the massacres, the plagues, the slavery, the kidnapping, the violent erasure of language and culture. We need to open our eyes to the racist policies that right now see Aboriginal and Torres Strait Islander people experience far poorer health outcomes and far greater rates of incarceration.

As a nation, we have the power to change this. A future where First Nations communities thrive with sovereignty, safety and opportunity is ours for the taking, we just have to reach for it together.

Until we do, our country remains broken. Our policies will remain racist. I truly believe that the Australian people are capable of compassion and sensitivity towards refugees and asylum seekers, people living in poverty, immigrant communities and religious minorities. But not unless we as a nation and as a collective consciousness confront the violence and dispossession Australia was built on. Not just learn about it briefly at school, I mean really confront it. Centre it. Make genuine reparations to Aboriginal and Torres Strait Islander communities and authentically dismantle the systems of oppression our country has been built on. But you shouldn't need me to tell you this – First Nations activists have been saying this for more than 250 years.

Ask yourself: What am I doing to actively support First Nations' movements? How can I be a better ally? How am I using my power to hold governments accountable for racism?

As we move on to the next section of this book, I am going to teach you about campaigning.

Maybe you will put it to use.

4

Actually, It's a Postal Survey

You'll notice we're only about a fifth of the way through this book, which in and of itself is a spoiler that parliament voting down plebiscite legislation isn't the end of this story. Even without the conspicuous remaining pages, though, it's likely that you know that the triumph of defeating a national vote on marriage equality didn't last very long at all.

This is because, as you may be sick of me repeating, marriage equality was very popular. The people loved it! It was a big risk for Malcolm Turnbull's Liberal government to go into the next election with marriage law still discriminatory. Polling showed that while marriage equality on its own wouldn't swing enough votes to change the outcome of an election (with people voting on the issues of health, education and the economy), the country knew Prime Minister Turnbull was a strong supporter of it. Facing an election when he hadn't been able to deliver on a policy he'd long publicly called for would make him look as weak and compromised as, I would argue, he was.

Turnbull's Achilles heel was that he was perceived by the public as being elitist and out of touch with what ordinary Australians wanted. Inaction on popular things like allowing gay people to get married fed into this perception. Turnbull only just scraped through the 2016 election with the plebiscite policy but there'd be no way he could win another election without passing marriage equality.

Because of this reality, both advocates for and most opponents of marriage equality were now eager to see the law change – for the first time in forever the two camps agreed! The point of difference between them was whether we'd have to do Tony Abbott's big public vote first. On that particular detail, the two sides remained at war.

In July 2017, a number of people in the Liberal party and in the Canberra press gallery told me that Liberal Senator Dean Smith was secretly planning to break ranks and introduce a private member's bill for marriage equality and push once more within the Liberal party room for a free vote on the bill. If Malcolm Turnbull still refused to allow a vote on the floor of parliament without a plebiscite first, Dean Smith would cross the floor of the Senate, that is, vote against the Liberal party and with Labor, the Greens and Independent senators to make up the numbers to pass the bill through. Then, should the bill pass through the Senate, according to the insiders I spoke to, there were at least four Liberal MPs in the House of Representatives who were gearing up to cross the floor – Warren Entsch, Tim Wilson, Trevor Evans and Trent Zimmerman. Their four votes meant there would be enough for the bill to pass and the law to change. We'd have marriage equality.

I need to emphasise how huge this was. Government MPs and senators were planning to defy their leaders, break rank and vote with the Opposition on an issue that could, if the Liberal– National Coalition agreement was upheld, blow up the government. A coup of this size was almost unheard of; even crossing the floor was almost unheard of. My intel was good but still, we couldn't be sure that Senator Dean Smith was going to do it. It would be extraordinary, but would he *actually* do it? A few days after I'd brought GetUp this intel the front page of *The Sunday Times* had a picture of Dean's face on it and the giant quote, 'Yes, I will do it!' which felt like a pretty compelling confirmation.

The newspaper announced that Dean would 'Do It' and after a year of fighting off a plebiscite, a parliamentary vote was back in reach, and my beloved, dysfunctional GetUp family and I were ready to push for it. We needed to demonstrate to Liberal MPs and senators once more that legalising marriage equality would be an electoral benefit for them so they were 100 per cent clear on that by the time Dean Smith introduced his private member's bill to parliament.

•

Let me tell you a little bit about working at GetUp. Without being a member or on staff, it's very difficult to understand the sheer scale of what goes on there. Over the years, I've observed journalists and politicians alike dismiss GetUp's power and influence, and I've always found it exceptionally strange because a quick glance beyond the tired trope of 'fringe lefties getting outraged at things' reveals incredibly sophisticated and strategic work. GetUp's activities range from local groups of volunteers in every electorate across the country, right the way through to a team of world-class developers who build open-source campaign technology that they make available to activists around the world.

A colleague at GetUp once described working there as like being on a relentless rollercoaster: soaring highs, devastating lows and sometimes you just really want to get off because you feel sick and miss the life you once had before you got on the damn ride. We worked ourselves to the bone, driven by activist guilt.

I have some very fond memories of my time there; some of the things we did were big and public, like helping to organise seven candlelight vigils in seven cities in just 24 hours to protest the migration and refugee crisis in late 2015. These vigils helped to push the Abbott government to announce they would take 12,000 new Syrian refugees. Some were small and lovely, like receiving emails from members saying that they were grateful for being part of GetUp because it gave them hope. Some were absolutely silly, like dancing on the tables in the middle of the day to Justin Bieber's 'Despacito' because my colleagues Henny, Kirsti and Emily decided that, in order to keep our spirits up, we would have a very loud, obnoxious dance party for three minutes at 1pm every day, before sitting back at our desks in grim silence.

My colleagues at GetUp were like family, in the good way and the bad way. We were there for each other, and we really did love each other, but we also weren't afraid of conflict. Each day, we'd have to negotiate which campaign would have access to the organisation's shared resources – the email list, the staff capacity of the graphic design team or the media team, the national director's feedback – so, as you can expect when you put a bunch of expert campaigners who are obsessively committed to their causes in direct competition with each other and in a pressure-cooker activist environment, things could get a little fraught. Plus, as is common in not-for profit organisations where all salaries are dependent on fundraising revenue, we lived under the existential threat that if we weren't working the hardest and the smartest then it would be our job at risk.

My colleagues and I at GetUp launched a series of target-centred campaigns. A target-centred campaign involves mobilising large numbers of people to exert the power they have as voters, consumers, community members in an organised way, so that their collective power applies pressure to a powerful decision-maker. We decided to pick eight target MPs who were on margins of 8–12 per cent in their electorates: not so marginal that they were the target of every activist campaign under the sun, but marginal enough for them to be thinking ahead to the next election and hoping to keep their constituents happy.

For ease of organising offline, that is, mobilising volunteers and helping members set up meetings and poster-runs, we chose to focus our resources in two states, Queensland and Western Australia (WA). We targeted MPs Steve Irons, Ben Morton, Ken Wyatt, Andrew Laming, Andrew Wallace, Steve Ciobo, Michael Keenan and Jane Prentice. The aim of our campaign wasn't to get them to support marriage equality (though they were all on the record as 'undecided') but to convince them they'd lose their seats if the Liberal government didn't pass marriage equality so they would support a free vote on Dean Smith's bill. IF you pass marriage equality, THEN you'll be re-elected.

Our eight target-centred campaigns involved localised polling on marriage equality, organising GetUp members in the area to email and call their MPs and then get together in groups to set up constituent meetings with them. We also plastered these MPs' electorates with posters asking why the MP was standing in the way of marriage equality, which were designed to frustrate and publicly shame the MPs in front of their voters. When Dean Smith announced that he was going to Do It, GetUp staff, including myself, began meeting and working with moderate MPs Trent Zimmerman and Tim Wilson to bolster their efforts pushing for marriage equality within the Liberal party. Both MPs deny these meetings took place, which might be explained by president of the Liberal party Michael Kroger's reaction to the collaboration when it was exposed in *The Saturday Paper* in early 2017. Kroger told *The Australian*, 'It is fair to say that people in the organisational wing are furious. They consider GetUp! as a mortal enemy of the Coalition. It was unknown to office bearers that these secret meetings were taking place. If the party's base wasn't on fire, it certainly is now.'

Five Liberal politicians gearing up to cross the floor on marriage equality was the talk of the town for weeks. And by 'the town' I mean #auspol and the marriage equality sector; the saddest town there is. Senior Liberals were briefing journalists that if these five men were to cross the floor, they'd move a spill motion against Turnbull and kick him out of the prime ministership. They warned that the conservatives within the party would call for Dean Smith's resignation and the removal of the others from their seats. An anonymous Liberal MP told *The Daily Telegraph* how the right would get their revenge, 'Tim Wilson is gone, [Trevor] Evans is going to get disendorsed, and [moderate leader Trent] Zimmerman will probably get challenged anyway.'

This is one of the super-nerdy reasons why the plan to cross the floor was particularly exhilarating, because the five rebel MPs were part of the Liberal party's moderate faction and supposedly loyal to Turnbull, their factional friend, and their plot was a spectacular display of belligerence that put his leadership and the entire government in jeopardy. It had become ordinary for the hard-right faction of the Liberal party to ignore the prime minister and make whatever mess they liked, but for Turnbull supporters to run amok in this way showed just how little control the prime minister had over his party. He couldn't even get first-term MPs in his own faction to behave themselves. It was absolutely wild.

A few days before the five politicians were going to Do It, Tiernan Brady asked me whether GetUp would publicly thank and celebrate the Liberal MPs who crossed the floor for marriage equality. I told him, 'Mate, I'll get their names tattooed on my forehead.'

•

This chapter is full of spoilers. Here's another one: I have no tattoos.

This isn't because I chickened out of getting the names of five Liberal politicians on my head, although I absolutely would have. It's because politicians lie to you. They just do.

I'm not saying all politicians are liars, but as part of executing their jobs to the best of their perceived ability, they will absolutely lie to you to get you off their case. They'll lie to you to win an election.

They'll also chuck ridiculous tantrums, like Nationals MP Andrew Broad did when he threatened to 'blow up the government' by quitting the Nationals and moving to sit on the cross bench as an independent MP if the parliament legalised equal marriage. What a cool guy.

Politicians will lie to you and throw their toys out of the pram if it's part of a bigger political play, which may have been what happened next.

To deal with the threat of rebellious Liberal MPs pushing a marriage equality bill through parliament by crossing the floor, Prime Minister Turnbull called an emergency party room meeting, the second of its kind within two years. In that meeting, Dean Smith and our rebels each spoke in favour of a free vote on marriage equality but, to our dismay, agreed to not cross the floor to pass it. Despite the promises to advocates, the announcements in the press, and the intricate plan that was set, they would not Do It.

Instead, the government announced they would try to pass plebiscite legislation again, which, because the majority of the Senate had reaffirmed they'd vote against the bill, was a little bit like trying to make 'fetch' happen. Gretchen, it's not going to happen.

I'd like to take this opportunity to introduce a super-villain to our story. His name is Peter Dutton. In 2008, when the Australian parliament formally apologised to the Stolen Generations of Aboriginal and Torres Strait Islander people who were torn from their families and forced into brutal assimilation programs, Peter Dutton boycotted the apology. He joked about people in the Pacific Islands being drowned by rising sea levels. He refused to allow a young refugee who had been raped while detained on

Nauru to come to Australia to terminate her pregnancy. He's said that immigrants are innumerate and illiterate in their first languages. He was voted the worst Health Minister in memory by Australian doctors. He called journalist Samantha Maiden a 'mad fucking witch' in a text message that he accidentally sent to her. In my opinion, he is racist, sexist and a cruel homophobe.

Yet all of a sudden, Peter Dutton was the man pushing for marriage equality to be passed as soon as possible. Not because he believes in justice and dignity for LGBTIQ Australians – this is Peter Dutton, remember – but because he knew the Liberal party would be absolutely walloped at the ballot box if they hadn't managed to change the law in accordance with the public's wishes.

In early 2017, which is where we are at this point in our potted history, Peter Dutton started spruiking a solution. 'There is this option of a postal plebiscite, which doesn't require legislation as I understand it,' he told the listeners of 2GB radio. 'It may achieve, in some ways, the same outcome to a plebiscite that you would think of in the traditional sense.'

When Dutton brought up a postal plebiscite, it really felt like nobody could possibly be interested in this idea. Not marriage equality campaigners, who were toiling day in, day out for a free vote; not the LGBTIQ community, who had accepted we might have to wait for a Labor government to see the reform. Not the invested public, who'd traversed a pathway to understanding that putting marriage equality to a popular vote was unkind, unfair and totally unnecessary. Certainly not the organised adversaries of marriage equality like the ACL and the executive of the Catholic and Anglican churches, who presumably were very happy with the stalemate Tony Abbott delivered them by proposing an unworkable policy as the only path forwards.

And yet, here was Peter Dutton – flagrant opponent of marriage equality, power-broker of the increasingly extreme hard right of the Liberal party, with an appalling disregard for minorities' wellbeing to boot – pressing for progress on the issue.

When Peter Dutton mentioned the thing on the radio, it was the first time I'd heard of a 'postal plebiscite' (are you surprised I was able to do my job to a reasonable standard with such lacklustre knowledge of plebiscites?), but Prime Minister Malcolm Turnbull knew all about them. In fact, he identified a key problem with voting by snail-mail while working on the campaign to make Australia a republic in 1997:

> What will voters do when confronted with a package of material they cannot understand and there is nobody around to explain it? They will throw it in the bin and their vote will be lost.

Wow, good point, Malcolm!

The government knew the original plebiscite would fail the second time, and they were fine with it. Emerging from the crisis meeting when the rebels promised not to Do It, Acting Special Minister of State Mathias Cormann told the press, 'There are two choices now. Parliament can either vote for a compulsory plebiscite at the ballot box, or we will hold a non-compulsory plebiscite by postal vote.'

A compulsory plebiscite at the ballot box was voted down by the Senate, as the government knew it would be. As the plebiscite bill went down for a second time, Senator Penny Wong told the Senate:

> This motion is not about giving Australians a say. This motion is about weakness and division on that side of the Parliament. This motion is about a government so divided that they have to

handball a hard decision to the community to make it because
they can't make it in their party room.

Once again, we were within reach of parliament just passing a bill
and changing the law so that LGBTIQ couples could get married
only for the Liberal government to pull it away from us and shove
some sort of ridiculous 'postal vote' in our faces – how was this
fair? How was this acceptable? Parliament had blocked a public
vote and the Liberal party were just going to . . . force one anyway?

There was very little information about this 'postal plebiscite',
but what we did know was that it was projected to cost over $100
million and we were fairly sure that was actually illegal? See, the
government can't just spend public money willy-nilly – they've got
to get the approval of the parliament first, because the Australian
public should get a say via their representatives on how their taxes
are spent. As such, the government announcing it was planning to
spend $122 million on something that parliament had now twice
rejected felt unconstitutional, to say the least.

The Australian constitution says the only time a government
can spend public money (which is the only money they have – it
comes out of your pay packets each fortnight), without first
passing legislation is when a situation is 'urgent and unforeseen'.
I couldn't see how they could justify this exception for marriage
equality? When I think of the words 'urgent and unforeseen' it
makes me think of someone shitting their pants, which was a
little like what the government was doing.

Building upon my pants-crapping analysis Anne Twomey, an
actual constitutional law expert from the University of Sydney,
pointed out that there had literally been allocations in the 2016
and 2017 federal budgets for a national vote on marriage equality, so the government couldn't really classify this situation as

'unforeseen'. Twomey also questioned whether the Australian Bureau of Statistics (ABS) were technically allowed to do a survey on people's opinions (rather than collect demographic data, which is historically their only role).

It seemed, almost certainly, unconstitutional. So we took the fuckers to court.

•

It was a freezing September morning outside the High Court of Victoria (the High Court of Australia building in Canberra was getting its air conditioning fixed, so we were relocated to Melbourne). The line to get into the court building was immense and winding, with hundreds of activists from as far as Perth flying over for the hearing. The long queue coiled in on itself like a sleeping snake as we shuffled past each other, round and round. It felt a little like a speed dating exercise, except all my potential suitors were nervous colleagues from the marriage equality sector and I didn't really want to make out with any of them.

That morning, everyone in line could agree that we needed to stop the vote from going ahead and shared an immense anxiety over the finality of the court's ruling, but that was pretty much the extent of agreement between the divided marriage equality sector. We couldn't even agree to work together on taking the government to court, so we were there to hear two almost-identical High Court challenges against the postal survey. A great look for the campaign.

One case was brought by Rodney Croome's just.equal and Rainbow Families, and the other was brought by Alex Greenwich's AME and the Human Rights Law Centre (HRLC), for which GetUp members crowdfunded $30,000. The High Court decided they would hear them both on the same day, because the High Court really doesn't have time for the petty infighting that resulted in two near-identical cases. How embarrassing.

The court case from the HRLC, which is the case I was involved with, centred on two arguments that Anne Twomey had flagged earlier: the government wasn't authorised to spend the $122 million needed to conduct the survey as it (thankfully) wasn't 'ordinary annual business of government', and the circumstances in which the government could spend the money – if something was 'urgent and unforeseen' – didn't apply.

The viewing room for the hearing was floors beneath the actual courtroom and was filled by familiar activists. Sharyn Faulkner, a leader from PFLAG, had travelled from Geelong that morning to stay for the duration of the case. I recognised a few younger activists from marriage equality rallies in Melbourne and people from the group Equal Love. BuzzFeed reporter Lane Sainty sat by the wall, her laptop re-charging after a long day.

When the judge entered the courtroom upstairs, we all stood up and then bowed at the television screen as if we were actually in the room, which was delightfully absurd. Without any legal expertise, it was very difficult to tell whether the trial was going in our favour. My only clues lay in the vocal confidence of Katherine Richardson SC, the lead barrister, and in the tone and frequency of questions from the judges on the bench. During adjournments, we shuffled into the lift anxiously asking each other, 'How do you think it's going?'

One thing I did understand as clear as day was when Solicitor-General Stephen Donaghue, who was there defending the government and the survey, told the High Court that the postal survey actually had 'no immediate consequences', and 'no effect on rights' of Australians in order to help justify the planned $122 million expense. My head felt like it was going to explode.

Not only had the government lied about the necessity of the postal survey, saying they couldn't hold a parliamentary free vote without it, they were unashamedly arguing in court that it was procedurally pointless. It was the most absurd, frustrating situation. In order to pull $122 million from the public purse, they were forced to admit that the survey was redundant. Was this real life?

But beyond the exclamations of vindication from a few of us, the solicitor-general's admission was of very little consequence. Really, nobody cared. It felt like the public were so worn down at this point and saw the postal survey as a way to finally get it done. While campaigners and the LGBTIQ community were desperately trying to beat the survey, the public had resigned themselves to it. It felt like, with rolled eyes and a scoff at the uselessness of Malcolm Turnbull, they were willing participants.

Prime Minister Turnbull, who had so comprehensively slammed the idea of a postal vote while campaigning for Australia to become a republic, started spruiking the thing, telling the House of Representatives during question time that 'there is no greater virtue in a free vote here or a plebiscite. They are each means of resolving the matter – one, I grant you is more expensive but, nonetheless, it is a very legitimate and democratic way of dealing with it.'

When the High Court announced that spending $122 million on an 'unforeseen' and 'urgent' 'postal survey' was constitutional, I was absolutely stunned. But beyond that, I was absolutely, knickers-shittingly terrified.

It was happening. We were to face the gloves-off horror of a No campaign and a general public given a platform to say whatever the hell they wanted about us and our families. The country was going to hold a national vote on LGBTIQ Australians' right to be treated the same as everyone else under the law.

5

The Numbers

There's an episode of the TV show *Friends* where Ross, Chandler and Rachel are trying to carry a large sofa up a flight of stairs to Ross's apartment. Critical feminist theory tells us that Ross is an objectively shit bloke: homophobic, fatphobic and controlling of the women he dates. Because he is a shit bloke, instead of paying a moving company to bring his sofa up the stairs (he is a very wealthy professor!) he forces his mates to carry it up the stairs for him and shouts at them the whole time. As the Friends struggle under the weight of the giant sofa and attempt to navigate a tight corner in the stairwell, Ross bellows, 'Pivot! PIVOT! PIVAAAAATTTTT!' to try to get them to move the sofa in a different way.

One of the lessons I've learnt from campaigning is that to do good work, you must not be precious about it. To be a good campaigner, you must be responsive to factors completely out of your control and constantly re-evaluate whether the idea you had this morning or the direction you gave last week is still the best course of action. If your tactics are no longer relevant and your strategy no longer applicable, you've got to drop everything you've created and start again. You've got to pivot.

You'll find the results of campaign pivots in the boxes of newly incorrect leaflets under the desks of activists and in the refunds offered for TV ads that never made it to air. They're the reason I've called polling companies begging to change the questions in a poll five minutes before it's due to hit the field. Campaign pivots have seen my weekends cut short, my holidays cancelled and my painstakingly crafted strategy documents left discarded, now useless.

Learning how to abandon work has taught me pragmatism and humility. It doesn't matter how clever something is or how much time and energy has gone into it; if it's no longer useful, then it's just a vanity project. The attachment you have to your ideas and strategies is at best futile and at worst destructive, if it's derived simply from the fact you came up with them.

When the High Court ruled that a postal survey on marriage equality was technically allowed and thus going ahead, all I could hear was shit bloke Ross's voice, shouting in my head: *Pivot. Pivot. PIVOT.*

All our work setting the scene for a parliamentary free vote, all of our lobbying of moderate Liberals to cross the floor, all our strategies to force Liberal backbenchers to agitate in the party room for a free vote. No longer relevant. In the bin.

What lay ahead didn't involve convincing a handful of very powerful politicians that they'd be more likely to lose the next election if they ignored us and continued to obey their fac-tional overlords. This was no longer about galvanising collective action to exert upward pressure on specific decision-makers. This was not a target-centred campaign fuelled by tens of thousands of people. To win the survey (who knew you could 'win' a survey?), we'd have to organise millions of people to engage in a process they weren't familiar with, that they weren't legally compelled to do and that we'd been telling them for the past twelve months was useless and harmful. The task felt enormous and the activists campaigning for marriage equality were staggeringly exhausted.

At the end of the *Friends* episode, the Friends chop the sofa in half out of frustration and then attempt to return it to the shop and get their money back. Do extend and decipher this metaphor as much or as little as your heart desires.

The government's plan for the Australian Marriage Law Postal Survey, as it was so catchily named, bore little information about how the process would actually work and what it would mean. The scant and contradicting details available to us felt like part of a big government conspiracy; they were deliberately obfuscating crucial details about how the survey would run in order to disadvantage campaigners! You'll forgive me for thinking this, because the survey in and of itself *was* a huge conspiracy to circumvent parliament and it felt impossible that the government didn't know the answers to very simple questions like, 'How will people get their ballots posted to them?'

It turned out that the government wasn't avoiding details because of a secret conspiracy, they genuinely didn't have them. They were just making it all up as they went along, filling in the details retrospectively. From what we could put together, we knew that they were planning to make the ABS run the vote, rather than the Australian Electoral Commission. You may recall the ABS from the time they colossally messed up the 2016 Census, leaving thousands of people unable to complete the survey and #censusfail trending for days. In one of the more ridiculous tales from the survey, the government told the ABS they'd have to run the national operation just 24 hours before they announced it to the country. Do you laugh or cry? How can the prime minister just casually tell the ABS they'll be running a completely redundant opinion poll expected to yield millions of responses about gay marriage, with 24 hours' notice before the plan goes public? It's like the government suddenly calling up the Bureau of Meteorology and asking them to divert every scientific instrument they have in the field to record what the weather says about 'Virgo season'.

'That is crazy,' BuzzFeed reporter Lane Sainty agreed. 'The idea that you would inform this government agency that they would be running a vote on arguably the most contentious issue to dominate politics over the last at least two years is crazy.'

The things we knew were that ballot papers would be posted to people and they could post them back if they wanted to (but it wasn't compulsory), and that if the Yes vote won, then the government would allow parliament to debate and vote on a private member's bill (but we weren't allowed to see the bill), and if the No vote won, they wouldn't. It really wasn't a lot to go by!

We couldn't begin to make plans because we didn't know what was going to happen. We didn't know how the results would be counted; whether it would be first past the post or like a referendum, where either side needs a raw majority as well as a majority of states to win. We didn't know if the votes would be reported in federal electorates and whether we'd have to win a majority of those. We didn't know who was eligible to vote – would Australians who were overseas, incarcerated or without a fixed address be able to participate? What would the accessibility measures be for people with disabilities that would make casting a vote difficult? We didn't know what we were even voting for; the government hadn't released any legislation for review or confirmed whether it would be Dean Smith's private member's bill that would be put to parliament, so nobody knew if the bill would be a Trojan horse for new ways to discriminate against LGBTIQ people. What would happen if ballots went missing, were stolen or tampered with? How would we know people weren't voting twice? If we gave ballots unique identifiers, how would we keep people's votes anonymous and secure? Would the question be written in different languages? What would the question even be?

Details continued to appear over the next week, but the most crucial fact for our planning came within 48 hours: we found out that the winning side would simply need to secure a raw majority of the votes and that we wouldn't have to get a majority of states as well (like in a referendum), or majority of electorates (like in an election). This was going to just be a straight-forward, 50 per cent + 1 vote.

With this information, and in the spirit of our urgent Ross Geller inspired pivot, we went back to the drawing board. Even the very best and most experienced campaigners will begin mapping out campaign strategies with a clear, agreed articulation of what the campaign goal specifically is (and what it is not). You are a campaigner now, congratulations, and so when you set out to create change in your community, you must first define exactly what it is you want to achieve.

One checklist I particularly like is from The Democracy Center, a US-based organisation that undertakes research and offers training in campaign theory, which says that to build a successful campaign you have to figure out the following things:

What do we want? (goals and objectives)

Who can give it to us? (audiences)

What do they need to hear? (messages)

Who do they need to hear it from? (messengers)

How do we get them to hear it? (delivery)

With the survey in our laps and mounting pressure on our shoulders, we had to ask ourselves – what do we want? What is the goal here? Is it 'win the survey with as big of a margin as possible'? That goal is quite different to 'ensure every electorate returns a Yes vote greater than 50 per cent'. The goal of protecting against a victory for No isn't the same as 'progress a positive public narrative around LGBTIQ rights'. The campaign goal needed to be specific and defined.

Two days after the survey was announced, my colleagues Kajute O'Riordan, an expert organiser and director of GetUp's volunteer network; Henny Smith, GetUp's chief of staff; and Ben Raue, GetUp's data analyst (and Australia's next Antony Green) and I met with Tim Gartrell, Patrick Batchelor and Wil Stracke. Gartrell and Batchelor are veteran Labor campaigners who ran the 'Kevin 07' campaign and, upon confirmation we were headed to a national vote, had been brought in to the Equality Campaign for their mass mobilisation expertise, displacing Irish campaigner Tiernan Brady to a 'spokesperson' role. Wil Stracke, the elected industrial and campaigns officer at the Victorian Trades Hall Council, would be overseeing the union movement's work on the Yes vote. It was up to us to develop the strategy for the Yes campaign's field effort that would be executed on the ground by the Equality Campaign, GetUp, the union movement, a raft of smaller LGBTIQ organisations and thousands of volunteers. Together, we interrogated the question: what is the Yes campaign's goal?

When we landed on it, the decision wasn't just about marriage equality but about the LGBTIQ community as a whole. We wanted a goal that would minimise lasting damage to Australia's LGBTIQ community in terms of our acceptance in society and future government policy agendas about other LGBTIQ reforms. Ultimately, we decided that the best outcome for the happiness and safety of our community would be to get the highest percentage Yes result possible. We were forced into this horrible situation and felt that a clear win with the biggest majority possible was the most important thing for the LGBTIQ community.

We were now clear on the first item on the Democracy Center's checklist: What do we want? To secure the highest Yes vote possible.

The implications and consequences of that decision are felt to this day. They lie in the ground we ceded in our fight against the misinformation surrounding the Safe Schools program. They rest on the LGBTIQ community members who live in the pocket of Western Sydney electorates disproportionately targeted by our opponents who returned No majorities, and who felt like the Yes campaign wasn't present enough. We will talk about both in chapters to come.

We laid our resources out on the table: GetUp could pull fifteen full-time staff onto the survey and activate our volunteer action groups, Unions across the country were to deliver 45 staff, working from their own offices or seconded to the Equality Campaign and to Victorian Trades Hall, and Equality Campaign were in the process of hiring about 50. The Equality Campaign were working closely with business leaders, who we hoped would chip in money to power the campaign. GetUp and the union movement would fundraise too, in small online donations. GetUp would bring the tech, the Equality Campaign would bring the brand, the unions would bring the community-organising oomph.

The people and organisations working in the marriage equality campaign sector each had their strengths. Whether it was political lobbying, legal work, media and communications or organising protests, our power was derived from people with different areas of expertise working together. The people in that room that day – from GetUp, the union movement and fresh to the Equality Campaign from the Labor party – were the experts in organising tens of thousands of volunteers and using cutting edge technology to strategically impact national votes. Now that we had landed on the campaign goal – get as many Yes votes as possible – it was down to us to crunch the numbers on how we'd get there.

'Okay, so the adult population of Australia is about sixteen million people and we need fifty per cent plus one to win,' Henny kicked us off with an enthusiastic clap.

'How many of those adults will actually vote though?' Patrick questioned.

'Hopefully no one,' I answered, still reeling from the biggest pivot I'd ever had to do and deciding that sarcasm would be most helpful to the cause.

'Yeah, definitely not all sixteen million, but what turnout can we expect, do we think?' Henny persisted, ignoring me. 'Ben?'

'We'll have to find that out, but our first priority will need to be making sure everyone updates their address on the electoral roll,' Ben pointed out. 'And that we get everyone who turned eighteen since July last year to enrol – they'll be key.'

In 2010, GetUp members raised more than one hundred thousand dollars and took the Australian Electoral Commission (AEC) to court, arguing that only giving people 24 hours to update their enrolment after an election was called was unconstitutional, and disproportionately disenfranchised young people and people experiencing marginalisation. We won, which is why you now have ten days to update your enrolment or enrol for the first time after an election is announced.

In the years that followed, GetUp called for the AEC to allow people to update or join the electoral roll online, but the AEC dragged their heels. They kept saying the technology would be too difficult to build, so in 2013 GetUp developers built the technology for them, offering the tool to them for free. The AEC declined and within months had built an online form on their website. So we had chops in this area.

Making sure everyone was enrolled to participate in the survey was the democratic thing to do (even though the process made a dog's breakfast of democracy) but it was also good for our campaign. The folks least likely to be correctly registered on the electoral roll are young people, who overwhelmingly support marriage equality because millennials are empathetic and socially responsible and fabulous.

'Yes, there'll be massive enrolment drives,' Tim confirmed. 'The Equality Campaign have ads out already. But we do need a pretty accurate prediction about turnout before we can even start to map targets and resources.'

Working out what we could expect in terms of voter turnout for a marriage equality postal survey was uncharted territory. In the United States, participation in elections is optional and they see an average of about 55 per cent of people voting in presidential elections, but that's also in-person voting at the ballot box on a specific day (and something the country is used to). That wasn't really a good measure. In the 2015 Irish marriage equality referendum 61 per cent of people voted for or against the reform, but the result of their referendum was binding and our survey wasn't, so their referendum had a far more compelling theory of change (IF we win the referendum, THEN the government is forced to change the law). Plus, it wasn't a postal vote. Voluntary postal votes, however, are conducted within the Australian union movement, so Wil had some sobering expertise to share from her time working with unions.

'You will stand in front of a room of cheering, enthusiastic unionists who swear they will all vote, and I'm telling you, you'll be lucky if 60 per cent of them actually follow through,' she warned us, her arms gesturing wildly and her eyes wide open with conviction.

'These unionists are completely committed to the cause,' Wil continued. 'They are fired up. They will put their hands up and cheer in a meeting and then they will go home and not post their vote. I've seen it happen again and again,' she concluded, shaking her head.

It wasn't exactly a rousing Sorkin-esque pep talk, but we needed to be real and we needed to be precise. Our strategy had to be informed by the numbers.

For hours we went back and forth, round and round, up and down, trying to pinpoint the exact numbers that would inform our strategy. We knew we had a starting point of about 62 per cent raw public support for marriage equality, numbers that had been settled for the last decade. We considered the attrition of support for the Yes vote over the course of the upcoming campaign, which was inevitable. Though plebiscites were almost unheard of in Australia, we've had a few referenda and those votes here at home and in comparable democracies overseas repeatedly show that the side of the status quo has a significant advantage over the side of the proposed change. People get irritated at the process, and that irritation combined with opposition campaigns spreading fear of change causes support to drop.

We analysed the data from the Irish referendum with particular attention to when and where the votes were cast, and by whom. We studied the patterns of voting behaviour in Australia and the state of the electoral roll. We tested theories about rates of participation in the union movement's postal votes by polling different groups of people, measuring their propensity to participate in the survey and whether that aligned with their political leaning. We cross-referenced each factor with years of research on public sentiment towards marriage equality, focus group findings that indicated the sturdiness of support of various demographics, and which people our organisations were going to be able to reach over the following months.

This process was vital. Once we knew precisely how many millions of votes we needed to secure, in terms of how many people we predicted would actually vote, we could work backwards from there on every other metric of the campaign, breaking our work down into daily, weekly and monthly targets. We were able to map out exactly how many people the Yes campaign would need to reach with multiple points of contact, and who those people were.

Perhaps you're familiar with the meme of a man in an office shirt and tie with frazzled hair, who's frantically pointing at a wall covered in pinned-up papers, photographs and stretched coloured string. He's manically explaining how the scraps of information pinned to the wall all fit together. I imagine if you'd been looking at us while we did our calculations and devised our organising plan, we'd have looked a little like this guy.

I googled the meme, a thing that very cool people do. It turns out it's from an episode of *It's Always Sunny in Philadelphia* and the frazzled guy is trying to explain an elaborate conspiracy theory about strange letters coming in the post. Sounds about right.

Hours went by, and eventually we had a number. According to our calculations, IF we pulled out all the stops and could pull off the biggest national campaign in the shortest amount of time in Australian history, we decided we could secure a turnout of 65 per cent, at a starting point of 62 per cent public support that we expected to dramatically fall in the face of a No campaign, THEN the highest number we could get to in the survey was winning it at 55 per cent. To hit those numbers, we'd need 5.5 million Yes votes. Five-point-five *million* people receiving a ballot to their correct address, choosing to fill it out with a Yes vote and then remembering to take it all the way to a post box and send it off. It was huge. It was unprecedented.

To give you a sense of how big that number is in terms of organising people to Do An Optional Thing for a cause, the biggest petition delivered to federal parliament in Australia has about 1.3 million signatures. It's estimated that one million Australians marched on 15 February 2003 to protest the imminent invasion of Iraq, in lockstep with 600 cities around the world.

In 2010, four million Australians watched the grand finale of *Masterchef*. I can't find any other voluntary activity that out-numbers this participation. We had to organise *Masterchef*-level engagement, and then some.

It might be tempting to think, after the fact, that the massive groundswell of support for the survey happened organically and that Australians in their millions simply took it upon themselves to respond so enthusiastically. While I think there certainly was considerable goodwill from large sections of the population, this just wasn't the case. The public response to the postal survey and the resultant Yes victory was significantly due to organised campaigning. It wasn't coincidental to the conversation we six were having in that room that day, or the similar conversations happening in meeting rooms around the country between activists huddled over calculators and calendars. Five-point-five million Yes votes was an overwhelming, exciting, terrifying prospect, but we had an advantage. We already had the majority on our side.

•

Here's something you might be surprised to hear: during the Yes campaign, we weren't trying to convince anyone to support marriage equality. Not one person.

As much as critics of equality would like people to believe that LGBTIQ activists are 'ramming everything down our throats' (almost as much as they like using innuendo when discussing our community), we really weren't. Sure, our campaign tactics sometimes occupied public spaces, but we had done everything we could to avoid a big public campaign on this issue. We weren't interested in persuading anyone who, by the year 2017, in modern, secular Australia was still unconvinced that LGBTIQ people should have equal rights. The reality was that if someone hadn't got on board with marriage equality after decades of campaigning then we couldn't spend a single minute on them in the final hour of the campaign. We didn't have time. This approach wasn't broadcast publicly, but it ultimately underpinned the development of our campaign organising strategy.

Let's consider the Australian voting population of sixteen million people as five separate groups, distinguished and categorised by their attitudes towards marriage equality. We'll refer to them by their numbers, 1–5, as this is exactly what my colleagues and I at the Yes camp did behind the scenes of the campaign.

The 1s are huge supporters of marriage equality. They've supported equal marriage rights for years and want the government to pass the law as soon as possible. If their circumstances allow it, the 1s have probably been to at least one rally at some point over the last decade, shared a video or an article on their Facebook page, and are willing to engage in a bit of debate around the dinner table about why they believe in the issue. Most (but definitely not all!) LGBTIQ people are 1s, enthusiastically or reluctantly. 1s who aren't queer are allies. 1s step in when they hear a homophobic joke and correct their mates if they're misgendering a trans person. You have bought a book about marriage equality and are now wading with me into details of our campaign strategy – there is a very good chance, my friend, that you are a 1. Hello, I love you.

The 2s support marriage equality but don't really think about it very much. You'll find a rainbow-filter profile picture a few clicks deep on their Facebook page from when the United States achieved the reform, but they probably couldn't tell you why the feature went viral. They have gay friends but might feel a bit uncomfortable if left alone with them in case other people thought they too were gay. If asked, they'll agree that LGBTIQ people should be allowed to get married, but they're probably unlikely to get into a discussion about marriage equality with people who disagree with them. They'd absolutely vote Yes if it were a compulsory, in-person vote at the ballot box but can't be counted on to go to the effort of filling in their form and remembering to post their ballot by themselves. If you think you are maybe a 2, I'm very excited that you are reading my book. There is so much potential within you, dear 2. Perhaps, by the end of this book, you will join us 1s and continue to fight for the safety, acceptance and celebration of the LGBTIQ community. I do hope so.

The 3s are undecided. They don't think LGBTIQ people are bad or anything like that, they're just used to marriage being between a man and a woman and don't really understand why LGBTIQ people are making a big deal out of it. Then again, they did shed a little tear watching Mitch and Cam finally get married on *Modern Family* and in that moment thought, *What the heck – let love live!* They want people to be happy and do think LGBTIQ couples have legitimate relationships, but they're not sure about what a change to marriage laws might mean for them, and they kind of wish they didn't have to think about any of this at all. If you are a 3 who is simply reading this book for the rumoured sex anecdotes and parliamentary gossip, I'm sorry in advance for the things I will soon say about you.

The 4s don't agree with marriage equality. They conceptually agree that LGBTIQ people should be treated with respect but believe that homosexual relationships are fundamentally different from heterosexual relationships. When pushed in a debate, they'd be quick with public assurances that they want LGBTIQ people to live happy lives but, privately, they don't want queer people in their immediate families or social circles. 4s likely feel the need to express revulsion about same-sex kissing on television to the people around them to signal that they think being gay is gross. They don't like the idea of two men raising a child. They've seen transgender people on a BBC documentary once but really have little comprehension of transgender experiences and would probably pull their child out of school if they had a transgender teacher. If you're a 4, please reflect on how harmful your choices are.

The 5s think LGBTIQ people don't and shouldn't exist. Most 5s don't want those LGBTIQ people who are already here to die – although some definitely do – but they do think diversity in gender or sexuality is wrong, and that it's either a sick choice or a result of childhood trauma. Whichever it is, it should be stamped out. They don't believe being transgender is real (which is kind of like saying you don't believe tall people are real). 5s will go out of their way to inflict cruelty on LGBTIQ people, whether it's harassing us online, misgendering us in shops and restaurants, spreading rumours about us in the workplace or spending their time and energy keeping LGBTIQ people fearful of living our lives openly. Some 5s actually dedicate their lives to upholding discriminatory and oppressive policies against LGBTIQ people, including LGBTIQ children. Some 5s beat and kill us. If you're a 5 reading this book, thank you for the $32.99. Go fuck yourself.

Our 1s, 2s, 3s, 4s and 5s don't exist separately. In fact, people from the five cohorts can share many things in common: churches, hobbies, sports teams, workplaces, parents. A 1 can work in an office full of 3s. A 4 can go to the same gym as a 2. An immediate family can contain 1s, 3s and 5s.

The Australian public aren't usually divided into groups based on their feelings about other people's marriages, but the country was now forced to divide themselves (and vote) based on exactly that. So, to develop the strategy for a campaign that had to consider sixteen million people rather than, say, a few thousand swing voters in a dozen marginal seats, dividing people into five distinct groups was vital. And here's where our crucial advantage lay: these five groups weren't evenly split. Not even close.

Research commissioned by the Equality Campaign the month before the survey was announced confirmed the numbers we'd seen for years. Conducted by Essential Polling, they were: 61 per cent of people supported marriage equality (the 1s and 2s), 13 per cent were unsure (the 3s) and 26 per cent were opposed (the 4s and 5s). Previous polling has shown that the 5s alone remain steady at about 12 per cent of Australians, which is sad and scary – but this number is now smaller than the percentage of people under 25 who identify as LGBTIQ . . . so, sucked in 5s.

Research conducted by GLAAD, an American media monitoring and accountability organisation, in conjunction with Harris Poll found that 20 per cent of American millennials identify as LGBTIQ. When that 12 per cent feels like it's more because the 5s are shouty and cruel, hold fast to the growing number of young people embracing their capacity to bend the gender binary and love whoever they love. They will run the world one day.

There is no point bothering with the 5s. Another lesson I learnt on this campaign is that you can't convince everyone of everything, and you shouldn't try to. When you're trying to make change, if your words aren't pissing anyone off, then you're not saying anything meaningful. If your work isn't forcing someone or something to fight back against you, you're not pushing power, you're reinforcing the status quo. If you're committed to saying something, believing in something or creating anything, you will have your own 5s who seek to tear you down. If you're pleasing everyone, everywhere, you must be sitting very still in an empty room, quietly whispering, 'I am in favour of breathing.'

We'd already spent decades on the 4s. Their number was roughly 14 per cent of the population at the time of the survey, but it had been diminishing drastically over the thirteen years prior. Activists had spent so much time working with 4s; cajoling them into seeing us as human beings, helping them to understand the consequences of their prejudice and making them feel warm, forgiven and welcome when they changed their minds to become 3s or 2s. I believe that the number of 4s and 5s will continue to diminish as time goes on, but the frantic two months of a postal survey when our goal was the highest Yes percentage possible was not the time for that work.

We also had to make the decision to let go of the 3s. It was hard. Activists are addicted to 3s. We campaign because we want to change people's minds about things that matter to us and our communities and because we believe in our capacity to do so. Converting a 3 to your cause is exhilarating. It affirms your work and it builds power for your fight. It confirms your faith that people are, in fact, capable of changing for the better and that we are right to hope for this change. But, as gutting as it was to shift focus from the 3s, we knew that in this survey, we wouldn't be able to count on them. The evidence we'd collected from the United States and Ireland, as well as focus group testing here at home, showed that we'd lose swathes of the 3s to the No side. Those wobbly, treacherous 3s. Glimmering with risk and potential, all 2 million of them. They were sadly too susceptible to the fear-mongering misinformation that other side would soon sell to them.

To make a 3 vote No, all our opponents needed to do was introduce the smallest element of doubt into their minds about the proposed change. While the Yes campaign would have to paint a detailed picture of why voting Yes would create a better future for every person, the No side didn't have to accurately articulate the status quo, they could simply tease the idea that there *might* be consequences. Your life could be negatively impacted by this change. How? Who can say. It remains unclear. Nobody can know for sure. But is it worth the risk? We don't think so. Surely things are fine the way they are? It's okay to vote No.

'Let go of the 3s' is probably a bit dramatic, actually. We didn't break up with them, we just could no longer prioritise them when they refused to prioritise us, you know? We spoke to the 3s through the advertising campaign that was running to promote a Yes vote – on TV, on the radio, on the streets and online – we just couldn't focus any volunteer energy on speaking to a relatively small group of people who hadn't made up their minds yet when there were 62 per cent of people who already supported marriage equality who needed organising.

The 1s and 2s alone were enough to win the Yes vote. Based on our prediction of 65 per cent turnout for both sides, if we could get everyone who already supported marriage equality to post back a Yes vote, we'd win. It was that simple. Plus, the best way for us to increase the final Yes percentage was to make sure that we were saving our energy and resources for people who already supported us.

This kind of campaigning has a name, it's called 'get out the vote'. Get out the vote or GOTV is an American phrase that means to encourage participation in elections, because voting in the United States is voluntary. To GOTV, volunteers will help political parties contact people who are registered as voters and likely to vote for that party to tell them where their nearest polling station is, prompt them to think about their 'voting plan' (which involves asking people what time they plan to vote, how they will get there, who they will go with) and to make a verbal commitment they'll actually go do it. In Australia, there's normally no need for get out the vote efforts because voting is compulsory. Instead, election campaigns assume that the people who support them already (their 1s and 2s, if you like) will definitely vote for them, so they focus their attention on speaking to the 3s and trying to persuade them to give them their vote.

But we weren't focussing on 3s, because we had our 1s and our 2s. We had to organise two groups of people who wanted to do their bit to make marriage equality a reality and one group of people who supported the reform but couldn't be relied on to actually vote. The 2s needed to be pushed to vote, and the 1s were willing to push. It was perfect.

The 1s were the campaign's secret weapon and our heart and soul. In my experience working on marriage equality, there's not much these 1s wouldn't have done to help the Yes side win, but fortunately all they needed to do was something they'd been doing for years: talking to people about why marriage equality matters.

Peer-to-peer voter contact is by far the most impactful way to shift a vote. Writing a Facebook post in your own words is great, but even better is a direct conversation with individual people: picking up the phone and making a call, sending a text or writing an email. Political advertising on television and the radio does work but is far less effective. Demonstrating in the street is useful if you're trying to keep a story in the press, and it can be good sustenance for 1s who enjoy the community and purpose of protesting. Placement of media stories can be very powerful if the tactic is consistent and speaks to new audiences. But the most powerful way to convince someone to support an idea or take an action is to have a direct conversation with them that draws upon shared values. Fortunately, again, the LGBTIQ community and our allies were no strangers to peer-to-peer voter contact. We've been doing it for decades. It's just that we call it sharing our stories.

Systems of power can only subjugate a group of people if they have been first objectified and then vilified, and our community is gravely familiar with both. For as long as LGBTIQ people have been criminalised, medicalised, pathologised and ostracised – largely by religious influence – we've been forced to work to humanise ourselves. Every inch of progress gained by the LGBTIQ communities is fought and won on a foundation of our personal stories. For as long as we've been fighting for our safety and our freedom, our community has opened up the most intimate parts of ourselves, greeting vilification with open vulnerability in the hope that those who stand by and maintain our oppression might just see their humanity reflected in ours. Our personal stories directly push against power.

We tell of our shame and fear from when we came out, in the hope that our struggle moves people enough to want to protect us. We describe the depth and breadth of love we have for our partners to patiently show that it's no different to anyone else's. We tell people about our communities and invite people to our parades. We write to members of parliament we've never met and tell them about our families. We take our children to parliament and put them on the television. We bare the intimacies of our love to strangers to prove that our relationships are just as worthy as theirs.

Every law repealed or written. Every rule changed. Every heart won. These are the fruits of our stories. While the organisations making up the Yes campaign had been making small preparations for a national vote for close to two years, the LGBTIQ community had been preparing for this campaign forever.

For the Yes campaign's voter contact strategy, the basic theory of change was that IF people who were strong supporters of marriage equality convinced people who were soft supporters to vote Yes, THEN we'd hit 5.5 million votes and win the survey at 55 per cent. The cheapest, fastest and easiest way for our 1s to connect with our 2s to have personal, persuasive conversations was over the phone, so we needed to figure out how to connect the two groups at a scale of hundreds of thousands in a matter of days. We needed to consider the fifth point in the Democracy Center's checklist: How do we get them to hear it?

So, we built a robot.

Obviously, I didn't build a robot. As a lesbian, I can build you some IKEA furniture, but I can't build a robot. GetUp developers Darren Loasby and Bridger Rossiter built the robot. And when I say robot, I mean sophisticated piece of digital infrastructure, which GetUp called Kooragang, after a nature reserve in northern NSW close to where one of the developers lived.

Kooragang is a tool that allows any volunteer to dial a special number from their own phone and be consecutively transferred to a series of total strangers for a chat. After each conversation, the callee is let off the hook and the volunteer is prompted to input data pertaining to the phone call, which is collected, measured and analysed, before being connected to the next caller for their next chat. This is the kind of technology used by your bank, your phone company, your electricity provider and anyone who calls you to try to sell you something. Now, it had been built from the ground up by activists to organise grassroots social change. Cool, right? This tool transformed the energy and enthusiasm of keen supporters of marriage equality into targeted, strategic action that had a tangible, measurable impact.

GetUp developers also custom-built a 'turf-cutter' map tool which was used in hundreds of volunteer-led door-knocks around the country. The tool maps every street in Australia and allowed volunteers, either in groups or individually, to input a few pieces of information before it spat out customised walk lists (like optimised routes) for the group, and a way for the volunteers to mark the street as knocked and feed back to the central team the kind of conversations they had. I don't know how to build sophisticated software from scratch so my colleagues handled that part, but for the rest of us the work was still finicky. We were recruiting volunteers to the big city door-knocks or helping them set up their own in their towns and suburbs, making sure people were sent their knock packs including street maps, scripts and reporting guidelines, arranging for journalists to cover the door-knocks and pushing out social media content to recruit volunteers for the day.

All of this work done by GetUp was released under the Equality Campaign logo. An agreement between GetUp and the chairs of the Equality Campaign – Anna Brown, Alex Greenwich, Tom Snow and their campaign director, Tim Gartrell – was that GetUp would be a bit of a quiet partner during the postal survey campaign, because the Equality Campaign's brand was neutral and more likely to have impact. Once the result was announced, the Equality Campaign was going to be open about GetUp's involvement and thank us publicly for the support. Maybe you saw this happen? I certainly missed it.

For years, GetUp had organised rallies, filmed videos and held press events and co-branded with the AME, before they became the Equality Campaign, because we were campaign partners. For the survey, GetUp developers built and serviced the technology, our analysts cut the data lists, our staff supported hundreds of decentralised groups and individuals to hold phonebanks and door-knocks as well as coordinated the grassroots LGBTIQ groups across the country to do the same. We built and designed the official Yes campaign organising website, we wrote every script used by volunteers.

GetUp did all of this under the Equality Campaign logo, which we had agreed to do because we knew that the Equality Campaign simply didn't have the infrastructure to win the campaign alone and they wouldn't work with us unless we were behind the scenes. It wasn't just GetUp, either. The union movement seconded their staff members to the Equality Campaign and drove much of the volunteer organising.

I want to personally, directly thank everyone who powered the marriage equality campaign but weren't given a public thank you. GetUp members raised hundreds of thousands of dollars for marriage equality over the years, pressured dozens of MPs to support the reform, turned out in their thousands on the streets and advocated within their neighbourhoods and online communities for equality. I see you. I know exactly what you did for the LGBTIQ people of Australia. You showed me what it was to be a 1. Working for you was an honour.

We had Kooragang, now we needed to make sure it was able to connect callers to the people we needed to speak to, the audience we were targeting. Finding 1s is easy. They tend to self-identify, their hands up in the air waving to help, or sometimes they've already started organising themselves without waiting for direction. Between GetUp, the Equality Campaign (which had the former AME and A4E mailing lists), the Victorian Trades Hall

Council, the Australian Council of Trade Unions (ACTU) as well as dozens of other organisations across the country – from Rainbow Rights WA to Sunshine Coast for Equality – the Yes campaign started with a strong list of people who'd taken action on the campaign in the past. Furthermore, as soon as the survey was announced, people flocked to marriage equality organisations wanting to know how to help. Organising the 1s took time, effort and sophisticated management, but we didn't need to look to find them – they were there ready and raring.

Finding the 2s, however, took a bit of research. We needed to be very clear about who they were, because they were the 'who can give it to us?' point on the checklist, so that we could tailor our campaign to our precise audience.

Who exactly were these people who supported marriage equality, but only a little bit? How old were they? Where did they live? What was their education level or income bracket? At the beginning of trying to answer this question, data analyst Ben Raue analysed years of polling, campaign research and publicly available data from the Census and the AEC and found that almost every attribute grouping, such as income, education level and postcode had a majority Yes vote.

'There were practically no groups who had a majority No vote, just evangelical protestants and men over 65 years old,' Raue explained to me. The dominant demographic of our federal parliament. Cool stuff.

It turned out that soft supporters of marriage equality came from all walks of life. Our 2s are employed and unemployed, Catholic and non-religious, live in rural towns and metro areas, some have children, and some do not. They live in every state and territory in the country.

'Religion played a small role; education, income maybe had a small role,' Raue went on. 'But, overwhelmingly, the biggest factors were gender and age. When I built a model based on the data we'd collected, I found that gender and age were the most predictive things to the point where a young, religious woman in a very conservative, rural area or the heart of Western Sydney was still considered more likely to be a Yes voter than an old bloke who lived in a Greens seat in inner-city Melbourne.'

The model told us that soft Yes voters – our 2s – were likely to be women 35–55 and men 18–35.

We considered these two groups and their respective propensity to perform the medium-barrier ask of remembering to post a letter. We found that it didn't matter if you lived in a rural town or a city, if you were a brickie or an engineer, or what political party you voted for – if you were a man under the age of 35, you were likely to support marriage equality but were unlikely to actually get it together and post your vote. Sorry, my dudes, you just can't be trusted in this regard. Polling conducted by the Equality Campaign just after the survey's announcement, as well as research commissioned by GetUp, confirmed this, showing that only 44 per cent of men under 34 were planning to actually vote in the survey. What the fuck, you guys? (And, you know, we'd still have to see it to believe it.)

When we were looking at voting propensity, women 35–55 can generally be relied upon to post a letter. More than the young guys, in any case. But still, a quick phone call from a Yes campaign volunteer reminding her to pop the letter by the front door so she can take it to work the next morning was an extremely effective way of helping to secure votes.

The focus of our energy became clear: if we could convince enough of these young dudes who support marriage equality but who wouldn't normally go out of their way to do anything about it to post back their ballot, as well as these busy women who likely appreciated the prompt, the Yes win was in the bag. The Yes campaign accessed these anonymised phone numbers through a commercial database, which is kind of like temporarily renting a phonebook, and our strategy began to come to life.

I imagine you could be reading this and feeling a bit icky about profiling and targeting people based on their demographics, behaviours and opinions? That's understandable. We don't tend to like to think that we're being personally marketed to, but the reality is that it's been happening to us for our whole lives.

I'm a 29-year-old woman and in the internet age, the online advertising I'm served consists of teeth whitening products, pregnancy tests, skin care and period-wicking underpants. Broadly applicable to my demographic, and I did buy that teeth whitening thing once. When I'm in a shopping complex, the advertising that appeals to me (ads featuring beautiful young women doing cool things) tends to be for makeup, clothes or cosmetic treatments like laser hair removal, which actually are all things I'm inclined to spend my money on. These companies know that and are specifically targeting me and people like me.

Beyond commercial products, communicating optimised messages to a target audience is how people have sold ideas and belief systems to other people since forever. Before the internet came along, you can bet your bottom dollar that the political rallies that MPs and senators were holding in the town halls in far north Queensland sounded very different to those held by the same people in conference centres of inner Melbourne.

In terms of galvanising mass action when we're working with limited time and resources, campaigners must make sure that they're speaking directly to their target audience in a way that's clear, relevant and tested for success so that they're not pissing resources up against the wall (especially since those resources are pooled together from ordinary people who are trying to make change).

We crunched the last of the numbers: the task at hand was to mobilise thousands of eager volunteers to join a phonebank and have persuasive conversations with hundreds of thousands of men under 35 and women under 55 about posting back a Yes vote. Working backwards from 5.5 million Yes votes, we estimated how many volunteers we could recruit and the conversion rates of our volunteers' conversations, and we set a target: we needed to make half a million calls and send 100,000 personal text messages. There was a matter of weeks to make this happen, and the consequence of losing would be lasting and profound.

We had pivoted. We dropped our target-centred campaign without so much as a second glance. It was time to do what is rarely done in Australia – it was time to get out the vote.

•

Two days after Tim Gartrell, Patrick Batchelor, Wil Stracke and my GetUp colleagues and I modelled the data, analysed the research, crunched the numbers and laid preliminary plans for what would become the centrally organised Yes campaign, I spoke to a room full of LGBTIQ activists and community members. I was sitting on a panel at the NSW Teachers Federation with Andrew Bragg, former president of the Liberal party and newly appointed head of Liberals and Nationals for Yes, along with Alex Greenwich, Tiernan Brady, Penny Sharpe from the NSW Labor party, Jenny Leong from the NSW Greens and Lauren Foy from the NSW Gay and Lesbian Rights Lobby.

Gathered in the room were the most dedicated 1s from the decade prior – community members who had many more years' experience working on the campaign than I did – who had come to the meeting to contribute to and be consulted on the campaign. *Their* Yes campaign. When it was my turn to speak, I explained the plan to organise hundreds of phonebanks to get out the vote. I told them we needed to make 500,000 calls and, if we worked as hard as we could, we could hope for a result of about 55 per cent because of the disadvantages against us in the process. I told them that if we were to get Yes over the line, we'd need to scale up our campaign like never before. The activists were invigorated, asking important questions about how the phone tool worked, whether the phonebooks would use scripts, how we got to the number 55 per cent. It was a community consultation, after all.

The following day, I got in trouble. A senior member of the Equality Campaign called the National Director of GetUp requesting that he chastise me (I should remind you that by this stage I'd been a campaign director at GetUp for several years and wasn't some sort of naughty junior on their first day). Apparently, I'd spoken out of turn and I shouldn't have revealed specific targets because 'no one wants to know how the sausage is made'. The concern was that the media might report on the numbers the Yes campaign were planning around and this was a problem because . . . then it wouldn't be a secret? I'm not sure. The media did report those numbers, and I imagine it showed people how ambitious and organised we were.

Here's the thing: I do think people want to know how the sausage is made. I think people deserve to know what they're being fed, and how and why it was put together that way. I think affected communities and people supporting campaigns with their time and money should know how their resources are being used, and if the risk is that the media might share that information wide then so be it – why is this information secret?

My personal theory of change as an activist hinges on communicating ideas to people. I am a communicator. I dedicate much of my time to speaking at events, on television, on the radio and at conferences. I tweet constantly, write articles and wrote this book in my spare time, alongside my full-time job. I believe IF more people understand the power they have to make change and the reasons why they must, THEN we will act together to create a fairer, kinder and safer society.

I don't think progressive social justice movements should replicate the secrecy and paternalism of institutions of traditional power. We are not a bank. We are not the police force. We are not the church.

I want to tell people in detail how we ran this campaign. I want people who donated to the Yes campaign to know that their donation powered the most effective, lean, cutting-edge tactics in a way that treated their donation with the utmost respect. I want to be scrutinised for using data to target specific audiences of people, or choosing the campaign goal of the highest Yes percentage rather than, for instance, the most equally spread-out Yes results. Those are the decisions my colleagues and I made, from the corner we were backed into, and those decisions should be transparent to the communities they're made on behalf of. If I make a wrong decision, which I have plenty of times as a campaigner, I want to be held to account because that's part of being a leader.

It is not up to salaried campaigners to hide tips and tricks and expertise from the general public, lest those tools are used against us. That's how dictatorships run. Some campaigners like me were at the helm of this particular campaign, but this movement is not mine and this information is not ours – it belongs to every person with a stake in this fight and, honestly, everyone else too. This is part of why I'm writing this book, so anyone who wants to can learn from some of my work.

The direct tension between my openness about campaign strategy and the Equality Campaign's eagerness to pretend the campaign was happy, organic conversations happening around the proverbial kitchen table continued for months, and probably to this day as this book lives and breathes . . . I'm still not sorry.

6
The Letters

When you're planning a campaign, it's useful to plot its crescendo around a 'moment'. A moment is a pillar to scaffold plans around, and it ideally happens without a campaigner's intervention. It might be the opening of a new store in a chain you're calling upon to treat its workers fairly, or the grand final of a sporting code you're pushing to make interventions in its players' treatment of women. It could be the anniversary of a high-profile death, or the Annual International Day of Whatever.

Sometimes you don't have the luxury of seeing your moment coming; it could be the day a news story breaks, and you don't have more than a couple of hours to launch a response. Or, it could be something you've been planning around for years, like an election or the release of a report that reviews the policy reform you've been campaigning for. Whatever it is, building your campaign around an external moment means that you're taking advantage of energy that something else has created for you. You don't have to drum up interest from scratch because on that day, the media and the community are already talking about it. Your campaign's moment, or series of moments, creates energy and urgency, and you'll need both for your theory of change.

The problem with our postal survey campaign was that it wasn't going to have a moment. Ballots were going to slop into people's letterboxes in dribs and drabs over the course of a few weeks and their arrival would be a wholly private affair. Shuffling junk mail out of the way to dig up your electricity bill reminder and a letter from the ABS as you get home from work thinking about what you've got in the fridge for dinner is hardly an inspiring exercise in collective action. A photograph of Dave in his underpants, standing gormlessly at the letterbox first thing on a Saturday morning as the sprinklers come on just doesn't stand up against the other iconic images of change-making history.

After crunching our numbers and devising a skeleton strategy, the GOTV crack-team of Wil Stracke, Tim Gartrell, Patrick Batchelor, Henny Smith, Kajute O'Riordan, Ben Raue and I turned to the issue that the survey was moment-less. It was a real problem. For a second, I found myself wishing for a ballot-box style vote like Tony Abbott's proposed plebiscite that my colleagues and I had taken down in 2016. At least that steaming pile of shit had a moment.

If there wasn't a moment for us to use, we'd need to create one. We considered announcing a National Day of Action and plastering that specific date on every advertising space we could find. We toyed with the idea of putting on big Yes events in capital cities, with bands playing and kids' rides and food trucks, where people would hand in their ballots to get entry. But this was logistically complex and we didn't have much time to organise events of this size. It also just wasn't very practical in terms of paper and pens and securing the ballots. Too big, too hard. We just needed people to tick the form and put the thing in the letterbox; any other asks, such as attending an event, felt like we were creating unnecessary barriers to participation.

Stracke's experience with postal votes in the union movement meant she had first-hand experience about how things could play out: she told us the majority of total ballots returned in a postal vote would arrive back within the first week. If people didn't post their form back straight away, chances were it was destined to be buried under bills in the 'to do' pile, or stuck to the fridge and forgotten about, or left to gather muck at the bottom of a handbag only to be found weeks later when you realise your salad has leaked balsamic vinegar throughout your bag. These scenarios are purely imaginary, of course, for I am extremely good at 'life administration' and have never let my driver's licence expire or had my power cut off. Not me.

We knew that the campaign needed to motivate people to send back their ballot as soon as possible because every day that went by made the task harder. We realised that we couldn't wait to create a national campaign moment once everyone in Australia had received their letters because we needed each individual to vote almost immediately. The only moment the majority of the voting population of Australia would share would be getting the letter in their letterbox. That had to be the moment. Or rather, that had to be 16 million individual, mini-moments.

We needed to engineer people's experience of the postal survey such that receiving their ballot in the post was the pre-climax of their journey; that finding that letter in their letterbox triggered immediate action, immediate participation in the process and an immediate return of the form. The moment had to be powerful enough to trigger a high-barrier action like posting a letter, it had to create the urgency that would see the action taken as soon as possible and this message had to reach as many people as possible in the short time we had before ballots arrived. The only way we could do this was with words.

When I say that Lube Mobile will come to you, what do you feel compelled to do? If your house is on fire and you're trying to escape, what are the steps you need to follow? Do you remember? What if you're trying to loosen a really tight tap and can't remember which way to turn it, or you want to know whether you can have a glass of shiraz after a pint of lager?

If you grew up in Australia, you'd likely call 13 13 32; stop, drop and roll; turn lefty loosey, righty tighty; and remember that it's beer before wine and you'll feel fine! Or is it wine before beer and you're in the clear? I can never get that one quite right.

These are funny little sayings that may or may not have burrowed their way into your subconscious, and the way they work is quite obvious: with these obvious phrases, you might recognise how their assembly interacts with our cognition to spark thoughts in our minds, but even when it's not as blatant as 'lefty loosey, righty tighty', the words that we use affect us in unconscious ways. Every single little one of them, particularly when they're placed beside other words that have been deliberately and carefully chosen.

Words can do big things. They can give something a name, condemning it with the associated meaning. A word can ascribe history to a moment, a character trait to an object and an agenda to an accident. Words can be sacred, words can be banned. Nothing exists outside of language and so we craft the world around us with the stories we tell each other and ourselves. Words define, create and destroy. Words can start a revolution.

Consider the words 'marriage equality', instead of 'gay marriage' or 'same-sex marriage'. The former speaks to a shared value, rather than a minority experience (and is more accurate, too). They won't start a revolution, but they did power a movement.

From the very beginning, we made a deliberate decision to call people 'Yes voters', because the name gave people the identity of the action we wanted them to take. We weren't marriage equality supporters. We were Yes voters.

And then we chose the words that would create our moment. We repeated these words in every email, every post on social media, every comment given to journalists and every public speaking engagement anyone within the marriage equality sector had. Within days, the mantra was repeated by radio hosts, celebrities, community leaders and supportive politicians. It was all over my Facebook newsfeed and Twitter timeline from activists, allies and ordinary Yes voters. In the first week of the campaign alone, before ballots had even arrived, Yes campaign volunteers (our wonderful 1s) across five states of the country made more than 50,000 calls to men under 35 and women under 55 to ask them to commit to our mantra: *Post your Yes the day you receive it!*

It's a truly incredible experience to see the words of a campaign take a life of their own. Just like, 'unnecessary, expensive, harmful' took flight in 2016 when we were fighting the original plebiscite, when I heard those words spoken by people who didn't receive briefing notes or a messaging document, but who adopted the words because they had become so tied to the topic it felt like our message was cutting through. *Post your Yes the day you receive it! Post your Yes the day you receive it!*

Those were the words splashed across posters and jumping out from online advertising. Those words were spray-painted on a bed sheet and hung from a bridge over the M5. They were chalked on footpaths. That was the commitment that people across the country were making to complete strangers who'd called them on behalf of the Yes campaign.

And it absolutely saved our arses.

For years, I was the only person at GetUp working on the marriage equality campaign. People would help, now and then, but the campaign didn't have a dedicated team. When the High Court ruled that the survey was going ahead, GetUp pulled together a group of about fifteen staff to help run our part of the Yes campaign. Some were already on staff, working on other campaign teams (GetUp has four: environmental justice, human rights, economic fairness and democratic integrity) or service teams (a media team, a design team, an organising team, a digital team, a data team, an operations team). Because the temporary team was new, one of the big meeting rooms in the GetUp office was converted into a 'war room' (despite my insistence it must be called the love room). We dragged in whiteboards, video-call equipment and the boxes of campaign collateral we already had on hand. It was in this room we held compulsory 1pm dance parties to one song per day and spent what felt like years sitting around the long desk strewn with laptop chargers and crockery that hadn't quite made it back to the kitchen yet.

It was Tuesday, 12 September in the war room (love room) when GetUp's head of campaigns Emily Mulligan suddenly cried out, 'Oh my God. My friend just received their survey!'

The rest of us were in utter disbelief. The forms weren't meant to arrive until 19 September! That was the date communicated by the ABS and reaffirmed by every media outlet, every insider and every instruction we had from the government. Not 12 September – 19 September!

We started to panic. We weren't ready for the forms to arrive! There was so much left to do – we had organisers to hire, collateral to print and distribute, events in universities, media appearances and one more week of our volunteers making direct contact with voters. This was too soon!

Within the hour, news of surveys arriving began to pop up all over the place. A text message from an activist let me know they'd been delivered to a street outside of Ballarat. A friend living in a suburb north of Perth posted a picture to Facebook. Someone on Twitter living in a row of townhouses in inner-city Sydney got theirs too. There was no pattern or logic to their arrival. The only thing we knew for certain was that they were here, and they were early.

My team and I began barking orders at each other: someone needed to quickly update our volunteer call scripts, we should put something on social media – no wait, let's check what the Equality Campaign are doing – has anyone called Lane Sainty from BuzzFeed yet?

Our worry wasn't about looking silly because we had the date wrong; we were worried because our campaign moments were here a week before we had expected them. Had we done enough to make sure people returned their ballots straight away? Would enough Yes voters know to post their Yes the day they received it?

As I waited to see whether our get-out-the-vote slogan would yield the results we needed, I took small comfort in knowing that even though the Yes campaign were caught with our pants down (and not in a sexy way) so too were the No campaign.

•

Allow me to introduce our opponents. The No campaign was a well-funded, well-oiled machine. The main organisation of the No side was the Coalition for Marriage, which was similar to the Equality Campaign in that it was a newly formed group incorporating existing organisations that came together. The official Coalition for Marriage was made up of Australian organisations, several large churches and a few notorious overseas groups, including the US-based World Congress of Families, which is classified as a hate group by the Southern Poverty Law Center. At the helm were anti-LGBTIQ groups the Marriage Alliance, a lobby group that made a TV ad in 2015 that claimed children raised by lesbian mothers were more likely to be rapists than children raised by different-sex parents, and the ACL, whose campaign videos have titles like 'Is transgenderism real?'. Official campaign videos from the Coalition for Marriage included claims that same-sex marriage would lead to the eradication of the terms 'mother' and 'father'.

The Coalition for Marriage had far, far fewer volunteers than we did, but what they lacked in volunteer power they made up for with expert communication staff and massive spends on powerful advertising. The rumour mill has it that hundreds of thousands of dollars poured in to Australia's No campaign from evangelical Christian churches and anti-LGBTIQ groups in the United States. We know the Anglican Archdiocese of Sydney – under the direction of Archbishop Glenn Davies gave the No campaign $1 million. Financial documents seen by Fairfax Media report that the ACL had a tax-exempt income between 2007–2017 of over $20 million. Donations to GetUp, by the way, aren't tax deductible.

The Coalition for Marriage's organisational structure was broadly unclear to me, with many spokespeople and seemingly few publicly identifiable staff, which was very different to the Equality Campaign, where staff who came on board for even a few months were publicly proud of their contribution, and rightly so. You might remember a lot of women as spokespeople for the No campaign, yet the four directors of the Coalition for Marriage were all men: Lyle Shelton, Damian Wyld, Kieran Walton and Michael Stead. Aside from Shelton, these men were rarely heard speaking by anyone other than their own supporters, leaving the women to front up to the public. I doubt this is cowardice and I suspect many men from the anti-marriage equality camp would have loved the limelight. I imagine this was a careful decision: they knew that men are statistically more likely to oppose equal marriage rights, and so women were the audience they needed to win over. Let's go through a few familiar faces of the No campaign who, to my understanding, worked at senior-to-executive levels of the Coalition for Marriage.

You might have heard of Wendy Francis, who in 2010 said, 'Children in homosexual relationships [their parents, not the children themselves] are subject to emotional abuse. Legitimising gay marriage is like legalising child abuse' and then went on to become the Queensland Director of the ACL. Wendy is the woman who first described the children of same-sex couples as another Stolen Generation, a vile blow to both the LGBTIQ people and Aboriginal and Torres Strait Islander communities.

There's Karina Okotel, federal vice president of the Liberal party and spokesperson for the Coalition for Marriage, who once stood in front of the Australian National Press Club and spun the well-worn lie that a Jewish school in the United Kingdom was facing closure for teaching their students that marriage is between a man and a woman, despite the claim being unequivocally false.

Kirralie Smith, another spokesperson for the Coalition for Marriage, in a Facebook video repeated claims from a United States anti-equality campaigner that the 'end game' of marriage equality 'was to redefine marriage so that polygamy and eventually paedophilia would become legal'.

Who could forget Sophie York, a former Liberal candidate, who suggested LGBTIQ people simply use the word 'garriage' instead of advocating for our rights under the law (why didn't we think of that?) and described supporters of marriage equality as a 'pagan caliphate'.

Before becoming the face of Coalition for Marriage TV ads during the survey, Marijke Rancie or 'Political Posting Mumma' on Facebook (carefully styled on the United States social media figure 'Activist Mommy') posted low-tech, selfie-videos announcing that schools are bringing dildos into the classroom as part of the Safe Schools program (they're not). She told her YouTube channel that marriage equality 'actually meant transgender marriage' and that it would become 'discriminatory not to teach homosexual sex acts at school'.

But we mustn't forget about the men. There's president of the Australian Marriage Forum and No campaign spokesperson David van Gend, a family doctor in Toowoomba who told a radio interviewer that homosexuality is 'a disordered form of behaviour', who described a young gay male patient he saw in his general practice as experiencing the 'depressing and degrading effect of his compulsive sexual encounters', and who wrote an entire anti-marriage equality book called *Stealing From a Child: The injustice of 'marriage equality'*. Another Liberal, van Gend unsuccessfully ran for LNP Liberal Senate preselection in 2012.

Then there's Lyle Shelton, who I've dealt with personally many times. Lyle is masterful with words and, from what I can glean, truly believes his own spin. In my experience, he approaches his work attacking LGBTIQ rights as tactical sparring. Like a debate or a boxing match, I perceive Lyle to engage with the fight for marriage equality as if each side has started on equal footing, should play by the rules of 'civility' and 'respect', and then should have a friendly handshake at the end. I imagine him going to bed at night after arguing with people on Twitter about LGBTIQ justice thinking, *That was fun*. When we speak in person, he is relentlessly friendly to me, and I can only conclude it's because for him, it's just a game. No harm, no foul. I never let on during the survey campaign, but each time I speak with him on television or the radio I am left feeling like I might have an anxiety attack. I always cry.

In a casual reference to the Holocaust, Lyle Shelton wrote that moves by politicians to progress on marriage equality were causing 'unthinkable things to happen, just as unthinkable things happened in Germany in the 1930s'. Six million Jewish people were murdered by the Nazi German government. Gay men were persecuted, arrested in their tens of thousands and sent to concentration camps to be castrated and often murdered. In an interview I did with Lyle on SBS's *The Feed*, he doubled-down on the idea first raised by Wendy Francis that marriage equality would create another Stolen Generation.

Until the Australian Marriage Law survey, many of the hurtful, hateful words from these people only reached the 5s on the groups' email lists or people like me who were working closely on the decades-long marriage equality campaign. When the survey was announced, these words were given a platform and a legitimacy. They were suddenly given a stage, a spotlight and a microphone. Their lies and their slander were legitimised as part of 'the debate'.

Research commissioned by the *Guardian* from media analysts Isentia Research and Insights found that Lyle Shelton received more media coverage than Alex Greenwich, Tiernan Brady and myself combined. BuzzFeed News commissioned similar research from media monitoring and analysis company Streem and found that in the week ballots arrived in people's letterboxes – the week of the crucial *Post your Yes the day you receive it* moments – the No campaign featured in the media four times as much as the Yes campaign. Analyst group Ebiquity found that in the first two weeks of the survey, the No campaign had spent five times more on advertising than the Yes campaign.

Words mean things. Words do things. And when one side's words are in the media four times more than the other side's words, the effect on the public consciousness cannot be ignored.

Human rights lawyer and anti-racism activist Nyadol Nyuon explained it well on *Q&A*:

We know, as people in minority groups, that people who want to hate you don't just want to sit on their television stations and call you stuff. They want those hate ideas made into public policy, and that results in real life consequences for minority groups.

Nyuon, of course, is right. Words aren't just words, they're seeds. The postal survey meant hateful words were propagated far and wide, sewn as poison in our soils, strangling the roots of our communities. The words that became acceptable in public discourse during the survey campaign will provide fertile ground for future attacks against the LGBTIQ community.

The Coalition for Marriage were very good at using words. During the survey campaign, the aforementioned spokespeople toned their anti-LGBTIQ rhetoric right down and constructed arguments using simple, vague language. The No campaign's slogans 'You can say no' and 'It's okay to vote no' are very clever collections of words. Without naming any reason for opposing equality or articulating a vision for what a No victory would achieve, the simple phrases tell a powerful neurolinguistic story. 'You can say no' is the whispered resistance between dissenters of a conformist regime. The slogan speaks directly to people and empowers them with a feeling of quiet defiance. You – yes, you – can say no.

'It's okay to vote no' implies that voting Yes is something irrationally and unfairly enforced upon people. It creates the idea that Yes is a socially enforced norm and those who want to vote No are socially shamed for doing so. We say to new mothers, 'It's okay to bottle-feed.' We say to men, 'It's okay to talk about your feelings.' We say to our colleagues, 'It's okay to take a sick day.' These words describe voting No as a small but brave stand against the norm. They position Yes as the poisonous Kool-Aid.

The spokespeople for the No campaign repeated the assertion that it was 'okay' to actively participate in the attempted oppression of LGBTIQ people. It's no big deal. You're not homophobic, it's okay. You're not doing anything cruel or unnecessary, you're not getting involved in something that has absolutely no effect on you. It's okay. You can say no.

I'm an activist and I'm committed to an open democracy. I believe people deserve the right to exercise their power as citizens to engage in our democratic processes and the equal opportunity to organise around issues. I'm mad for activism and deeply believe in the redistribution of power away from a small pocket of politicians and interest groups to the ordinary people who wish to participate in the decisions made about their lives. I also fundamentally believe that it's not okay to vote No.

It's not okay to cast a vote on the lives of your fellow citizens. It's not okay to think of yourself as superior to LGBTIQ people and thereby allow yourself to dictate their dignity. African American writer James Baldwin wrote, 'We can disagree and still love each other unless your disagreement is rooted in my oppression and denial of my humanity and right to exist.' Equal marriage rights for LGBTIQ people is a different struggle to the systemic racism Baldwin was describing, but the sentiment applies. It's not okay to decide against simply staying quiet and abstaining from the exercise in favour of actively trying to prevent the legislation of human rights. Voting No is not a right, but a cruel, opportunistic exercise in the oppression of your neighbour. Voting No might not make you a homophobe, but it does make you mean.

'You can say no' was a deftly smart slogan from the Coalition for Marriage, but the action it demanded was simply ticking the box – only the first step to getting your vote counted – and that's where they made their mistake. When ballots began to arrive across the country a week earlier than anyone expected, countless people took to social media sharing photos of themselves with their forms re-sealed and ready for the post box with the words, 'Post your Yes the day you receive it!'

Although there were many other factors at play, I am confident that our carefully chosen and oft-repeated mantra had a role in 9.2 million ballots being returned in the first week of the survey – that's 57.5 per cent of the entire voting population. (Remember, we were aiming for an overall turnout of 65 per cent!) The figure was massive, but it was no wonder: in the same period of time, 2569 volunteers signed up to join the phonebanks, who then made 295,998 calls – spending 2132 hours connecting with potential Yes voters over the phone and asking them to commit to posting their Yes vote the day they received it. The day before the first official numbers were released, a ReachTell poll of 5000 people commissioned by *Sky News* indicated that of the people who had returned their ballot, 64 per cent of them had voted yes. It was also my 29th birthday and these numbers were the best present I could have possibly received.

•

It sounds ridiculous, but I think I tricked myself into thinking that the postal survey wouldn't happen to me. Reviewing data, projecting numbers and devising communications plans behind closed doors had perhaps lulled me into the comfort of thinking that the survey was something that would simply happen to the other people we'd set out to organise. I was in the control room, so it couldn't affect me.

If you knew me personally, you'd know that I'm meticulously organised with my time (though please don't confuse that with being punctual, which I am not). I like to know what my calendar looks like weeks ahead of schedule, blocking out the hours in the day in the most efficient way. If you knew me personally, you'd know I suffer from emetophobia, a severe and sometimes incapacitating fear of vomit. I've spewed only once in my life, as a young child. If you knew me personally, you'd know that even the thought of hallucinogenic drugs, being pregnant or doing some sort of off-the-grid trek through the wilderness stresses me out.

What I'm trying to convey here is that I very much like to be in control of myself: my body, my actions, my environment and my life. You could probably extend this character trait to explain why I don't like being told what to do – so much so that even though I don't want to ever get married I spent five years of my life absolutely incensed that the government told me I wasn't allowed to. I suspect this desire to feel in control and the fact that I was working directly on the campaign was what gave me a subconscious fantasy that I was somehow personally exempt from having to participate.

I'd been doing nothing but talking about the postal survey for weeks, and I must have known deep down that I'd have to vote, but nothing could have emotionally prepared me for the feeling of nauseous shock when that little letter arrived at my house.

It was a Friday night and, as per usual, I'd come home late from work. My housemate Leah greeted me at the front door both solemn and tender.

'Guess what arrived today,' she winced, as if I'd received a conscription letter for war.

I gingerly walked down my hallway and there, on my dining table, sat three envelopes, one with my name on it. How dare this thing enter my house, I thought to myself. How dare this thing sit on my dining table. This was the table where my friends gathered around vegetable feasts to celebrate graduations, interstate visitors and birthdays. This is where I sit to Skype my far-away family members and to write out my shopping lists on the weekend. This is where I held hands with a woman by candlelight and said, 'I love you.'

The flimsy denial of the reality that I, too, would get a survey ballot began crashing down, and I was furious. Who gave the government any right to put a survey on my worth on my dining table, in my house, with my name on it as if it belongs to me or I want it?

After what was probably only a few minutes, I managed to pick up my survey, turning it over in my hands. Leah pottered around in the kitchen, giving me space. I gave the envelope a shake so that my name and address fell squarely in place behind its plastic film window. Leah had already opened her envelope and the letter inside was splayed out across the table. The folds in the paper thrust to the ceiling the question: Should the law be changed to allow same-sex couples to marry?

Those words might seem fairly neutral, but I'm here to tell you that, linguistically speaking, they were absolutely rigged against the Yes side. In fact, had this question not been written (or at least overseen) by Attorney-General George Brandis, a supporter of marriage equality, I would've been certain it was crafted to suppress Yes votes. It was so wordy, so procedural, so individualistic. It wasn't as complex as the one put to the Irish people, asking whether to add to the Constitution that 'marriage may be contracted in accordance with law by two persons without distinction as to their sex' (yikes) but it could also have been feasibly used in a push-poll by the No campaign.

In 2016, AME commissioned research by Crosby Textor, a political communications firm, that tested respondents' reactions to various questions on marriage equality in preparation for a

potential plebiscite. It showed that any mention of technical legislative process, for instance 'amend the Marriage Act', 'put a bill
to parliament' or indeed 'a change in the law' saw Yes responses
drop a whopping 8 per cent. At the outset of the campaign we
were hoping to secure a 55 per cent Yes vote; an overly technical
question that disadvantaged us by 8 per cent would have dashed
our hope of success.

Then there's the word 'allow', which immediately assigns
authority to the individual person casting their vote. Had the
question been written, for instance, 'Should same-sex couples be
able to get married?' it wouldn't have created a hierarchy between
the same-sex couple mentioned and the person voting in the same
way that invoking the word 'allow' does. To allow is to grant a
request, to relinquish a previously held rule, to take pity. Only the
powerful can allow, while the marginalised must plead.

And then there was the phrase 'same-sex couples', which
explicitly excludes some intersex people, some transgender people
and couples where one or both people have a non-binary gender.

In August 2016, as part of consultations with the LGBTIQ
community on the original, defeated plebiscite legislation, Attorney-
General George Brandis assured me and other marriage equality
advocates that the use of the term 'same-sex couples' wasn't
designed to exclude gender diverse and intersex couples, and that
the final legislation would use the inclusive language 'two people'
instead. During this same meeting, the attorney-general called us
all 'fools!' after we each confirmed our unconditional opposition
to the plebiscite, which I found to be a strange way to engage
with the stakeholders of an issue. It turned out that Brandis was
telling the truth and the marriage equality bill put to parliament
used the words 'two people', but that didn't stop his parliamentary
colleagues from using the wording of the survey question to

attempt to defeat the bill on its second reading, the stage at which parliament debates a bill before it formally passes into law.

The wording of the question really mattered. Before we knew that the official question would be the one initially proposed in 2016, I wrote out a list of ideal questions we could put to the nation:

Is it likely that marriage equality will negatively impact your life?

Do you enjoy voting on strangers' ability to fulfil their dreams?

Is your relationship more precious than your cousin's?

You feel icky when two men kiss; is this enough to deny people their rights?

Are you jealous of our joyful pride parades and multiple, multiple orgasms?

I was just spitballing, to be honest, but I think some of them could have really popped.

Although we were served the words that Australia would vote on, we created the words that defined our campaign.

Thalia Zepatos is the former Director of Research and Messaging at Freedom to Marry, an organisation dedicated to delivering marriage equality nationally across the United States. In 2016, she explained in a podcast interview with *Berkley News*, 'There's kind of a campaign truism, which is whoever defines the campaign will win it. If you get people to say this is what this is really about, you're setting the terms of the debate.'

Zepatos' work, among many other things, involved moving the discourse surrounding same-sex marriage in the United States from the ideas of rights and benefits to the values of love and commitment. In Australia, we had the same task, but the words that worked in America weren't necessarily going to work for us.

Take, for instance, the name of the organisation that Zepatos worked for: Freedom to Marry. It's a gorgeous name for an organisation in the United States. Freedom is a fundamental value of their nation, and many people understand individual liberty as a cornerstone of their society. In the US, the concept of freedom is far more important, or culturally resonant, than equality.

The same word isn't as powerful down under. Maybe because Australia is still technically a colony owned by the imperialist British Crown, maybe because we don't actually have a bill of rights that sets out any specific freedoms at all, maybe because our public systems of health and education are so strong and our sense of community so precious that the concept of individualism seems largely flawed from the outset. Australians don't love freedom the way Americans love freedom, but we do love fairness. Fairness backs the underdog and gives a mate a leg up. The 'fair go' is Australia's answer to the US's 'American dream', except while their dream tells a story of a rise to riches, Australia's more understated fair go seeks to simply live comfortably without too much fuss. It describes a relationship between people as a community, not as individuals. Fairness spoke to the heart of Australian values.

This was more than a tummy compass thing. Ours was a data-driven campaign, remember, so we performed significant message-testing research, and fairness far out-performed any other value or concept.

But back in my home, at my dining room table, nothing felt fair. It felt like every moment of homophobia I'd experienced in the past decade and every bad word I'd heard about LGBTIQ people was inside that envelope, bristling to get out.

I didn't expect my ballot to get under my skin the way it did, but I found myself walking to my bedroom and blu-tacking the envelope to my wall. It sat there at eye-level right next to my door, opposite my bed. I burst into tears. Beyond the injustice of the government bypassing parliament to hold the survey, beneath the worry for the wellbeing of my community and the fury that their lives would be put to a popular vote, that envelope felt like the most shameful, activist-guilt ridden personal failure. I didn't stop this from happening.

I cried the same distraught tears I'd cried two years earlier when we had been so close to a free vote, and then Tony Abbott announced this policy. They were the same hot, angry tears that would spill over my clenched jaw in the coming weeks in the desperation of the campaign. They were the same gasping, afraid tears I cried the week earlier when I marched with 50,000 people through the streets of Sydney for the Yes vote, full of hope and celebration.

'Don't they understand,' I'd silently sobbed under my sunglasses, marching in step with the excited, determined crowd of enthusiastic 1s. I had told myself, 'We aren't going to win this. This isn't going to be okay.'

I was right, sort of. We eventually passed marriage equality – but for the next two months, we weren't going to be okay.

1
We Are Family

In late 2012, two young women shuffled into a brightly lit TV studio in Ultimo, hiding a secret under their jumpers. Just like every Monday night for the prior decade, members of a studio audience had gathered to ask questions to a panel of politicians, journalists and community leaders on everyone's favourite talk show, the ABC's *Q&A*.

I don't often watch it live: the program doesn't conclude until 10.35pm, which is well past my bedtime, and I don't like to work myself up into a situation where I'm shouting at my laptop livestream before going down for the night.

Maya Newell and Charlotte Mars listened quietly to the panel, biding their time, until moments before it was Maya's turn to ask a question, when they slid off their jumpers, revealing t-shirts printed with a URL and the words '*Gayby Baby* the movie'. Visibly branded clothing is strictly forbidden by the show. So too is any form of political stunt, but over the years the *Q&A* audience has been blessed with unfurled banners, chanting students and a shoe pelted at a sitting prime minister, so it's fair to say #qanda rules are made to be broken. Measured and charismatic, Maya addressed the panel.

'Thanks to the Labor government, I can now have the names of both my mothers listed on my birth certificate,' she began, the mention of two mothers pricking the ears of the nation. Here was one of those hypothetical kids we'd all heard of, right there in the flesh. 'I've been interviewing many kids from same-sex families over a year for a documentary I'm making,' Maya continued, the prohibited URL for the film crinkled into her t-shirt but still legible for the millions watching at home.

'To them, their parents' right to marry means a lot. It would mean the world. It means they might not get teased in the playground as much. It means their families would be validated. It means they'd be on equal footing as their friends,' she went on as the camera flitted to the panel to catch Penny Wong, Labor senator and lesbian mother, gently smiling. 'My question to the panel is: have you ever thought of kids in same-sex families? And how do you think a change in the Marriage Act might change their lives?' she finished.

Maya's articulate question was first met with a convoluted answer from right-wing columnist Janet Albrechtsen, who said, 'I don't think that children of gay relationships are going to win out in a debate where those who oppose it get hectored for having that view.' Albrechtsen presumably would prefer it if oppressed peoples simply asked for their rights patiently and politely until those exerting the oppression had an independent change of heart. Except that's not how change happens, Janet.

The second person to answer the question was the leader of the National party at the time, Barnaby Joyce. Joyce let out the trademark sigh of exasperation he exhales every time he's asked a question he doesn't have an answer to, as if reporting back to the people he's paid to serve is a pain in his backside. He reiterated his opposition to same-sex marriage in a long-winded answer that managed to dodge the question.

'I think that many politicians use the excuse that marriage is about children in their arguments, and they say that we need a mother and a father,' Maya levelled with Joyce. 'Everyone seems to have an opinion about our families, like you, Barnaby. But it doesn't seem that anybody's asking the kids what they feel.

Because we're proof of our parents' successful relationships. My mums have been together for twenty-seven years, why is their relationship worth any less than anyone else's?'

The audience burst into rapturous applause. This young woman had put her face to the unnamed children of same-sex parents, and given them a voice through her own. As the applause died down Senator Penny Wong looked up at Maya and said, 'We will achieve marriage equality, even if that takes a while. What we shouldn't have in the meantime is people using their views on marriage to have a go at our families – I think that is unacceptable. I think the worst aspect of the marriage debate has been the people who chose to make this about parenting.'

I agree with Senator Wong. For as long as LGBTIQ people have pushed for our right to marry the person we love, opponents have retaliated by saying marriage equality would deny children a biological mother and father and that this would harm the child. Apparently it hasn't mattered that children aren't actually conceived by the exchange of vows at a wedding or that LGBTIQ couples already raise children, like Maya, because when it comes to LGBTIQ rights, homophobic and transphobic creeps are always there with a counter-argument about protecting children.

The idea that LGBTIQ people are preying on children to hurt or convert them has long been the most abhorrent, devastatingly effective weapon used by groups seeking to discriminate against us and make our lives hell. And it's textbook moral panic: a social phenomenon engineered by powerful institutions to isolate a group of people as 'deviants' and paint their existence as threatening to the safety of vulnerable members of society.

Prominent psychologist Professor Gregory M. Herek, who's known for his work researching social prejudice towards sexual minorities, explains that, 'Members of disliked minority groups are often stereotyped as representing a danger to the majority's most vulnerable members. For example, Jews in the Middle Ages were accused of murdering Christian babies in ritual sacrifices. Black men in the United States were often lynched after being falsely accused of raping White women.' Children are frequently used at the epicentre of moral panic engineering, because they're small and precious and societies are usually designed with their protection in mind. People panic when they're told children might be at risk.

In the twentieth and twenty-first centuries, Christian faith churches are the key peddlers of the myth that LGBTIQ people are a danger to children, and not because it says so in their bible (because it doesn't). The vast majority of victims of child sex abuse perpetrated by members of the clergy are boys. As such the church has historically defended rape allegations levelled at priests by suggesting that homosexuals have infiltrated the clergy and that it is actually homosexuals, not priests themselves with their unquestioned power, forced celibacy, access to children and God complexes, who are responsible for priests' heinous crimes. In 2002, the Vatican – an organisation responsible for child sexual abuse on an industrial scale – directly responded to ground-breaking, harrowing revelations of the widespread perpetration and cover-up of child abuse by priests by declaring that gay men should not be ordained.

It shouldn't need to be said, but to be very, very clear: there is absolutely no correlation between sexuality and crimes against children. The same cannot be said of priests.

This moral panic and social fear is why in 1973 Macquarie University told Penny Short she was 'medically unfit' to become a teacher and revoked her scholarship after they found a poem she had written about being a lesbian. It's why around the same time openly gay teachers like George Weir were explicitly refused work by the Queensland education department. It's why, during the push to decriminalise sex between adult men in NSW in the 1980s – which at the time could land a man in jail for fourteen years – Nationals MP Jon Brewer argued that parliament 'should do all they can to prevent homosexuality penetrating our schools or being inflicted on the community generally.'

It's why in 1985 the Queensland government under Joh Bjelke-Petersen made it illegal for 'perverts, deviants, child molesters and drug users' to purchase alcohol or enter licensed premises, a law blatantly written to target LGBTIQ people. The law was even referred to as the 'homosexual deviance' law and allowed bar owners to quite literally call the police if LGBTIQ people came into their pub in the name of child protection. Children don't tend to frequent bars, but invoking child protection to introduce new ways to discriminate against LGBTIQ worked a charm for Bjelke-Petersen. It's why in 2019 religious schools unashamedly lobbied the federal parliament to uphold their ability to refuse and terminate employment of LGBTIQ teachers. Yes, that's right – religious schools are still allowed to do this.

It's the fear in the bellies of parents in the 1990s when they watched the Grim Reaper plough down a tiny child with a bowling ball in a crude metaphor for HIV in one of Australia's most controversial public health advertisement ever televised. Like hurting children is a sport for gay men with HIV. It's the same irrational worry that Jim Wallace, former Managing Director of the ACL, invoked when he said, 'adoption is about children, not adults. About finding mothers and fathers for children tragically denied them – not children for adults,' and 'children are not pets to be had at a whim,' implying that LGBTIQ couples might treat a child like an animal. It's the same prejudice that prevented LGBTIQ people from being able to adopt children in every state and territory of Australia until April 2018.

It's the reason the delightful documentary film *Gayby Baby*, made by Maya Newell, who spoke so bravely from the *Q&A* audience, was briefly banned from being shown in high schools by the NSW education department in 2015. Despite the film being a wholesome, PG-rated documentary about kids and their families, NSW member of parliament and prominent homophobe Reverend Fred Nile warned it's 'quite dangerous to promote homosexuality in schools to children'.

It's the reason why the innocuous Safe Schools resource for teachers, which was introduced under former Prime Minister Tony Abbott, approved by his education ministry and independently reviewed to be entirely age-appropriate, was completely shredded in the Murdoch press before having its funding cut. There is no sane, evidence-based reason for the destruction and removal of the Safe Schools anti-bullying program. It was destroyed as the result of deliberately engineered anti-LGBTIQ hysteria hiding beneath the façade of protecting children.

In early 2016, Queensland Nationals MP George Christensen described Safe Schools as akin to 'the grooming of a paedophile'. Christensen warned, 'This material is putting children at risk of being sexualised at an early age', a classic homophobic dog whistle that taps into a bigoted fear designed by people who hate me and my community.

The implication that LGBTIQ people, particularly gay men, are seeking to harm children is weaponised in campaigns to uphold discriminatory policies in Australia, but it's also used in the form of personal attacks. Notably, in 2002, Liberal Senator Bill Heffernan accused High Court Justice Michael Kirby of using

Commonwealth cars to procure young men for sex, claiming that Justice Kirby is therefore unfit to judge criminal trials involving paedophilia. Justice Kirby slammed the accusation as homophobic, false and absurd. A week later, Bill Heffernan resigned as parliamentary secretary after it was revealed the documents Heffernan had presented as evidence of the claim had been forged and the story entirely made up. Ask yourself: would those false accusations and the confected association to an inability to sentence paedophile criminals have made it to the front page of the paper if they were levelled against a straight man or woman?

Even the suggestion of fictional LGBTIQ characters in proximity to children can spark outrage. Consider the reactions of conservatives at the suggestion that puppets enjoyed by children may be perceived by adults to be gay. Bert and Ernie. TinkyWinky from the Teletubbies. It's vicious, pervasive and completely hysterical.

LGBTIQ people aren't immune from the pervasiveness of this cultural narrative. From childhood we're inundated with homophobia and transphobia, subtle and explicit, through the conversations we hear, the reactions we observe, the stories we're told and the people we see – or don't see – in our communities. The understanding that LGBTIQ people are unnatural, sinful, sick and a danger to children is ingrained within most of us, which is why it is too difficult for some people to even admit to themselves that they're gay or bisexual or transgender. With the love of our families and friends, support from our schools and workplaces, and outreach from the wider LGBTIQ community, some of us can unlearn some or all of that internalised homophobia and transphobia, but you shouldn't underestimate the power of these deeply ingrained ideas.

Award-winning comedian, writer and beloved lesbian Hannah Gadsby explained to Fairfax media in 2017 that 'You don't get to avoid your cultural upbringing.' Speaking about growing up in the 1990s in Tasmania, which didn't decriminalise homosexuality until 1997, she said, 'When I heard people saying that homosexuality should be legalised, I remember thinking "But how do you stop paedophiles?" I subscribed to the idea that homosexuals are subhuman.'

I'm proud and grateful to be queer. It really is the best, so if you feel like you've got it in you, I really recommend you let it shine. I advocate for the rights of LGBTIQ people because I know that we deserve equal rights under the law and in society, but Gadsby's words resonate with me. Not because I carry that internalised homophobia with me daily but because there are moments in my life where that unconscious bias against LGBTIQ people pops into my head, as if someone stitched it in there when I was too young to notice and I haven't been able to fully unpick it, even though I know it's completely untrue.

A week after the postal survey was first announced, I wrote a tweet and then deleted it. It was book week, one of my absolute favourite times of the year, when kids across Australia dress up as a character from a book (or AFL player, which I suppose is acceptable too) for a school assembly. I love all my friends' kids so much, and I get so much joy from seeing them dressed up for their parades. I'd written, 'Please subscribe me to your kids' book week pics!' but I deleted it immediately because I was afraid that trolls on Twitter, who were all over my account because of the campaign, would call me a paedophile. I was scared Miranda Devine would quote me in one of her columns to scare people into voting No.

This is not an ordinary thought to pop into your head when thinking about how proud you are of your friends' cute kids and how book week costumes get progressively more hilarious as the interpretation of what is and isn't a book character is allowed greater artistic license. This is internalised homophobia.

Nowadays, even though anti-LGBTIQ campaigners consistently imply that LGBTIQ people will hurt and convert kids, they do so while speaking in code. It's no longer acceptable to mainstream Australia to suggest something so prejudiced and nasty about LGBTIQ people – unless you are Miranda Devine, who was quite happy to call marriage equality campaigners like me 'rainbow fascists' in News Corp columns, likening us to ISIS militants and Nazis who systematically groomed children. Where homophobes and transphobes of yesteryear would unashamedly decry that the queers were preying on children to hurt and convert them, modern-day bigots instead use the words: 'Kids deserve a mum and a dad'.

Kids deserve a mum and a dad. Do they? Why? Many of us probably had a mum and a dad – I did for a while there. I don't think the presence of one mum and one dad in a child's life is any more than just that. Kids need affection, attention and affirmation. Kids need safety and sustenance. Having a mum and a dad isn't a compulsory precursor for a child to play, learn and grow.

The idea that a mum and a dad is essential for optimum child raising is also some archaic gender bullshit that suggests all people belong in one of two categories, and that the members of these groups have an identical set of traits. It says that all women are the same and, as such, all mothers are the same. All men have the same attributes therefore every father brings identical attributes to the table. If children are not raised with 1 x man-parent and 1 x lady-parent how will they possibly know how to be nurturing *and* how to kick a ball? In this model of binary thinking, no man can replace the attentive care and gentle nurture of a mother, and no woman can . . . what are fathers meant to do again? Take you fishing? Show you how to throw a punch? Be emotionally distant? I am being silly, obviously. So diverse are fathers that they boast the full gambit of human character traits. As do mothers. Because parents are people and there are more than two identical types of people.

When I hear the phrase 'kids deserve a mum and a dad' you may as well be saying to me, 'kids deserve a Sagittarius and a Leo'. I don't believe in horoscopes and I don't believe that you can classify the entire human population into two categories, let alone use that quackery as a justification for the state to intervene in how families raise their children.

'Kids deserve a mum and a dad' is only ever weaponised by anti-LGBTIQ campaigners. There aren't multi-million-dollar lobby groups seeking to prevent kids living with their grandparents or trying to remove children from single parents.

Breaking down the prescriptive structure of a nuclear family so that other kinds of families can exist doesn't mean that the nuclear family is wrong or bad. Families with two parents of the opposite sex will always be the most common type of family, because the majority of people are heterosexual, often make babies together, and in our Western society that's the way we tend to organise our families. And that's great. But when these families flourish and thrive – as they often do – it's not simply because of the gender of their parents, it's because of the tireless dedication of these parents to creating the best lives for their children and for their partner. The work that goes into supporting each other, caring for each other and strengthening bonds as they grow together; that's what makes a family. Love makes a family.

And yet, research confirms time and time again that the most effective message to persuade people who are undecided on marriage equality is 'kids deserve a mum and a dad'. And as the No campaign shouted it from the rooftops, the consequences of their words were felt hard on the ground.

'We knew the focus of any plebiscite would be on us and our families,' lesbian mother of three Jac Tomlins told me. 'The [ACL] and their counterparts had long since given up trying to persuade people that two consenting adults shouldn't be able to marry – they'd lost those arguments. So, they focussed on other things, like children with same-sex parents. Those are my children and that felt very direct and very personal.'

Jac tells me that 'your first and most fundamental instinct as a parent is to protect your child'. I believe her, because I can imagine it, and because I saw it in the eyes of every queer parent I spoke to during the survey. Jenny Joy, a lesbian mother living in Castlemaine, Victoria, told me that the survey campaign coincided with their first months with their tiny baby, a child they had always dreamed of. She told me that her partner felt very scared at night when she was up breastfeeding him, like every noise was an angry man coming in to take the baby away or hurt them in some way. 'I fell into a pretty deep depression,' Jenny said. 'It was a deeply traumatising, frightening time for our family.'

Susan, a lesbian mother who lives in Barnaby Joyce's regional electorate, told me of her frustration that No campaigners blustered about keeping children safe and their best interests, because she believes this actually demonstrated a reckless disregard for the wellbeing of her kids. She said, 'It was really tough for me as an adult to see how hated we are by some . . . I can't begin to imagine how it feels for a child.' Reflecting on the No campaign's attacks on same-sex parent families, Susan explained that 'while our little one is too young to ever remember this time, our impressionable ten-year-old has been exposed to lies and outrageous claims made by the No campaign, that were even aired during children's programs. He's heard himself described as disadvantaged, and a "stolen generation". His parents – my partner and I – have been called everything from paedophiles, perverts, and sick scum to inadequate and causing him long-term damage.'

When campaigners sought to stop the plebiscite from going ahead, it wasn't just to prevent LGBTIQ people suffering through the process; it was to prevent an entire generation of people hearing anti-LGBTIQ messages as if those words and the ideas that underpin them were totally acceptable. We knew, 'kids deserve a mum and a dad' would be weaponised, because for the No campaign it communicated their main frame: children.

A frame is a concept that evokes ideas, images and values. For example, when we think of a hospital, we might think of sickness and injury, imagine medicines and diagnostic equipment, picture doctors and nurses hurrying about with clipboards and feel a sense of emergency. We already have those associations in our head, and when we group them all together, this is a frame. In campaigning, we apply frames to our communication of issues so that the ideas, images and values that are automatically attached to the frame are evoked. For example, to use a hospital frame we might say, 'the Great Barrier Reef is on life support', or 'let's nurse the economy back to health'. Communications expert Anat Shenker-Osorio says that progressives should use a 'car' frame for the economy, because we should encourage people to think about the economy as a man-made thing we build and steer rather than an autonomous living body.

The way an issue is framed will change the way it's perceived by your campaign's target audience, even though the facts of the issue remain the same. It's a deliberate packaging of information in a way that reinforces the idea you're trying to communicate. Put simply, it's spin. But it's not simple; good campaigners will make sure the way they're framing their issue has been tested, measured and adapted so that it yields the very best results from their audiences. From that work, campaigners know which frames work well for their issue, and which frames don't.

When it came to the issue of equal marriage rights, the No campaign relied on a 'children' frame rather than, say, a 'sin' frame. I can't imagine saying homosexuals are abominations destined for hell and evoking fire and brimstone imagery testing well in the No campaign's focus groups. Somebody should tell Israel Folau. Reminding ordinary Australians that your anti-LGBTIQ hatred stems from contested interpretations of scripture just doesn't resonate quite so well. When we think about children, however, we might think about families or classrooms, we might picture little smiling faces, grazed knees, pigtails, school uniforms. We (hopefully?) feel fondness and a sense of protectiveness. Saying 'kids deserve a mum and a dad' simultaneously evokes this frame and taps in to generations of engineered social panic regarding LGBTIQ people and children. The message is incredibly persuasive for 3s and 4s (and, sometimes, even 2s).

Just like the No campaign used frames that worked for their goals, the Yes campaign also stuck to frames that worked best for us. This brings us to the third item on the Democracy Center's campaign checklist. We have established what we want (to get the highest Yes vote possible) and who can give it to us (the 1s getting out the vote of the 2s, who are dudes 18–35 and ladies 35–55), and how we will speak to them (over the phone). The penultimate point is, 'What do they need to hear?' (messages)

Different frames work for different audiences, and so as campaigners we had to be deliberate about how we were framing voting Yes for the specific audience we were targeting (the 2s).

Here are some frames I used during my work on the campaign depending on who I was speaking to. Think about how these words work for you, how they might work for someone undecided on marriage equality or how an opponent might hear them.

Frame: Rights

Message: *LGBTIQ people should have equal rights under the law.*

Frame: Activism

Message: *This is the civil rights fight of a generation; together we can make history.*

Frame: Families (modern)

Message: *Every family is different, but we all deserve equality.*

Frame: Families (conservative)

Message: *Marriage creates stability for families, the building blocks of our communities.*

Frame: Love

Message: *Love is love, and everyone should be able to marry who they love.*

Frame: Fairness

Message: *Your neighbour shouldn't be treated differently to you. It's only fair to treat all loving couples the same.*

Frame: Commitment

Message: *The institution of marriage is the foundation of our society – every couple should be able to commit to each other.*

Just as different frames work for different audiences, different frames can also favour one side of an argument. Let's use a non-marriage example. In a debate about energy policy, the fossil fuel lobby might apply the frame 'reliability' to the issue of whether to build a new coal mine. They use messages like, 'coal fire power is dependable, every hour of the day' or 'people can rely on coal to keep the lights on' and other iterations of apocalyptically reckless spin. Campaigners trying to end the burning of fossil fuels would know that making their argument for renewable industries using the frame of 'reliability' isn't useful or compelling for their target audience (even though renewable energy technologies are very reliable). They would know that 'reliability' is a frame that favours their opponents, the coal lobby, so instead of trying to argue that renewable energy is actually *more* reliable, they'd package their message in a different frame that they know is compelling for their audience. Maybe they'd talk about creating employment opportunities in future-facing industries (a 'jobs' frame) or clean, breathable air ('health').

When we pick up our opponent's frame and make our case through it, not only do we disadvantage our own message but we can inadvertently bolster their argument. George Lakoff, who many call the Father of Framing, explains in 'Framing 101: How To Take Back Public Discourse' that when you're arguing against an active opponent, 'Do not use their language. Their language picks out a frame – and it won't be the frame you want.' People campaigning for renewable energy don't want to be banging on about reliability when doing so actually makes their audience less willing to move away from coal.

Tiernan Brady from the Equality Campaign explains frames by asking you to imagine a campaign as a game of football, where it's up to campaigners to create the pitch they want to play on. Our opponents will try to force us to play in their frame, because they know that that's where they have an advantage.

Your opponents want you to fight in their frame, so they'll often describe an issue in a way that's so controversial that it acts like a rabbit hole: a provocative distraction to jump into, wasting our time and covering us with dirt. It's our job as campaigners to avoid this and stick to our steady ground.

The temptation to argue with your opponents in a frame they've built that is offensive or incorrect is often irresistible, but it's something I'm getting much better at. Except for sometimes on Twitter when it's very important that @egg_loser_75 is taught a lesson.

Campaigners for marriage equality had to learn how to not be pulled into the rabbit holes of arguing about whether marriage equality would increase the spread of HIV (no), create a new generation of children who turn gay because they saw two women kissing (not how sexuality works) or destroy the very fabric of our society (queers love fabric?). If we agreed to talk about the issue of equal marriage rights within a bad frame, by arguing that our opponent's assertions were false/stupid/insulting, we weren't helping our cause – we were actively hindering it. Negating your opponent's frame ('it's not true that kids deserve a mum and a dad!') actually strengthens it. It's kind of like that serpent in Greek mythology where cutting off one head means three grow in its place – fighting it just makes it stronger.

Resisting the urge to argue with your opponents about the false, harmful things they say is hard! During the survey, Liberal politician Kevin Andrews casually explained to a stunned *Sky News* host, 'Optimally, you've got the input from both [a mother and a father] and the children brought up in those circumstances are, as a cohort, better off than those who are not . . . whether it's in terms of health outcomes, mental health, physical health, whether it's in terms of employment prospects, in terms of how this is generated from one generation to another, the social science evidence is overwhelmingly in one direction in this regard.'

His remarks were in a similar vein to anti-LGBTIQ rights group the Marriage Alliance's press release proclaiming '[c]ontinuing to raise children in a same-sex parent household amounts to child abuse,' and quoted a study in the journal *Depression Research and Treatment*.

Except neither Andrews nor the Marriage Alliance's claims have a shred of evidence or truth. I went online to read the study referred to by the Marriage Alliance for myself but in its place is now a retraction, a statement of concern and apology from the publisher.

While it felt vital in both instances, and every other, to correct the record, the best way for us to counter the message that 'kids need a mum and a dad' is to reject that frame, not try to disprove it. Especially not with a slew of facts.

Facts bounce off frames, and academic studies rarely shift strongly held, emotionally charged personal beliefs. Most people will deliberately (and actually more intensely) push back on information that directly threatens their core beliefs, because as Anat Shenker-Osorio says, 'people like to say they'll "believe it when they see it" but actually, people only see it when they believe it'.

I haven't been able to count the number of published studies into whether the children of LGBTIQ parents are okay or not. I've seen studies that measure the adult child's educational achievements, income, any problems with relationships, criminal behaviour or illicit drug use. Studies that go back and forth trying to prove or disprove the hypothesis that queer people aren't good enough parents. This research is maybe useful in terms of science (but is it? really?), but it's not useful for campaigning. And if we as campaigners continue a vicious circle of trying to prove or disprove whether LGBTIQ people are good parents, we continue to reinforce the *legitimacy of the question*. We are locked into our opponent's frame.

You simply cannot persuade an anti-vaxxer that vaccines do not cause autism by throwing studies at them; they are impervious. But now we're talking about vaccinations and autism and I have repeated the words 'vaccinations and autism' and the neurolinguistic connection between those words is once again reinforced. (By the way, the hysterical anti-vaccination conspiracy movement is now listed by the World Health Organisation as one of the greatest health risks to humanity. If people want to talk about parents wilfully putting their kids' lives in danger, setting them up for a life of poorer health outcomes and risking the safety of their entire communities, they best start with anti-vaxxers.)

The same rule applies when prosecuting a defamation case. Yes, the judiciary may find that what was said or written is indeed defamatory, but the fuss of going through the legal battle tends to cement the defamatory statement into people's minds. For example, what do you think of when I say Chris Kenny?

Marriage equality campaigners did try to disprove the assertion that kids need a dude parent and a lady parent in the earlier years of the campaign, but by the time the survey came around many of us had learnt to resist being drawn into that fight. Instead of talking about 'children' we shifted the frame and made it about 'modern families'. When the No campaign wanted us to talk about whether or not kids with same-sex parents are or are not going to harm children, we talked about celebrating all kinds of families, and how wonderful it is when families are welcoming. We told stories of how every family is unique and just as good as the next one. We explained that every family, no matter what it looked like, deserved respect and dignity. We told the country that it's love that makes a family.

The idea that it's love, not opposite-sex parents, that makes a family is powerful and persuasive. Just ask then-Opposition Leader Bill Shorten.

'For my personal journey,' he told me on a sunny morning in Sydney, 'when I formed a blended family in 2009, I realised that there's a lot of judgements about families and that, in fact, narrow 1950s definitions of families cause more hurt than they cause positivity.'

Bill Shorten was a vocal supporter of marriage equality before many of his Labor colleagues, despite being part of the right faction heavily influenced by the Catholic church and the SDA union. When the LGBTIQ community pleaded with the Labor party to block plebiscite legislation, not only did he listen to us and vote against the bill, he also went out of his way to make the case for a fair process for our community. During the survey, he campaigned passionately for a Yes vote. Bill Shorten is not perfect, but I will always be deeply grateful for his allyship and work to achieve marriage equality.

'Families come in all shapes and sizes,' Shorten went on. 'I felt that when there was a judgement about LGBTI Australians, the judgement was about more than just them; it was a sort of a very narrow definition of what it takes to raise a family.'

The No campaign loved talking about parenting almost as much as they loved to talk about LGBTIQ anti-bullying program Safe Schools. Both are messages within the same, powerful frame of 'children'.

Research conducted for the Yes campaign showed that linking marriage equality to Safe Schools saw potential Yes votes haemorrhage, even though there wasn't and isn't any connection between the two. But after two years of bellowed hysteria from the Murdoch press and some within the government that culminated in an unceremonious scrapping of the tiny funding it enjoyed, being drawn into debates about Safe Schools was unstrategic at best and irresponsible at worst. Our goal was to get the highest Yes vote, our audience were the 2s, and to allow the discussion to become about Safe Schools meant that our 2s could become 3s or even 4s.

Benjamin Law, who wrote a Quarterly Essay on the media destruction of the Safe Schools program, agrees:

> By the time the postal survey came around, I could see how discussing Safe Schools would become an absolute liability for the Yes campaign. You saw the No campaign weaponise Safe Schools, because they knew community sentiment was overwhelmingly in support of same-sex marriage. It hurts to say, but they'd won the debate over Safe Schools by then and knew it. All they needed to do was mobilise community fear.

Ben was right, as he usually is. It took extraordinary, miserable discipline to not talk about Safe Schools during the campaign. Many times I wanted to scream the truth – that Safe Schools saves lives and harms nobody – but was instead forced to smile and give some sort of saccharine line about how marriage was a precious day everyone dreamt of, in a refusal to engage in the issue of marriage equality through the No campaign's frame. That was my job, and I was at work.

I'll give you an example, one of many. When the No campaign released their first advertisement saying that marriage equality would mean that 'radical sex education' and gender fluidity would become 'widespread and compulsory' in schools, the campaign faced a tough moment. As experienced activists, we knew that trying to quell fears with facts didn't work, that jumping into our opponents' frame was unstrategic, and that negating their argument would only strengthen its linguistic association in people's minds. We had the focus-group data that showed discussion of the Safe Schools would bleed votes to the No side.

I wrote, filmed and edited GetUp's response to the No campaign's ad in the course of a day. It's still online, if you want to watch it. The video is a white, suburban, heterosexual mum getting her young daughter and son ready for school in their big, expensive house.

Research conducted by Thalia Zepatos using test cases from the United States told us that the best way to tackle fear and misinformation from anti-LGBTIQ campaigners is to simulate a 'reassuring hand on the shoulder'. The way to alleviate concern surrounding children (or anything, but we're talking about a quintessential moral panic here) is to treat that concern as understandable, and then explain why it's not true, and re-connect on shared values. The solution is not to mock concerned parents' fears, as many comedians immediately did – I love satire, but it's just not strategic during a get-out-the-vote effort when faced with a fear-mongering opposition. The solution is to treat those fears with respect and gently reassure your audience using a more effective campaign frame, in our instance, fairness.

Our final item on the Democracy Center checklist is 'Who do they need to hear it from?' (messengers), and for our men under 35 and our women 35–55, the messengers that were most effective were, you guessed it, straight people. Not just vaguely straight people, super straight people. Parents and grandparents in domestic, gendered family settings. With this in mind when we responded to the No campaign's TV ad choc-full of lies about Safe Schools, the suburban mother in my ad spoke a carefully crafted message to the camera:

In this house, we believe in fairness and kindness, and we're teaching our kids that everyone deserves to be treated with respect.

There's a lot of misinformation out there at the moment, linking marriage equality to what these two will learn at school. It's just not true. Marriage equality has nothing to do with the curriculum.

Kids learn their values at home, from their parents. That's why we'll vote Yes in the upcoming marriage equality survey. And if they ask, we'll tell them it's about fairness and kindness.

GetUp and the Equality Campaign focus group tested this ad, and it was a powerful antidote to the No campaign's ad. I love effective campaigning, but making the ad and seeing the positive focus group response was a strange kind of torture. During the attacks on the Safe Schools campaign of 2016, I organised community meetings, spoke at rallies, wrote opinion pieces and spoke out time and time again about how the program likely saved young lives, and that all young people would benefit from a bit of education about LGBTIQ inclusion. I couldn't say any of that during the survey, because of the votes.

But in not saying it, because of the votes, my colleagues and I allowed the misinformation about Safe Schools to spread unchallenged in the consciousness of our society, particularly within the immigrant, working class and religious communities targeted by the No campaign. Those fears live on, long past the survey, and I suspect will make it incredibly difficult for any state or federal government to re-introduce the program in its current form.

Many LGBTIQ activists and community members were critical of the decision from those of us at the forefront of the campaign to sidestep debates about Safe Schools. I understand that.

Rodney Croome, then director of just.equal, publicly criticised public-facing Yes campaigners for this strategy, which seemed a peculiar choice as he has all of our phone numbers. Writing on behalf of just.equal in Junkee, he said '[W]e are proposing the Yes campaign pivot towards countering the No side's negative campaign. It's vital principals and teachers have the chance to explain publicly that the priority for schools is dealing with the prejudice faced by LGBTI students, not "radical sex education", and that the Marriage Act doesn't affect this.' Croome continued, 'We know some people will say, "Don't chase every nonsense argument down a rabbit hole." That's true, but some No case talking points are more compelling than others and demand a reasoned response.'

Within the specific parameters of the postal survey campaign, I disagree with Croome. I think that when every adult in the country gets a vote on the most significant cultural reform in a decade that will impact the lives of LGBTIQ people for generations to come, it's negligent to engage in arguments that demonstrably lose Yes votes. I believe that a No victory, or a very close call, would have been catastrophic and that we simply did not have the time or resources to do everything all at once. However, I include Croome's criticism here because though I disagree with it, he raises a valid point that is worth your consideration. Perhaps you will disagree with my position, and that's okay too. It's certainly not a position I held or a decision I made without significant inner turmoil, which I will tell you about a little later when everything begins to fall apart.

•

If you ask someone why they support marriage equality, chances are they'll give you an answer that explains their values. They value their own marriage and the happiness it's brought. They value fairness, kindness, self-determination, a non-interventionist state, family stability; whatever their previously held values were, they now see marriage equality as aligning with them. When the No campaign came at us with coded language seeking to spark fear in the minds of people who've been conditioned to worry about LGBTIQ people's proximity to children, we didn't argue whether kids deserve a mum or dad or not. We spoke to the values of children and parents, uncles and aunts, godmothers and grandads, and reminded them that it's love that binds us, not the configuration of our households and our genitals.

When I say we, I do mean the Yes campaign and I do mean marriage equality activists across the country, who repeated these messages over and over. But the people who really made millions of Australians understand it, believe it and vote Yes for it were the parents and children in rainbow families. These loving parents and their precious children taught Australia to be more open-minded and open-hearted, whether in the national press or at the gates of the school drop-off. For this and more, I want to pay tribute to the LGBTIQ parents, who in the face of smears and prejudice against them fought for their families' rights.

I pay tribute to Felicity and Sarah Marlowe who campaigned for marriage rights and empowered rainbow families across Victoria to access support and advocate for their rights, all while raising the kind of kids who can proudly stand in front of their school assembly, thank their teachers and friends for supporting them through the survey and reassure them that even if it's a No vote, they know they are loved.

To Jason and Adrian Tuazon-McCheyne, who raised their son, Ruben, while spending their evenings and weekends pushing for marriage equality in every way they could think of: through an organisation, as a political party, in the courts and in the media. Ruben's spent his whole life learning that injustice isn't someone else's problem to solve and that it's up to all of us to do what we can to help.

To Kerryn and Jackie Stricker-Phelps who welcomed their daughter, Gabrielle, into their lives as a nine-year-old foster child. Kerryn and Jackie fought for years to become Gabi's legal mothers and finally became the first non-relative same-sex couple to adopt in NSW. As a family, they've been campaigning for marriage equality all her life with them.

To Tom Snow and Brooke Horne, who brought their passion, patience and leadership to the Yes campaign and supported dozens of campaigners to be the best they could be: skills that make them amazing fathers to their three beautiful young children.

To Shelley Argent, who has poured years of her time, tens of thousands of her own dollars and all of her heart into fighting for equality not just for her gay son, but for every LGBTIQ person who needs a mum in their corner.

I pay tribute to the parents across the country I'll never know, who know more about persuading people to support marriage equality than I ever will. Who model that love makes a family every day, leading by example to everyone around them. Who've spent the entire lives of their children protecting them from a homophobic and transphobic society and empowering them to be strong and forgiving. Who advocate for their children every day and, in doing so, teach their entire communities to be kinder, fairer and more understanding. They're not just raising their families, they're raising the country.

•

My friend Miriam, a queer parent in a blended family, once sat across from me in a Sydney cafe and told me and my audio recorder about what it's like raising a rainbow family in Australia.

The fight we are forced to put up just to make the basics of these families happen – our names on certificates, our zygotes on ice, our hearts on the outside – and all of the extra hoops we jump through to prove that we've got the right to do so: this is what no parent should ever be required to give their precious kid-loving energy to. We should be at the park with our smalls. We should be showing them how to make slime out of borax. We should be making investments in the webbing of our communities so that we can hold each other up when the state fails to. When our schools fail to. When the courts fail to. We should be busy learning our kids how to care for their elders, because it's gonna be their job. We should be enjoying the magic that is being there for a child, that is guiding them into this complex headfuck of a world, that is holding their trust and growing their goodness. Whether you made a child for yourself to love, or whether you fall in love with one who'd already gotten here, I see you pushing shit uphill, queer parents. And I see you falling all over yourself not to let any of it get in your kids' hair.

The No campaign and their friends in parliament and the press pretend that they preach that kids deserve a mum and a dad because they care about children and want what's best for them. As if LGBTIQ parents haven't fought tooth and nail to create the precious families they have and would do everything they can to protect them. These people feign concern for hypothetical, future children from rainbow families, but it's the same cohort of people who unashamedly bully and victimise children who are LGBTIQ themselves. Children who suffer extraordinary rates of mental illness. Children who are discovering who they are or who they will one day love and learning that the world is hostile towards them.

Children who may emotionally isolate themselves from their parents out of shame. Children who daily hear the word 'gay' as a slur.

Anti-LGBTIQ campaigners will happily screech, 'Won't somebody think of the children?' Why won't they think of these children?

8
Won't Somebody Think of the Children?

Please note that this chapter discusses suicide.

When I was a teenager, my dad would often tell me that no parent should have to bury their child. It just wasn't natural, he'd say emphatically in his fading British accent, flicking a cigarette onto the pavement outside his little Fremantle terrace. People aren't built to be capable of it, he'd explain.

On reflection, it was a strange thing for my dad to have repeated to me. But he was a man of many mantras. Whenever he would pull out his wallet at the shop counter, he would open it to show strangers a picture of me and my sisters telling them, 'I'm the richest man in the world'. When I used to try to trick him into giving me money, or that there would be parents at a party, he'd laugh and say, 'Sally, my name's Rugg, not mug!' 'A parent should never bury their child' became one of those mantras he liked to repeat.

Fortunately, for everyone, really, he never had to bury any of his children. A few weeks after my 21st birthday, my dad killed himself.

The morning of the day his body was found, I woke up and I knew he was dead. I don't believe in a sixth sense, and I am not a spiritual person, but the feeling was present and clear. I just knew. I got ready for work and headed to the city, pushing the thought out of my mind. I didn't want it to be true, so I was choosing to ignore it. I wouldn't let myself call him to check, because if the phone rang out that would confirm it, and I wasn't ready. I wanted the day to unfold as it would, and I needed to brace myself for when everything came crashing down. That afternoon, my dad's girlfriend called me and said she was worried – she hadn't heard from him in a few days. It was then that I left work early to go to his house, expecting to be the one to find his body. 'I have to go,' I told my bewildered team, 'I think my dad is dead.'

As I drove down Stirling Highway in silence, my phone started to ring. It was my mum, who'd been separated from him for a decade by then. She rang again and again, and I ignored the calls because I didn't want to hear the words. I was driving to his Fremantle terrace because I didn't want anyone else to see what I thought I was going to see – I felt that it had to be me. The calls from Mum kept coming so I texted, 'driving'. We hadn't spoken that day, but she simply replied, 'Don't go to his house.'

The rest of the story spans from that moment until now, and it will continue forever. But the story didn't start with a death: the tragedy was not his death but his life. A life of darkness, of nightmares, of addiction and of hopelessness. Dad used to also often say, 'Put on my gravestone "I told you I was sick!"' His story isn't just his now – it's mine, too. It's written differently, but it's in my bones. It's retold in my trauma. It's etched into sobs of grief, gasps of panic and silent moments of despair. His, mine, my sisters'.

As a young person, the suicide of a parent is a destabilising grief. I found myself in shock, overwhelmed with both guilt and the childlike anger of abandonment. I was furious that the man who was supposedly meant to protect my young sisters and me from this kind of harm had hurt us so much. His death brought to the surface 21 years of the unique neglect felt by a child let down by a caregiver.

Nobody ever wants to bury their parents, but I think there was truth to his mantra; that parents should never have to bury their child. I'm not yet a parent, but I am an aunt and I have kids in my life who are like family. Losing a parent to suicide was, is, deeply painful. Losing a child to suicide would be incomprehensible agony.

Even in the abstract, it's difficult to fit the two concepts together; people usually end their lives because they're unable to imagine a future for themselves without unbearable pain and suffering. Children shouldn't ever feel this way. Kids shouldn't experience that kind of sorrow and hopelessness. But as we know, they far too frequently do.

•

On Tuesday, 22 November 2016, Wayne Unsworth returned from work to his property in north-west Queensland with the expectation he'd find his thirteen-year-old grandson skipping school again.

Tyrone had just taken a month off from Year 7 to recover after being brutally attacked by a group of kids the year above him. They'd beaten him with a fence paling, breaking his jaw and putting him in hospital for emergency surgery. It was the most violent attack he'd suffered from the bullies he saw daily at Aspley State High School, but by no means the first.

Tyrone had been due back at school the previous day, but he instead went fishing with his family friend Gypsie-Lee Edwards Kennard. While they were out, Tyrone suddenly broke down in uncontrollable tears and told Gypsie-Lee that 'The kids at school keep telling me to go kill myself.'

Wayne, Tyrone's grandfather, couldn't see him when he got in the door. Heading through the house, Wayne checked the child's empty bedroom before wandering out the back. There he found his grandson's body hanging, lifeless. At thirteen years old, Tyrone Unsworth had ended his life.

In his short time, Tyrone, who was Aboriginal, developed close and loyal friendships. He played rugby league, had an Instagram account and fabulous taste in music. He was also violently, relentlessly bullied for being gay. In the days after his death, Tyrone's mother Amanda told the media, 'the boys always picked on him, calling him gay-boy, faggot, fairy; it was a constant thing from Year Five.'

Tyrone's death broke the nation's heart. The news of his suicide sent shockwaves across the country, and for weeks it felt like everywhere I looked I saw this boy's beautiful golden curls and cheeky smile. Most of us had never heard his name until we were mourning his loss, and yet our grief was profound.

LGBTIQ communities and Aboriginal communities across the country organised candlelight vigils in Tyrone's name, to honour his memory and to come together in our sorrow. My friends and I cried in Sydney's Taylor Square and held each other close. Our tears fell for Tyrone and for the others we've lost before, those who we couldn't save. We wept for the people whose pain became insurmountable, for those where any light at the end of the tunnel had flickered out. We mourned every child taken from us before they could blossom and bloom. Losing people to suicide is our collective trauma – we know it too well because it happens far too often.

Tyrone could have been our brother, our classmate, our nephew. To many in the LGBTIQ community, Tyrone felt like our son. He probably didn't know it yet, but he was our family, too. We'd lost a child.

And within many of us there was a whisper . . . Tyrone could have been you. He could have been me. *Remember when you felt that afraid*, it whispered. Dark, painful memories were pulled to the fore and we cried by candlelight for Tyrone, for each other, for our past selves who've lived to stand with community today.

Before he died, Tyrone posted to Instagram: 'If I just killed myself, would anyone cry, would anyone care? I wonder if they'd even notice.'

I ache when I think of what the outpouring of grief and sorrow at Tyrone's death would have meant to him. He had no idea that so many people cared about him, because he was taken from us before he could find his community. Before we could find him. I wonder if other young LGBTIQ kids struggling with suicidal thoughts saw the reaction to Tyrone's death and realised just how valuable their lives are to so many people. I hope so. I hope that if you are one of those young people and you are reading this book, you believe me when I say that you are loved, you are family and we want you to be here. I want you to be here.

Suicide is very, very rarely reported in the news. There are strict guidelines on it, in fact, in an effort to prevent influencing vulnerable people to also commit suicide or providing any incentive to people who might see value in having their name in the news. Only suicide deaths with significant public interest, that is, special relevance to the public, make the news. So why was the death of a 13-year-old in a regional Queensland town in the public interest? The reason is damning: the public interest lay in the fact that the LGBTIQ community had been sensationally bullied by political leaders and sections of the media for an entire year, which drew to a close with a 13-year-old gay boy literally bullied to death.

Tyrone died at the end of 2016, the year right-wing engineered hysteria surrounding Safe Schools meant that unchecked homophobia and transphobia were spewed relentlessly from the mouthpieces of power. It was only two weeks before his death that the Senate officially blocked legislation for a plebiscite on marriage equality, after it had passed the House of Representatives, following a year of heated national debate on whether individuals deserve a say on the rights of LGBTIQ people, and whether the Safe Schools program was actually a Trojan horse for the terrifying Gay Agenda.

Activists, commentators and politicians alike pointed their fingers at the Christian far right and the trolls posing as columnists who spent a year vilifying young queer people and the advocates trying to support them. In those same parliamentary chambers where plebiscite legislation was read, politicians of all stripes paid tribute to Tyrone. His death transcribed into the Hansard as 'heartbreaking' again and again.

Michael Koziol, political correspondent for the *Sydney Morning Herald* and *The Age* told me that Tyrone's death had a very clear message about public policy. 'We'd just watered down this program in response to vocal demands. Tyrone was like proof on the platter that this program was something that was so needed. There was a clear public policy dimension and that's why his death came to prominence and shook people up.'

My unqualified guess is that Tyrone was probably not following complex passages of legislation or the daily minutiae of political discourse (I could be wrong, he could have been even cooler than I already think he was). But he certainly would have picked up on the debate raging about whether the government should hold a $122 million national vote on his right to ever get married. He would have known about the attacks on Safe Schools.

Maybe he heard that some politicians were threatening to quit their jobs if marriage rights for LGBTIQ people were legislated, or that a married couple in Canberra planned to get a divorce because they felt their marriage would be tainted by same-sex couples accessing the same right.

Maybe he saw pictures of those homophobic flyers distributed in the letterboxes of Western Sydney that say 'homosexuality is the curse of death', or the pamphlets sent home with kids at a school in Tasmania saying that gay people 'abuse and neglect' their children. Or the advertisement warning of LGBTIQ workplace inclusion showing a woman with her neck in a rainbow noose. Maybe he saw Lyle Shelton on another prime-time TV slot saying there would be severe social consequences if someone like him married who they love. Maybe he heard the Attorney-General George Brandis argue that everyone should have the right to be a bigot.

Comments vilifying and humiliating LGBTIQ people had become canon from Australia's Liberal government, and instead of thinking about the harm that these words might cause and refraining from this kind of hate speech, they were simultaneously trying to remove protections for racial and ethnic minorities in the Racial Discrimination Act so they could dish out even more.

Maybe Tyrone saw or heard none of this behaviour directly. I really hope he didn't. But people at his school would have. People posting to social media would have. His extended family, some of whom dispute that he was gay, would have.

When homophobia and transphobia are repeatedly modelled by the powerful and influential in our society, that behaviour becomes not just permissible but *en vogue*. How can we expect teenagers not to pick on a kid for being gay when everything around them says it's okay to do just that?

Tyrone was thirteen, in high school and on the internet; he would have known the way LGBTIQ people were being treated in his country. How bullying, vilifying and humiliating LGBTIQ people was not only accepted by those with power, it was condoned. And the bullies at his school would have known this too. Tyrone would have heard those ideas turned into punch-lines repeated in the playground. He would have known that if something was uncool, it was 'gay'. If someone was doing something unpopular, they were a 'faggot'. If a situation was unpleasant or bad, it 'sucked arse'.

In his brilliant essay 'Moral Panic 101: Equality, Acceptance and the Safe Schools Scandal', Benjamin Law observes when he was growing up being gay was one of the worst things you could be in Australian schools. 'Some would say it is the worst', he ventures. On a macro level, things have undeniably improved for queer kids since the 90s but LGBTIQ teenagers still face extraordinary bullying and exclusion.

Tyrone had only been dead for six months when the Liberal government announced once again that they were going to take the country to a national vote on marriage equality, but this time by force. His death and everything it represented meant nothing to the Liberal government who were willing to put kids like Tyrone in harm's way to hold on to power for themselves.

LGBTIQ people and the people who love them were terrified. We knew a national 'debate' on our identities and our families would lead to extreme levels of distress for the community and, inevitably, more deaths like Tyrone's. We knew that people who were already vulnerable, whether it be because they were young, or from other pressures in their life such as poverty, mental illness, isolation from family or the intersecting marginalisation of other aspects of who they are, such as their race or ethnic background, would be put at even greater risk.

When the High Court confirmed the postal survey would go ahead, parents of transgender children panicked. These parents knew that despite not having anything to do with same-sex mar-riage, their children would have targets painted on their backs by the lobbyists, commentators and campaigners who'd now assembled to form the No campaign. That's why they'd fought alongside marriage equality campaigners to stop the plebiscite and the postal vote from happening. The tabloid-led assault on the Safe Schools program in 2016 had pulled private, personal decisions made about their transgender kids' care into a hostile spotlight and this would certainly happen again in the national debate.

The No campaign were already pushing the 'kids deserve a mum and a dad' message, but they also knew they could tap into a 'children' frame by engineering a campaign around the mere existence of transgender children to make other parents afraid of 'radical gender theory'. 'Racial gender theory' seems to be a combination of a 'reds under the bed!'–style Marxist scare campaign and your standard 'sex education is sexualising our children!' weirdness, piggybacked on the emerging visibility of transgender children (who, remember, have always been here).

In 'radical gender theory', anti-LGBTIQ activists warn that explaining to kids that different people have different experiences of gender – though it remains unclear when and where they'd be taught this, as the Marriage Act doesn't have anything to do with the curriculum – might turn them transgender and therefore destroy the world as we know it.

'I think another reason they come after the trans children is because being transgender is something not many people understand yet,' author, advocate and mother of a trans child Jo Hirst explained to me. 'The No campaign can misconstrue what being transgender as a child actually means. They seemed to be able to twist people and make fake news look like real news so easily, because there's not enough education out there with regards to transgender children. That's the weak link.'

A widespread lack of understanding meant that the public could easily be convinced that LGBTIQ activists like me were trying to sneak into schools and trick kids into deciding they were transgender and undergoing reassignment surgery without the knowledge of their parents. A conspiracy theory to rival the flat earth.

It's always baffled me that some people genuinely think that you can influence a person's gender or sexuality by informing them about LGBTIQ people, or restricting their exposure to anything other than straight and cisgender concepts.

Let's take me for example. I grew up solely with stories of heterosexuality: my parents were heterosexual, everyone in my extended family was heterosexual (not anymore!), the (limited) television, film and pop culture I consumed all reinforced heterosexuality. When I learnt about sex in primary school sex ed, it was about male penises in female vaginas. When I learnt about sex in high school sex ed, it was about labelling fallopian tubes on diagrams and watching slideshows depicting graphic symptoms of various untreated STIs. I don't think I really knew what being gay was until I heard it as slang for 'uncool'.

I was sixteen when I first saw a bisexual character on TV, Alex from *The O.C.*, and I was very much already kissing girls by then, so it's not like she was an influence. I was even having actual sex with actual boys by the time I was about fifteen – a fully immersive 'heterosexual' experience! But in spite of all this – in the face of being raised and socialised in an overwhelmingly heterosexual culture – my homosexuality prevailed.

My best friend Rebecca Shaw says it's obvious that people can't choose their gender or sexuality, otherwise we'd all be lesbians. Noted homosexual Darren Hayes from iconic band, Savage Garden, also believes you can't control or choose your sexuality, so that settles the matter. If you're still unsure on both counts, consider the amount of heterosexual men and women who watch lesbian porn and don't turn into lesbians by exposure.

If you could influence or change someone's gender or sexuality, LGBTIQ people simply wouldn't exist. Too many people for too long have tried to stop us from being here, and yet here we are. Still, this is the logic and ideology that continues to underpin dangerous, unscientific attempts to change LGBTIQ people through 'conversion therapy' practices. Our scientific understanding of sexuality has evolved since the times when we would perform lobotomies on queer people, but 'conversion therapy' is alive and well here in Australia.

Nowadays conversion therapy looks like forced surgeries on intersex babies and children, a culture of reluctance and diversion on the part of health practitioners when treating trans people, refusal from some states to allow trans people to amend their personal documentation without expensive and sometimes sterilising surgery, 'pastoral care' counselling within schools and twelve-step style programs run by churches that prey on people who feel the way I did when I first realised I was gay. These surgical, hormonal and psychological 'conversion' interventions usually 'fail' and leave LGBTIQ people picking up the pieces of their shattered selves and working the rest of their lives to put themselves back together. Some people don't survive.

You can't change someone's gender or sexuality by legalising same-sex marriage, or equipping teachers with resources about homophobic and transphobic bullying. If a young person, or any person for that matter, learns what it means to be transgender or bisexual or gay and then realises that's who they are then they *already were that way*. Giving young people (any people) the language to describe their identities and the support and acceptance to flourish in them isn't a recruitment program for the Gay Agenda, but even if it was, what's wrong with people feeling safe to explore their gender and sexuality?

Not one of the TV ads from the Coalition for Marriage made a case for 'traditional' marriage. They didn't even speak about marriage at all. Instead, they rolled out 'kids deserve a mum and a dad' and 'radical gender theory' scare campaigns. It didn't matter to the No campaign that there was no evidence to support their claims that marriage equality would lead to 'radical gender theory' being taught in schools or any truth to their assertion that kids learning about the diversity of sexuality and gender would make them gay or trans. Not satisfied with the kids in rainbow families being targeted by their messages, they went after trans kids too.

Take the main TV ad the Coalition for Marriage aired throughout the survey. I estimate it to have cost about $15,000 to film and hundreds of thousands of dollars to distribute to the prime-time commercial advertising spots, centred around a picture book written by Jo Hirst: *The Gender Fairy*.

The ad starts with a woman named Heidi McIvor – a pastor with an impressive job history working for Liberal, National and Family First politicians – saying, 'School has no place teaching my son radical gender ideas' as an image of Jo's gorgeous picture book appears on the screen. The cover of her book shows an illustration of two smiling young children looking up at a little fairy. Then a quote from *The Gender Fairy*, which is specifically written for families seeking to support their gender diverse children by reading affirming bedtime stories together, appears on the screen: 'Only you know whether you're a boy or a girl.' A sinister sound effect plays as the words appear and then fade.

Another mum, Cella White, enters. She's the woman who delivered the widely mocked line 'School told my son he could wear a dress' in an earlier Coalition for Marriage ad. She reacts to the onscreen quote pulled from Jo's book and worriedly asks, 'How am I supposed to protect my kids in the future from this stuff?' before the words 'Say no to these radical sex and gender programs' flash on the screen. The ad closes with the Coalition for Marriage's catchcry, You Can Say No.

Advertisements like this whipped up fear that children might be harmed by 'radical gender theory' and the only way to stop it was to vote No, with a wilful disregard of the harm these messages were causing actual, living transgender children. Because words mean things. Words do things.

Research commissioned by Telethon in 2016 found that in Australia, one in two transgender teenagers will attempt suicide. That's by far the highest risk of death by suicide of any group of people in our society. Furthermore, 80 per cent of transgender young people have self-harmed, which can involve cutting, burning or beating their bodies. People who self-harm describe the behaviour as a way to relieve mental anguish through experiencing physical pain. This figure is staggering compared to the 11 per cent of non-transgender kids who self-harm. Gay, lesbian and bisexual teenagers are five times more likely to attempt suicide than their peers.

LGBTIQ people suffer extraordinary rates of depression, anxiety and other mental illness, but we aren't more susceptible to mental illness and suicidality because of any inherent biological factor; we are not the problem. Being depressed isn't just something that comes part and parcel of being gay or trans. LGBTIQ people aren't inherently psychologically vulnerable. If you ask me, I think we are inherently strong, courageous and brave. Our experiences of mental ill-health arise from being born into a society that too often tells us that we don't or shouldn't exist.

During the crucial first week of the postal survey, a group of Australia's most influential mental health groups banded together to use their platforms and years of expertise to advocate for marriage equality. ReachOut, Headspace, Orygen, the Black Dog Institute and Sydney University's Brain and Mind Centre crunched the numbers and found that if Australia was to legislate marriage equality, we could prevent up to 3000 high school kids from attempting suicide every year. So, as responsible health professionals who dedicate their lives to improving mental health outcomes in our communities, they added their voices to the Yes campaign.

'[We] are encouraging Australians to carefully consider the real and devastating links between youth suicide rates and discrimination against young LGBTIQ+ people when they cast their vote over the next six weeks,' their websites read.

Their modelling was based on the research from the USA that examined representative data from 47 states and found that states with equal marriage legislation saw a 7 per cent reduction in LGBTIQ teenagers attempting suicide in the past year. I'm no expert but achieving a 7 per cent reduction in youth suicide by passing one single law sounds like a public health miracle.

The effort the five groups put in to conduct the research, and coordinate and execute the media push showed just how important they saw a Yes victory was to public health. The campaign was data-driven, measured and informed by years of experience.

The number was brought up on *Q&A* the following Monday, and Nationals senator cum No campaign cheerleader Matt Canavan immediately called it out as 'emotional blackmail'. Speaking on the panel, the senator justified his claim: '[t]hey accused people who support traditional marriage of causing 3000 suicides each year, when in fact there was only 2800.'

Only 2800. Silly marriage equality campaigners – that's not enough child suicide to worry about!

As we have established, I think suicide is horrifying. I think that reasonable people would consider the suicide of any person, but particularly a child, absolutely heartbreaking, and something to avoid at all costs. Preventing the suicides of children should be, in my opinion, the ultimate trump card on any policy argument. How could anyone argue for a process or policy that would inevitably cause the suicide of children? Right?

And yet, over the course of the survey, a fascinating pattern of rebuttal emerged: each time my colleagues and I spoke of the very real risk of children killing themselves during a public vote, we were accused of emotional blackmail.

In the prelude to the survey, Lyle Shelton told *The New Daily*, 'We shouldn't be allowed to have a plebiscite because someone might take their life? I think that's emotional blackmail in the extreme.'

Before the survey was called, Bill Shorten spoke in the House of Representatives against the idea of a public vote, saying, 'A "No" campaign would be an emotional torment for gay teenagers, and if one child commits suicide over the plebiscite, then that is one too many.' In response to Shorten's comments, Andrew Bolt wrote in his *Herald Sun* blog, 'This is the ultimate shut-up to stifle a debate – reckless, inflammatory and a grossly exaggerated scare. Shorten's suicide threat is emotional blackmail.'

When Greens leader Senator Richard Di Natale spoke about the survey's potential harm to vulnerable people in the LGBTIQ community, News Corp columnist Caroline Marcus labelled his comments as, you guessed it, 'emotional blackmail'.

In the second month of the survey, Nationals Senator Bridget McKenzie told *Sky News* that marriage equality campaigners using suicide statistics as a 'political tool' was unacceptable. I suppose we were all meant to just ignore them, then?

When the president of the AIDS Council of NSW Justin Koonin told the *Sydney Morning Herald* that being exposed to homophobic advertising harms LGBTIQ young people, David van Gend declared it 'shameless emotional blackmail designed to silence one side of a serious debate.'

It was perhaps the most disciplined rebuttal of the entire No campaign. Dismissing the urgent pleas for the consideration of children's wellbeing as 'emotional blackmail' meant that the discomfort of anti-LGBTIQ campaigners when presented with the statistics was somehow given equal or greater value than the actual mortality of LGBTIQ kids. 'Emotional blackmail' became a buzzword for anything that made a No voter feel bad. After all, bringing up LGBTIQ teen suicide rates was clearly part of our cunning plan to push our Gay Agenda of ... reducing LGBTIQ teen suicide rates? I mean ... yes?

For the No campaign, the suicide of LGBTIQ people was something they perceived to exist simply to make them feel bad, a thought pattern typical of narcissists who, funnily enough, are people who actually *do* perpetrate emotional blackmail and abuse. Using medical research and public health information to make a case for urgent policy reform is not emotional blackmail. Desperately trying to protect vulnerable members of our society from shameful political games is not emotional blackmail.

'Think of the children,' the No campaign wail from their soap-box. Protect them from 'radical gender theory' and make sure they each have a mum and a dad. Unless they are LGBTIQ children, of course. To think of the LGBTIQ children is 'emotional blackmail'.

In his Quarterly Essay, Benjamin Law writes that everyone invested in the discussion around LGBTIQ kids – from the ACL to activists like me – wants the same thing: to keep kids safe. 'The conundrum, of course,' he writes, 'is that our interpretations of what constitutes the safety of children differ wildly.' Law is a dear friend of mine and one of the kindest, most gracious people you can meet. Apparently, far kinder than me.

I don't think these people care about LGBTIQ children – I think that they're happy to use the spectacle of them to advance their campaign against our community. As such, I have a message for people like Cella White, Heidi McIvor and Marijke Rancie. To Lyle Shelton, George Christensen and Miranda Devine: if your advocacy for children's wellbeing is simply a fig-leaf for your cruel persecution of an already marginalised group, you are a doubly terrible person. Please reflect on what you're doing and why.

•

We discussed earlier how suicide is very rarely reported in the news. Because of this, we will never know exactly how many people died from suicide during the survey. We will never know how many people we lost in the months that followed or will lose to the trauma of the process so many of us still carry to this day.

I know of a girl in Melbourne, who was around twenty during the campaign and didn't make it to see the Yes result. She ended her own life halfway through the debate.

I know of a transgender man in Sydney, who over the course of the survey dropped out of university and then stopped going to work, as he was unable to leave the house. His best friend found him hanging in his home two days before the results were announced.

There's a girl in Western Australia who tried to commit suicide during her Year 12 exams. She'd been out since she was fifteen and came from a lovely family, but, according to her father, found the postal survey and public debate of her identity unbearable.

She's now left trying to put her life back together after failing her exams and spending months recovering from the process.

My friend Jonny Seymour walked a young gay man off the Sydney Harbour Bridge who was looking for a place to jump. The boy's strict Catholic family were campaigning for the No side and had forced him to go letterboxing with them. He believed that ending his life would be easier than living with his family's homophobia.

We know that during the survey, mental health service ReachOut reported a 40 per cent increase in young LGBTIQ people seeking support. LGBTIQ youth service Drummond Street were inundated with calls for help, unable to keep up with demand. So too were Beyondblue and Headspace.

We know that 2017, the year of the survey, saw a 9.1 per cent increase in suicide deaths on years prior. Suicide was the thirteenth leading cause of death, moving up from fifteenth the year earlier. Queensland, Western Australia, the ACT and NSW recorded the highest suicide rate in a decade.

A year after the survey concluded, the academic journal *Australian Psychologist* published research from the University of Sydney that conclusively proved that frequent exposure to negative media messages about same-sex marriage during the survey caused greater psychological distress for LGBTIQ people.

We know the postal survey had a $122 million price tag, but how much did it really cost? How can we calculate our individual distress or the fracturing of families and communities? Should we try to quantify the staggering loss of productivity and potential as scores of Australians struggled to go to work and school? How do we measure the aftermath of the process for LGBTIQ people and their families as everyone else just gets on with their life completely unchanged, just like we said they would. How can we mourn the people we've lost if their deaths aren't deemed newsworthy, despite the searing public policy dimension of their suicides.

How do the politicians who engineered and executed this process sleep at night knowing that they temporarily saved their government by sacrificing vulnerable lives?

They probably feel nothing. Our lives mean as much to those politicians as the refugees they've locked on Manus and Nauru, the Indigenous Australians who are murdered in police custody, and every one of our children who will face the catastrophic fallout of unchecked climate breakdown.

•

When my dad died, I blamed myself. I wasn't there for him. I didn't help him. I didn't love him enough.

I sometimes still believe those things to be true, but I'm working on not drawing a line between those feelings and his suicide. My rational brain tells me that I couldn't have saved him, and I'm working to unpick the feelings of responsibility for his death, slowly letting them loosen their grip on me.

Of course, I don't blame myself for Tyrone's death. I didn't know him or his family, to associate myself with his death would be narcissistic and silly. But I will feel a responsibility for Tyrone ending his life for as long as I live mine. I will keep asking myself the same questions.

If the kids in Tyrone's school who bullied him had learnt that being LGBTIQ wasn't anything to be ashamed of, would they have bullied him quite so much? If TV and radio hadn't blared the homophobia of politicians and shock-jocks, would these attitudes still be so pervasive? Had Tyrone and the other kids at his school grown up in a country where it was visible and normal for gay people to get married, would it be more socially acceptable for him to be gay? Would things have been different?

Tyrone likely wouldn't have wanted his life politicised, and that's the point. The obsession of politicians, church leaders and the right-wing media with LGBTIQ kids is killing them.

One day, I hope that the people who dedicate their lives to the preservation of discrimination against LGBTIQ people will begin to understand their responsibility for Tyrone's death too. But more than that, I want all of us to feel responsible for these kids' lives.

The research project from the University of Sydney that illuminated the mental distress LGBTIQ people experienced during the survey also found that LGBTIQ people who had the support of their families, friends and workplaces experienced little to no meaningful distress. The paper concludes:

> This study highlights how legislative processes related to the rights of stigmatised, minority populations have the potential to adversely affect their mental health. More importantly, however, the results also emphasise the role of social support as a potential protective factor against the mental health consequences of stigma.

Keeping our kids alive should be the easiest thing in the world. All they need is our love and our acceptance. They need us to listen to them. They need us to protect them from the voices that say they shouldn't be here while we do everything within our power to create a society that celebrates and loves them.

If you or someone you know is thinking about suicide, you can call Lifeline on 13 11 14, Kids Helpline on 1800 551 800, Mensline Australia on 1300 789 978 or the Suicide Call Back Service 1300 659 467.

9
The Headbutt

I've received a few phone calls in my life that have almost forced the contents of my stomach to an emergency evacuation. And I don't vomit, remember. I mean one of those 'urgent and unforeseen' situations. Of course, there are the calls announcing the death or illness of a loved one that are undeniably the very worst, but I'm talking about the tummy-drop calls informing you of a crisis that's entirely your fault, and entirely your responsibility to fix.

When I was a teenager I managed a Boost Juice in a city mall. At 9pm one night I got a call from centre management telling me that the entire underground arcade was flooded, and the water seemed to be coming from my store. I'd left a tap running. Once, I was texting my best friend about how I planned to break up with a girl I was seeing, when my phone rang – it was the girl I was dating. She said, 'I don't think that text message was meant for me . . .' Whoopsies! But one of the worst crisis calls I'd ever received was on Monday, 18 August 2015. It was GetUp's media advisor at the time, Adrian Dodd.

'Mate . . .' he said with an audible wince, 'one of the MPs you sent glitter to freaked out and called the cops. They called the fire department, and then they rang the HazMat unit. The entire street is shut down because of a chemical-weapons scare and the media are hounding me for comment.'

Fuck. It was bad. Lose-my-job bad, ruin-the-campaign bad, get-arrested bad.

Dodd continued, 'What are you doing sending glitter-bombs to members of parliament?'

In hindsight, his question wasn't entirely unreasonable. It was 2015 and when Tony Abbott's government announced plebiscite 1.0, it just felt like the sensible thing to do was to post every Liberal and National member of parliament glitter. What could possibly go wrong?

The MPs received one of two letters from GetUp, depending on whether they'd voted for or against holding a free vote on marriage equality. Those who spoke up in favour of a free vote received a thank you with a little packet of glitter to show our gratitude. Those who'd voted against received a letter saying, 'We are sorry that this glitter has made a mess of your carpet, but you've really made a mess of our plans. See, we were planning to hold a bunch of weddings this year – we bought all this glitter for the occasion, and we had to find a new use for it ...' The letter continued with some polling and electorate-specific figures like how many same-sex couples were registered in each MP's seat, and finished with the sentence 'Your prejudice will never take away our pride'. I should note here that these weren't real glitter-bombs; there was a tiny amount of glitter loose in the envelope, so it wasn't an exploding carpet mess (sadly).

This was designed as a media stunt. I'd given the story exclusively to BuzzFeed in advance who were ready to publish as soon as the letters started to arrive, but it was meant to be a 'GetUp members glitter bomb the Liberal party after they block a free vote on marriage equality'–type vibe. It was not meant to be 'Radical GetUp protesters cause bomb scare' or 'Idiot GetUp activist loses marriage campaign, professional standing, job, after glitter stunt backfires'. Fuck.

As the minutes passed, details started to come out. The politician responsible for the emergency services callout was Craig Laundy, the Liberal member for Reid at the time. Laundy had posted photos of the closed-down street outside his electorate office with the caption '6 police cars, 6 fire trucks and 1 Hazmat unit ... The emergency response today when my staff found a suspicious package in our PO Box was tremendous. It has since been discovered that it was a stupid stunt by GetUp.'

If I'm honest here, six fire trucks and six police cars and the HazMat unit did feel *a little overboard*. The envelopes were registered Australia Post, had glitter glued all over the outside of them and had 'love from GetUp' on the back. Out of the 123 letters we sent, we received quite a few letters back to us with the glitter, which we found quite funny, and a few thank you notes from Liberal MPs. Still, the optics – both visual and metaphorical – were not great.

'Leave it with me,' I told Dodd. I called Paul Oosting, GetUp's National Director. Paul is a formidable campaigner and has steered GetUp through some incredibly difficult times, including the relentless attacks from the far right of the Liberal party who've seemingly been tasked with trying to shut GetUp down. Despite Paul's gentle demeanour, I was terrified to call him and tell him what I'd done. I was certain he was going to be furious and that I'd be called into his office and dramatically fired. I would probably never work as a campaigner again. I'd set marriage equality back for years, the Murdoch press were going to come after me ...

I was wrong. 'This isn't ideal, but don't freak out,' Oosting reassured me. 'You can make this work in your favour. Whatever you had planned comms-wise, go harder.'

Like I said, the glitter letters were a stunt. The objective was to get the frustration felt by LGBTIQ people at the Liberal government in the media. Yes, it served as a tactical reminder to the MPs that GetUp members were paying attention to how they were voting on the issues and was meant to give the LGBTIQ community something to smile about after such a big set-back, but mostly it was a media hook, a way to get our message out so we could try to shape the public narrative. Better to give the media something new to write about that furthers our cause, rather than a retelling of the government's decision to block a free vote.

We wanted media attention, and we'd got it. It wasn't what we'd planned, but we needed to make it work. So, even though Laundy's Facebook post had only been seen by a handful of people and we'd only had one media inquiry, we sent out a statement of apology. We wanted to make sure as many journalists as possible knew that Craig Laundy's staff had called the HazMat unit on some glitter. The media release read:

> GetUp would like to express its regret for confusion that saw emergency service workers diverted to the office of Coalition MP Craig Laundy over a package of glitter. The glitter was sent to all Coalition MPs as part of the campaign for marriage equality in registered Australia Post bags with GetUp marked as the sender. The glitter was mistaken for a 'suspicious package' by office staff that called emergency personnel, according to a post on the MP's Facebook page. GetUp would like to express its regret for this misunderstanding and confusion. We hope nobody was unduly concerned for an extended period by the glitter.

The plan worked. For the vast majority of the media, our 'apology' was the first they'd heard of the incident. The story was reported widely, with most articles picking up the gentle mocking of our press release and running with that tone. *The Daily Mail* wrote '[t]he office of Liberal MP Craig Laundy have made an embarrassing blunder after mistaking a harmless envelope filled with glitter as a suspicious package.' BuzzFeed News reported the incident as a 'colourful misunderstanding'. Lisa Cox wrote in the *Sydney Morning Herald* what I maintain is probably the most important piece of Australian journalism in my lifetime. The article reads:

> The modern incarnation of glitter has been around for decades and, among other things, has featured in fancy dress, school projects, parades and make-up in the nineties. *Glitter* is also the name of a 2001 film starring Mariah Carey. Glitter has been used as a tool in a non-violent act of protest known as 'glitter-bombing'. It is unclear whether or not this is the first time glitter has triggered an emergency response.

In campaigning, you have to take risks. You can't do the same thing again and again and expect people in power to change their minds. You need giant carrots and even bigger sticks. Sometimes these risks pay off, sometimes they backfire; you just need to be successful often enough to justify the risk.

Oosting's suggestion to use this crisis as an opportunity to make the Abbott government look silly and out of touch worked. The reason this stunt worked is that the media wanted to tell a fun story, and we gave them one. But it also worked because of drastic, rolling changes to the media landscape.

In this chapter, we're going to talk about the media: how activists work with them, in spite of them, and how to use them for change. But first, we need to understand them.

As we approach 2020, the media as a collective group of publications and broadcasters in Australia is completely stretched and increasingly desperate. Newspapers used to make millions of dollars in advertising because people, potential customers, were looking at their broadsheets. Now, people are looking at the internet, so that's where the advertising money ends up and each year sees another round of journalists made redundant as traditional outlets struggle to find new revenue models to sustain their business.

More and more online publications form, serving stories and content designed to appeal to a specific audience, in order to secure advertising contracts for that specific audience. And so we consume our media in smaller and smaller bubbles of ideas as the content we consume is increasingly tailored to what we want to see and hear. Journalists and content producers working in every kind of publication or broadcast are under enormous pressure to deliver an exponentially growing number of interesting, exclusive stories, in order to move papers, pull mouse clicks or get the television switched on. The state of the media is . . . hugely depressing. Publishers and broadcasters are forced to sacrifice quality investigative journalism and localised reporting in favour of sensationalism and entertainment, in order to make the revenue to stay operational. As a result, the population are left with mostly information that's been hastily prepared with a specific audience and specific reaction in mind. That's not journalism, that's campaigning.

As an aside, this is why we must protect the independence and funding for the ABC. A fully funded ABC is absolutely crucial to the functionality and integrity of our democracy. The ABC can be trusted to hold power to account fairly and without bias; it's literally written in their charter. We are so fortunate in Australia to have such an incredible public broadcaster, you need only look at how partisan the reporting is in the USA to realise the value of the ABC.

I studied two years of a masters in journalism at the University of Technology Sydney before dropping out. I thought I wanted to be a journalist because I saw the media as the people and platforms that shaped ideas, influenced cultural narratives and impacted policy. I wanted to use investigation and storytelling to make the changes I felt were necessary for us to live in a flourishing society together. Eventually I realised that actually what I wanted to do wasn't journalism, it was campaigning.

Far be it from me to recite my incomplete academic record simply for the sake of it. My point is, while I'm not a journalist, I know a bit about how the media works, mostly from the outside but a bit from the inside. The media is not a person, nor is it a singular, homogeneous agent. The media is a collection of loosely associated publications forming amalgams based on their mode of communication. At their purest they serve to hold power to account, and at their worst they just make up stories to make money with no regard for consequence. Perhaps when media companies were profitable they had more noble agendas. In our digital age where mastheads deliberately editorialise their content to appeal to a specific audience, much of the media are increasingly partisan and do little, if anything, to hide their ideological and political agendas.

I also know a bit about the love/hate relationship between campaigning and the media. Back in the early twenty-teens, the media loved digital campaigning. An online petition in and of itself was enough to get a story up, because people were fascinated by this new type of activism. Nowadays, the media are very unlikely to report on a petition alone, which is why petitions that do make the news tend to do so only if the petition is on something that's already in the news, if there's a very well-timed public delivery of said petition to a newsworthy decision-maker, or as a bit of background information about someone with a compelling personal story of injustice or misfortune.

Grassroots activists need the media, because the media are still the strongest megaphone we have. We're not loud enough on our own, even with social media helping us along. Movements of ordinary people can't bankroll tens of millions of dollars' worth of advertising for our cause, unlike the fossil fuel industry, the gambling lobby, organised religion and the Murdoch media empire, or other bodies of power we're trying to push. We tend to be outmatched in terms of resources. We need the media.

There are different kinds of media campaigning (that is, working with or using the media to your campaign's advantage) on a sliding scale of collaboration with the media. An example of a tactic that's very collaborative with the media might be when animal rights activists break the law to collect footage of animals being mistreated in abattoirs or factory farms and then give it to the media, who report on it because it's in the public interest. I'd put whistleblowing up here too, as it's gifting the media information with the shared objective of publishing that information. Very collaborative (and extraordinarily brave).

Another less dangerous way to closely collaborate with the media in campaigning is to give an outlet an exclusive story, which means no other outlet will have the same story when the news breaks. At GetUp, we'd often crowdfund to commission our own polling and then give the data to a paper exclusively, or we would source compelling personal stories from our membership so that journalists could put a face to various depersonalised government policies.

A step back from intimate, planned collaboration might look like sending journalists a good media release that outlines new, interesting information about an existing or breaking story. Journalists receive hundreds of terrible media releases a day, so this is only going to work if the message is clear, holds new and unique information and will be helpful to the reporter. Ways to make your release stand out from the crowd include providing images the media can use or details of what visuals reporters could source, for example the photos they are likely to capture at an event you're trying to convince them to cover.

A step further back from collaboration is deliberately disrupting the media but knowing they'll kind of love it. These tactics look like the protests outside morning television shows that can be seen through their studio windows, or banner-drops at *Q&A*. One of the most memorable disruptions that comes to my mind is when 2004 *Big Brother* contestant Merlin Luck staged a silent protest on live television, with his mouth taped shut, holding a sign saying 'Free Th[e] Refugees'. It was an incredibly powerful image. Luck had planned the protest before entering the show, which was watched weekly by millions of people, and had sewn the sign into a shirt to smuggle it into the *Big Brother* house weeks before his elimination.

Then there's the Streisand Effect, which is where an attempt to hide, ban or censor a piece of information makes the original piece of information so much more newsworthy because of the media's attempts to hide it. The media don't necessarily love to hide information (unless they're protecting their powerful mates, which absolutely does happen) but are sometimes restricted on what they can report based on gag orders or viewing classifications. It's not not-cooperating with the press, but it's very deliberately taking advantage of two truths of the media: they are bound by certain rules and they love to report a conflict.

Knowing this, in the 2013 election, Paul Oosting and I made a television ad for GetUp's election campaign that called out Queensland paper *The Courier-Mail* for its shameless bias towards Tony Abbott. The ad showed a man collecting *The Courier-Mail* from his front lawn and then using it to scoop up fresh dog poo (we zoomed in nice and close on this) while he delivered the line,

'Political bias presented as news is misleading crap.' As planned, the ad was banned from appearing on commercial television and as a result was seen by many million more people than our small advertising buy could have reached because everyone rushed to see the banned ad online.

The Coalition for Marriage also used this tactic very cleverly during the survey, securing an MA rating for one of their ads by quoting a resource from LGBTIQ youth service Minus18. The ad quoted: 'Penis-in-vagina sex is not the only sex, and certainly not the ultimate sex' (I'm not here to diminish P-in-V sex, all sex is fun. But if you disagree with that statement, I do feel a bit sad for your sex life), which was enough to see it banned from being aired during the day. Maybe I'm giving them too much credit, but I suspect that the Coalition for Marriage did this deliberately, to make the point that the resource was inappropriate for children. It was smart; it got the coverage they wanted and they were able to get their lines about 'radical gay sex education' into the press. Of course, the fact that this resource from Minus18 wasn't part of the school curriculum and was designed specifically for school counsellors to give to teenage students struggling with their LGBTIQ identity didn't make the media coverage.

At the far end of the collaborative scale is where I'd put media hoaxes: tactics that deliberately mislead the media, knowing how they'll behave. Anti-coal activist Jonathan Moylan knows this strategy well. In 2012, Moylan sent out a fake press release from ANZ, announcing that the bank was withdrawing funding from the controversial Whitehaven Coal mine on ethical grounds. The story was reported by the *Sydney Morning Herald*, the *Australian Financial Review*, *Business Spectator* and *Australian Associated Press* and within hours, the share value of Whitehaven Coal plummeted by $314 million. At the time, Moylan said he didn't expect the company's share price to fall; he just wanted ANZ customers to think about where their bank was investing and saw the fake release as a way of getting that idea into the press. Moylan was charged with making a false and misleading statement under the Corporations Act but avoided prison on a good behaviour bond.

Then there's fake news, where special interest groups or groups with extremist views literally pretend to be the media in order to tell lies that will benefit their agenda or campaign. Or they're just trolls. This is definitely the least collaborative strategy with real media.

The media are hungry for stories, and not just any stories: they want conflict, they want drama. That drama is almost always created using the same structures as stories told since the beginning of time. It relies on a 'drama triangle' of three characters: the villain, the victim and the hero.

Within the 'drama triangle' many people have studied the 'hero's journey' in narratives and mythology. The hero's journey was popularised in the 1940s by Professor Joseph Campbell, who was inspired by Carl Jung, and looks like this: an unlikely hero is unhappy with the injustices of the world that they see negatively affecting those around them, the victims, but feels too disempowered to do anything; the hero meets a mentor, who gives them a special power or tool or piece of information; the hero goes on a journey of self-discovery before confronting the source of their world's injustice – the villain. They fight and the hero wins, of course, thus delivering justice to the victims.

The hero's journey makes for a cracking yarn every time, and it's applied far beyond the books and comics and movies that I'm sure you can think of that fit this structure. Campaigners use it constantly, so it's a useful tool to understand. We apply it to the issues that we're attempting to resolve in order to communicate to wide audiences the problem, the solution and the journey we'll need to go on together to get there. It's common, however, to see the drama triangle misapplied, when campaigners cast themselves in the role of the hero.

Consider this: a greedy property developer (our villain) wants to acquire a community park that's beloved by local families, sporting clubs and pet owners. If campaigners cast themselves as the hero of this story, someone who comes in to save the day, where does that leave the people who love the park? They're cast as the victims, which is terribly disempowering. Instead, good campaigners must construct a narrative where ordinary people are the unlikely heroes of the story. They're the ones who need to go on a journey, to harness their power despite their doubts and to bring justice to their communities. Campaigners must cast themselves in the supporting role: the mentor. We pop up to give our heroes the tools they need to win and cheer them on, and then fade into the background.

Consider marriage equality. Does the story of a victimised LGBTIQ community being rescued by a few high-profile gay men from the villainous heterosexual Marriage Act make us feel jazzed up? Or are we excited by coming together as a community, cobbling together all the power we have, to take on the powerful individuals who actively persecute LGBTIQ people, to create a fairer and more loving society for everyone? When written, hailing the individual reader as the unlikely hero of the drama triangle is called a reader-focussed theory of change; IF you reading this right now and take the action I'm asking you to, THEN together we can defeat the villain. This is not just a more empowering story, it's also an accurate description of how ordinary people won the campaign.

You'll notice I've clearly, albeit briefly, described exactly who our villain is. This is crucial. In the story, or public narrative, of your campaign, defining who the villain is also defines the path to stopping them, bringing justice to the victims. If the villain of your story is a greedy property developer, the path to stopping them might mean targeting the local council in a campaign to challenge their permit. If the villain in your story is a corporation exposed for underpaying their workers, the path to stopping them might be organising a consumer boycott. If the villain is a small pocket of hard-right politicians who hold our parliament in a stranglehold, the path to stopping them as a change-maker is to educate the citizens of their villainous behaviour in order to mobilise millions of people to use their power as electors to not only vote them out, but send a message to all political parties that people won't stand for factional bullshit that gives radical ideologues the ability to make decisions about our lives. A clear villain in the story also reminds us that injustices don't just happen, they're perpetrated by people.

How we construct the stories of our struggles and our successes matters in real time and was particularly crucial during the postal survey. In Jonah Sachs' book *Winning the Story Wars* he refers to the time we're living in as the Digitoral Era. 'Digitoral' sounds a bit like a staple of lesbian sex, but I digress. Sachs coins the phrase to refer to the way the internet and personal broadcasting devices allow people to actively produce, modify, challenge and retell the stories we share as a society. It matters in real time because controlling who the public views as the hero, the villain and the victim can significantly empower or hinder your campaign.

The fight for the roles of hero, villain and victim of the marriage campaign on the national stage reached fever pitch during the postal survey, and it was fuelled by the media. The media who want to sell papers and advertising space. The media who want to whip up a culture war in order to better appeal to their target audience. And in some instances, sections of the media who have a vested interest in how activists are perceived in our shared public stories.

During the survey, some commentators in the media became fixated not on heroes, but with a story of victims and villains. Or, as they wrote it, victims and bullies. They wrote column after column insisting that it was, in fact, the LGBTIQ community who were the true bullies of the postal survey, victimising poor, helpless No voters. It didn't matter that we didn't want a public vote and that we were working for our rights – the rights of a long-oppressed minority. To these commentators we were an angry mob ramming 'PC nonsense' down people's throats, persecuting those who disagreed with us and destroying society as we know it.

Andrew Bolt wrote in the *Herald Sun*, 'This gay-marriage cause is brilliant for bullies … For them, the real cause seems to be the freedom to bully, not the freedom of gays to marry.' Janet Albrechtsen wrote in *The Australian*, 'a No vote is an understandable protest against the daily bullying and intimidation by the activists. If their deplorable intolerance derails a campaign premised on tolerance, this Yes voter won't shed a tear or be surprised.' *The Daily Telegraph*'s Caroline Marcus described me and my colleagues as 'the rainbow lynch mob' up to 'dirty tricks', lecturing that 'Gay marriage activists are pushing many like me to "No" column.' Marcus qualified her opinion by claiming that she was looking forwards to the 'fabulous future weddings of her gay friends', which sounds a lot like 'I'm not racist, I have a black friend, but–' to me.

BuzzFeed reporter Lane Sainty explained to me, 'The idea of bullies and victims was a very useful narrative for commentators on both the Yes and the No sides to deploy, it was a point around which they could rally their readers. It also plays into a binary of how you see the issue; it allows you to think "the other side is bad, and I am good",' Sainty continued. 'It energised the No campaign to be able to think of themselves as the real victims. They were very upset that their stance had negative connotations; the word bigot became a slur, and the word homophobe became a slur even though those are words that mean things, they're not just thoughtless insults. It allowed the No campaign to evade their dislike of being labelled things like bigots and homophobes.'

Casting the Yes and No sides as bullies and victims respectively morphed beyond a narrative convention to help sell papers and too often became an editorial position to campaign for voting No. The idea was enthusiastically fuelled by the Coalition for Marriage.

'I think that narrative in particular really hurts LGBTI people because so many LGBTI people know acutely what it is like to be bullied. To be bullied by others but also to be bullied by yourself; to know that you are different and to punish yourself for that difference, usually when you are young, usually during your formative years and that feeling for many LGBTI adults does not go away. A part of it stays with you,' Sainty observed.

As you now know, many of the public-facing Yes campaigners had decided to remain relentlessly positive and not be drawn into conflict, down rabbit holes or into our opponent's frame. But as the survey went on, that became more and more difficult.

The closest that GetUp and the Equality Campaign came to taking the bait was about midway through the campaign, when the idea that No voters were the ones being persecuted by angry Yes voters really felt like it was gaining the upper hand.

It was excruciatingly difficult to ignore, not just because it was unfair and not just because those of us working on the campaign were receiving horrible online abuse, but because the community around us was suffering. Every time I saw a new hot-take about how No voters were being persecuted for their opinion on other people's lives I wanted to shout that my best friend's rainbow flag had been burnt on her front porch, that a young person I volunteer with at LGBTIQ youth service Twenty10 is couch-surfing in strangers' share houses because their parents are voting No, that my trans friend is going days without being able to leave the house because he's crippled by anxiety. How dare the very people inflicting such unnecessary trauma, who called for the vote in the first place, suggest they were the victims in this horror show?

Tim Gartrell came to GetUp one evening to have a serious discussion about whether we should chronicle the violence, vandalism and online harassment and give it to the press, with the goal of countering the No campaign's self-proclaimed victim status. This was the same time that Alex Greenwich and his electorate staff were being absolutely pounded with angry phone calls, emails and online abuse because Alex's name authorised a text message that the Equality Campaign sent to millions of people.

After the conversation with Tim, I screen-shotted a few dozen of the worst messages I'd received on Facebook and Twitter. Being a public face of the campaign, who was also young, female and gay, I had the dubious honour of copping some of the worst online abuse. Only once I'd compiled a selection of my death threats and abuse, and Alex his, we decided that nobody should have to read those words, and that repeating them in convoy would be counterproductive and distressing to LGBTIQ people. We also worried that highlighting the violence and harassment against key figures in the campaign might encourage more of the same.

I won't repeat any of the abuse I received then, or now, because it doesn't deserve to live in print. What I will say is that I've read every horrible message I've ever received, checking to see if anyone has found out where I live or says anything about my family. The first dozen or so of nasty messages are devastating, but then you become desensitised. The messages become pathetic, almost funny. Then, suddenly, after you've read hundreds and hundreds of disgusting messages, they reach a critical mass in your head and you live with the constant fear of being followed from your office, being attacked at public appearances or being hunted as you lie in bed at night. Congratulations to everyone who has tried to frighten or intimidate me, I guess.

Without a doubt, the outlet responsible for the majority of accusations that the Yes campaign were bullies was *The Australian*. Tiernan Brady, who's run campaigns all over the world, describes *The Australian* as one of the most dishonest publications he's ever come across and a danger to our society.

'It does what Fox News does,' Brady told me over Skype from Ireland. 'It deliberately extrapolates extremist voices and tries to say that's what an entire community looks like. And it does it for one reason: to poison that community in the eyes of the rest of society. It deliberately divides society.'

Tiernan warns, 'Going forward, people should just be so careful of the Murdoch Press and the division they are trying to bring to Australia, in the most dishonest way. They'll pick a person and turn them into a demon and then once they've turned them into the demon, they'll say, "This person represents one culture from society". It will really hurt society unless you start calling it out.'

There are some highly skilled, fair-minded journalists at *The Australian* who report valuable stories. I am lucky to call some of them my friends ('I'm not against The Aus, some of my *friends* work at The Aus!'). The newspaper also consistently publishes baseless attacks on marginalised people, shamelessly persecutes young women who dare to voice their political opinion and they, unquestionably, held a flaming pitchfork for the No side.

'There is a real mood that something has gone wrong,' former *Australian* journalist Rick Morton told students at a 2019 university event when speaking broadly about the paper, while still working there. 'People will tell you going back a decade it used to be a very great paper, and in many ways it still is, but some of the craziness has been dialled up.'

'I was surprised by how hard News Corp, and particularly *The Australian*, went out at the start of the survey campaign in terms of the extent to which they gave airtime to arguments that it would affect gender education of children,' *The Guardian*'s Paul Karp told me.

I was not surprised. I was in the thick of the paper's merciless demonisation of the Safe Schools program and the LGBTIQ advocates and academics behind it. I'd witnessed their violent, deranged campaign against my friend and former Queensland Young Australian of the Year, Yassmin Abdel-Magied because of an innocuous post on her personal Facebook page, which she apologised for and deleted. The newspaper stalked her, harassed her and assassinated her character until, at just 25 years old, she was literally driven out of the country for her own safety.

The media can be used as a powerful tool, if you know how to work it. But just like campaigners can play the media, the media can play us right back. A newspaper can put an editorial hit out on your organisation or wage war against your campaign. Some journalists just make up whatever they like, relying on 'unnamed sources', and whack the words 'allegedly' somewhere in the article.

If they want to, they'll try to trick you into saying exactly what they want to publish to further characterise you and your cause as villainous.

It's like when journalist for *The Australian* Remy Varga emailed me to ask if I was responsible for sending white powder to the ACL's office, despite there being no evidence that I was involved. It was a tabloid trap. No matter how you answer a question like that, you risk being demonised. To push back against the accusation is reported: 'Sally Rugg denies she sent suspicious white powder to No campaign', and to refuse to comment gets written up as: 'Sally Rugg refuses to rule out she sent suspicious white powder to No campaign'. Journalists know how to trap people into saying, or not saying, exactly what they need for the story they've already decided they'll publish, and for some reason that apparently constitutes investigation.

On the Yes side, outlets like Junkee certainly took the piss out of prominent No campaigners with headlines like 'Please Enjoy this Video of Mark Latham, Miranda Devine and Lyle Shelton Falling Over'. Junkee also described Lyle Shelton as a 'famous loser' and ran an entire article called 'Just A Bunch of People Telling Lyle Shelton to Eat Shit'. This is punch-up comedy; making fun of people in power who hold power and powerful views. Punch-up comedy explains why making fun of politicians is funny and making fun of poor people is extremely not.

Lyle Shelton is a middle-aged white man who is well-connected in politics, has the ear of the nation's media, is a loud advocate for the discriminatory status quo as the head of major lobby groups, walks the halls of parliament with government ministers and rubs shoulders with senior church officials, and has absolutely no personal stake in whether LGBTIQ people have equal rights or not. He is a very powerful man. Making fun of Lyle Shelton is not the same as villifying a community of marginalised people. I think it's cruel and kind of sick to dedicate your professional life to demonising and oppressing other people, particularly people from a marginalised community. That's what I would call bullying.

●

The media during the survey were in an absolute frenzy, which goes some way to explaining the single most stomach-dropping phone call I've ever received in my professional life. Far worse than the news of the HazMat unit being called on my glitter.

It felt like just an ordinary evening at the office on 21 September 2017. My team and I had ordered Thai to our desks and we were finalising logistics for the weekend's giant door-knock for Yes. There we were, working under fluorescent lights in the increasingly dishevelled GetUp war room (love room), thinking the biggest thing on our plate for the rest of the week would be the door-knocks. Little did we know that only a few kilometres away, Andrew Bolt and Steve Price were taking a phone call from former Prime Minister Tony Abbott, live on 2GB radio, who told them this: 'I was walking from the Mercury office across that beautiful docks area in Hobart towards my hotel. A fellow sang out at me, "Hey, Tony!" I turned around and there was a chap wearing a "Vote Yes" badge. He says, "I wanna shake your hand" so I went over to shake his hand and then he headbutted me!' Abbott's voice lifted in pitch and volume for emphasis, like he was still stunned it had happened. 'Now, he wasn't very good at it, I've got to say, but he did make contact,' Abbott continued. 'The only damage was a very, very slightly swollen lip. I was with a member of my staff, the member of my staff briefly grappled with this guy and he then ran off, swearing his head off basically. As he was scarpering away, amidst all the effing this and effing that it was, "you deserve it because of all the things you've said!" and I think it was pretty clear that this was,' he begins to laugh, 'to use the phrase, politically motivated violence.'

Ah, politically motivated violence. Hilarious.

Tony Abbott went on to appeal to 2GB listeners that if they didn't support the headbutt he received, they must vote No. I wasn't listening to 2GB because, as established with regard to *Q&A*, articles about insomnia suggest it's not good to get worked up before bedtime. Within moments my phone pinged with a notification of a tweet saying 'BREAKING: Tony Abbott has been assaulted in Hobart'.

I hurried through the office to find GetUp's chief of staff, Henny Smith. Her phone lit up with a call from Tim Gartrell who delivered the news, 'It's true, and Abbott's saying it was a Yes campaigner.'

We were absolutely incredulous. Who would do this? In a state of panic, Henny and I tried to get more details from Tim; what did he mean a 'Yes campaigner'? Does that mean someone on staff? Is Abbott hurt? The Equality Campaign's Tasmanian Field Director Alex West was on the ground and had no idea who this supposed 'Yes campaigner' could be.

At the beginning of the survey, my team and I had mapped out potential comms risks and how to mitigate them. They included things like, 'Yes voter caught stealing other people's ballots to vote Yes', or 'Yes and No protesters clash with each other' and even, 'Street violence increases'. We did not, however, predict that a 'Yes campaigner' would attack the former prime minister.

Before we knew it, an article was live on the *Herald Sun* website with the headline 'Tony Abbott Headbutted By Yes Supporter'.

I couldn't believe it was happening. It was a campaigner's worst nightmare and that campaigner was me, Sally Rugg. The disbelief quickly turned into a cold, sickening horror. If what Abbott said was true, it had the potential to not only ruin the survey campaign but be disastrous for all LGBTIQ-rights activism for years to come. It was an absolute crisis.

And as my colleagues and I were hearing the news, so were journalists across the country.

'I was at the theatre in Canberra that night when it all happened,' Michael Koziol tells me. 'I started getting texts from the Yes campaign and then got a call from an editor being like, "Are you jumping on this?"'

Kylar Loussikian, *The Daily Telegraph*'s national political reporter recalls, 'I was like . . . "What the fuck? Is this really the year 2017?"'

'The first thing I thought was "Oh, fuck just what we need",' Paul Karp from *The Guardian* told me.

'I was on Twitter,' BuzzFeed's Lane Sainty remembers, 'and I saw that there were reports that Abbott had been headbutted and the first thing I saw was from Andrew Bolt so I was like, "Is this reliable?" Then I saw that other people were reporting on it and thought, "Yes, this is probably reliable information."'

'My first reaction was, "This won't help the Yes campaign",' Phil Coorey at the *Australian Financial Review* told me. 'It's perfect propaganda.'

Punters, politicians, journalists and the social media accounts of news outlets were responding in rapid fire.

The Australian tweeted, 'BREAKING: Tony Abbott "headbutted" by Yes campaigner' and 'Tony Abbott says today's headbutting incident is a reminder of how "ugly" the same-sex marriage debate is getting'. The *Sydney Morning Herald* tweeted, 'Breaking: Tony Abbott headbutted by same-sex marriage campaigner in Hobart' while Jason Om, a journalist covering the story at the ABC, wrote, 'BREAKING Tony Abbott confirms he was headbutted by a same-sex marriage supporter in Hobart.'

It felt out of control; Abbott and the headbutt were trending across the country, and 24-hour news channels were riffing on the story freely. Before long, TV show *Sunrise* was spruiking its morning show, tweeting, 'Is Tony Abbott being headbutted likely to harm the same-sex marriage "yes" campaign . . . ?' The national affairs editor for the *Sydney Morning Herald*, *The Age* and *Canberra Times*, Mark Kenny, tweeted, 'Love might be love. But violence is violence. With despicable morons like this on their side, "yes" has again been harmed by this zealotry.' And I thought I had a dramatic reaction!

As the press chased him for comment and clarification, Abbott doubled down, giving a television interview saying the attack was 'just a reminder of how ugly this debate is getting, and the ugliness is not coming from the defenders of marriage as it's always been understood. The ugliness, the intolerance and in this instance, even the hint of violence, is coming from those who tell us in the name of decency, and fair-mindedness and freedom we've got to allow same-sex marriage. The "love is love" brigade aren't showing a lot of love I've got to say.'

In that first hour of the story breaking, the most urgent priority for me and other public-facing Yes campaigners was to immediately condemn the attack. I tweeted, 'SSM is about love and dignity. All violence happening during this plebiscite is abhorrent, including alleged assault on Tony Abbott tonight.'

We knew that if we weren't observed immediately and publicly condemning The Headbutt then we'd be written by some in the press as approving, or even complicit. We'd end up the villains.

I guess this is how Muslim leaders must feel every time someone commits an act of terrorism and they're forced to publicly denounce the crime (and then it so often ends up being a white supremacist or Incel anyway).

'*The Australian* would have been scouring Twitter to find someone connected to the campaign who said "hooray!"' Tiernan Brady said. 'But LGBT people were totally disciplined, they were brilliant. Yes, the leaders of the campaign got out fast, but ordinary people chose to take the line and run with it as well.'

'It was late in the day so it was a rush trying to get the facts,' Phil Coorey explained to me. 'It was being reported locally so we had to lift it from there and try to get on to Abbott. We really didn't have time to do anything significant on the day because we were just trying to make deadline.'

It must be said that much of the breaking coverage did say that at that point in time, the headbutt was an allegation and the link to marriage equality was a claim of Abbott's.

But, when I was up at 5am the following morning, I saw the following front pages:

SAME-SEX HEADBUTT: Tony Abbott assaulted by Yes activist
(*The West Australian*)
LOWERING THE TONE: Thug activist headbutts ex-PM (*The
Daily Telegraph*)
YES ADVOCATE HEADBUTTS ABBOTT (*The Australian*)
HEADACHE: Has one 'head-butt' knocked out same-sex mar-
riage? (*The Sydney Morning Herald*)

That last one particularly pissed me off. The speculation published in the paper's prime A3 real estate that the actions of one random guy in Hobart could somehow ruin the entire campaign and prevent the law from changing was, in my opinion, a pretty inappropriate thing to print. Especially because the question posed by the headline was answered in the article by Peter Hartcher on page five, in the negative.

'It was a really bad moment for the Yes campaign,' Lane Sainty lamented. 'It just gave this perfect example of the narrative that the No campaign had been spinning the whole time – that the Yes campaign were bullies, the Yes campaign were physically violent and that the Yes campaign are just crazy lefties.'

The morning after the headbutt, *Sky News* reporter Samantha Maiden was also up at 5am getting ready to host a morning of live television. She and the news producers were scrambling to get the details. Samantha made her way into the Parliament House press gallery and still didn't have a clear picture of what had gone down and, despite *Sky* reporter in Tasmania Katelyn Barry scouring the city until midnight, there was no CCTV to be seen.

Samantha rang Tony Abbott's press secretary and asked him directly for a blow-by-blow account of what had happened. He re-told the story: they were coming out of a meeting with the local paper, the guy comes up and asks for a handshake, he headbutts Abbott and then runs off saying, 'That's for all the things you said.'

Samantha was confused and asked, 'Okay, so, "That's for all the things you said" . . . said about what?' The press secretary replied, 'Well, for all the things he said, you know, about gay marriage.' By this time, Samantha was in the bathroom hastily putting on her makeup to go on camera, and pressed, 'Did he actually say "gay marriage?"'

The press secretary responded, 'Well, no, but he was wearing a rainbow badge.' Samantha was bewildered and asked, 'Okay, so I'm just checking: you're saying that the only evidence that he had anything to do with the Yes campaign or that the assault was linked to the same-sex marriage debate was the fact that he was wearing a rainbow badge?' The press secretary seemed to become annoyed, responding, 'Oh, well if you're going to be like that!' Samantha's line of questioning continued: 'Did the badge say "yes" on it or was it just a rainbow? Was it a badge or actually a sticker? Was the man wearing other badges, since we know people styling themselves as anarchists often cover their jackets with them?'

The press secretary started to get cranky, asking Maiden what her agenda was. Maybe he was getting cranky at the line of inquiry because – wait for it – the headbutter didn't actually say anything at all about marriage equality! The man just had a sticker on his jacket that Yes volunteers had been leaving stacks of at cafes and pubs along the dock strip earlier in the day in an effort to promote the campaign, and the man – who was drunk off his face – didn't even remember he was wearing one. Abbott's allegation that he'd been attacked by someone from the Yes campaign, the accusation that the Yes campaign were responsible for 'ugliness', 'intolerance' and 'violence' and the pounding our campaign got in the press was all because of . . . a sticker.

So, Samantha reported live on *Sky News* that, actually, there was absolutely no evidence to suggest that the man had anything to do with the Yes campaign or, indeed, assaulted Abbott because of marriage equality. Over the following hours speculation buzzed – had Abbott just made the whole thing up? Did the guy even have a sticker on at all? People on social media were zooming in pictures of Tony Abbott's mouth from before and after the attack, trying to figure out where this supposed swollen lip was. Hobart locals were spreading the word that the alleged headbutter was known in the area for being a bit of a knockabout and drunk – but who was he?

Before long, we found out who he was in what I maintain is one of the very best news interviews of all time. Less than 24 hours after the incident occurred, Australia was blessed with footage of a self-proclaimed anarchist by the name of Astro Labe, aka DJ Funknukl, claiming responsibility for the headbutt. Astro Labe is bald with long, bright-orange sideburns and a piercing that sits between his eyes on the bridge of his nose. He nonchalantly gave the interview while wearing a shirt with a skeleton character on it saying, 'Too weird, too rare to die'.

'I was quite drunk and I just decided I'm never going to get the opportunity to headbutt that cunt again, so . . .' he told Seven News, standing outside a pub. 'I hate Tony Abbott. It had absolutely nothing to do with marriage equality, it was just coincidental that someone had stuck a sticker on my jacket. I was just thinking, "There's Tony Abbott, I'm going to headbutt him."' When asked if he would do it again, Astro Labe shrugged and said, 'Probably. Depends on my level of sobriety.' He later told *The Guardian*, 'All it was is I saw Tony Abbott and I'd had half a skinful and I wanted to nut the cunt.'

The interview was delectable. Just as 'prominent No spokes-person headbutted by Yes campaigner' was the stuff of campaign nightmares, the appearance of Astro Labe as the culprit was a dream. He was such a hilarious villain in the story that in online discourse he briefly became a Ned Kelly-esque Aussie hero.

'The press conference was extremely funny,' Sainty chuckles to me. 'He was obviously so blasé about what he had done. He felt bad about hurting the Yes campaign but didn't feel bad at all about headbutting Tony Abbott.'

'If he looked like a reasonable person then maybe you could imagine him being any general Yes supporter. He just didn't really have any sort of credibility. I mean, if Alex Greenwich walked up to Tony Abbott and headbutted him there'd be a problem,' Kylar Loussikian agreed.

Phil Coorey added another interesting perspective, telling me 'I think if it had been anyone else but Abbott, you know, because he is disliked, he's not a popular person. That doesn't excuse what was done,' he quickly added, 'but I think there wasn't a great deal of sympathy for him. If it was someone less controversial than Abbott I think it would have been more damaging.'

What started with catastrophe quickly turned into something emblematic of the whole postal survey ordeal: a senseless, violent altercation without any lasting political impact, unnecessarily panicking the queers of Australia and working right-wing homophobes up into a gleeful frenzy to sell some papers and score some political points.

So, a drunken anarchist headbutts a former prime minister and the campaign for marriage equality cops the knock. Did the incident occur? No doubt. Astro Labe pleaded guilty to causing harm to a commonwealth public official and was sentenced to six months in jail. Did swathes of the media absolutely jump on the opportunity to spin the yarn that Tony Abbott had been headbutted by someone from the Yes campaign before there was any actual evidence to confirm Abbott's claims because they loved the drama? Absolutely.

'It's a tabloid newspaper – it's meant to sell copies, shift lots of copies,' Kylar Loussikian told me of *The Daily Telegraph*.

'I think by the end of the day it kind of, you know, the link was very tenuous,' the *Sydney Morning Herald*'s Michael Koziol admitted to me. 'But I think people sort of still had this great idea for how to sell the paper in their heads and were keen to press on with that. This is journalism, like, you know, it's, it's what we do.' Koziol laughed awkwardly. 'You've kind of got to beat the living daylights out of these things sometimes. Pun very much intended.'

Are the media to blame for reporting sensationalist allegations without proof? Also yes. Call me a purist but if someone says it's raining and another person says it's dry, it's not the job of the media to report that a Yes campaigner headbutted the former prime minister when that never actually happened.

'That's all well and good,' Phil Coorey says of the revelation that the headbutt had nothing to do with same-sex marriage. 'The fact is Abbott had already beaten [Labe] to the punch, if you know what I mean.' He laughs. 'He'd jumped on the radio and portrayed this as the sort of tactics that the Yes campaign condoned.'

When Astro Labe drunkenly lurched at Abbott, Tony Abbott didn't call the police to report an assault. He called 2GB. And the media did as the media does. Abbott called his mate Andrew Bolt and spun him a story deliberately free from facts but riddled with suggestion and implication, and the media dutifully reported what they were given because of the time pressure they were under, the fact that everybody else was doing it and, seemingly, because Abbott and his press secretary hadn't actually been pushed to tell a detailed account. Abbott's a skilled campaigner. He was able to play the media like a fiddle and got exactly what he wanted, for his own political gain and to the detriment of the Yes campaign.

Abbott calling 2GB after the 'headbutt' came the day after he told listeners of the same station his opinion of Yes campaigners, saying, 'You just can't trust these people given the way they're conducting themselves.' A couple of days before that, Abbott tweeted a video of university students clashing over the survey, writing 'So far, it's the supporters of change, not the opponents, who've been responsible for bullying and hate speech'. Abbott's comments to the media the day after the headbutt were, 'If you don't like the kind of intimidation that's creeping into our society, then the only safe thing you can do is vote No.'

I imagine Tony Abbott was delighted when Astro Labe hit him in the mouth, hoping he could use the incident to further the idea that LGBTIQ people were bullies.

Sean Kelly reflected in *The Monthly* on the visible leaders of the Yes campaign hastily making statements of condemnation about the headbutt and the tutting from journalists and commentators that it was a terrible campaign tactic (duh) and a bad decision from the Yes campaign to start headbutting people. He writes, 'The first, minor, point is the condescension in this – as though the organised Yes campaign, and the vast majority of Yes supporters, isn't aware that threats, shouting, and violence isn't the path to victory.' Kelly then cut through the noise of 'bullies' and 'victims'; and the sensationalist nonsense of whether 'one "head-butt" knocked out same-sex marriage?' He believes that a loss for the Yes side would be caused by large parts of the country resisting the concept of equality, not because of the campaign.

> Think about what the alternative conclusion means – this constant suggestion that if Yes loses it will be because of various undesirable incidents or the rhetoric used. It means that in a situation where the country votes to continue to deprive gay people of equality, *we will have found a way to blame gay people for that.*

> Or to put it another way: LGBTQI people only really deserve these rights if they ask nicely.

•

Institutions with a concentration of power, like media empires, don't like to have their power questioned or pushed. They don't tend to like minorities and don't tend to like activists. In conservative and tabloid media, activists are caricatured as hysterical and constantly outraged, or smelly barefoot hippies, or poorly educated attention seekers. Through this characterisation, we're positioned as villains in a drama triangle that newspapers and broadcasters construct to sell their wares.

But this is more than just turning current affairs into juicy stories. It's also a deliberate strategy that seeks to undermine and dismiss activists' work. The institutions that hold traditional power work in cahoots to maintain that power, which is why you'll see parts of the Murdoch media empire defending Catholic priests convicted of child abuse, or conservative governments giving tax breaks to the Murdoch media empire, who in turn write pro-coal propaganda while the fossil fuel lobby make massive donations to conservative political parties. And on it goes.

While much of the media are fixated on making activists villains and the powerful majority victims, the heroes of our story are too often overlooked. Ordinary people were the heroes of the marriage equality campaign. That is not only an empowering narrative device deployed to run a successful campaign, but it's also the truth.

10

It's Not Me, It's You

I'm at a cafe in the Inner West of Sydney with my friend, Gala, a 34-year-old queer woman. We've ordered coffees but we're skipping the smashed avocado. Gala is strikingly beautiful. She has a short, blunt fringe above an angelic face, and strong arms. She's also intimidatingly intelligent, both academically and emotionally. I think we must have met through friends years ago, but since everyone knows everyone in Sydney's Inner West queer scene, it's always hard to remember if someone was your friend's ex or your ex's friend or someone you smooched on a dancefloor before intensely talking about how the current popularisation of the term 'emotional labour' misappropriates what Karl Marx originally meant. Gala's probably all three, to be honest.

It's a month after the law passed, and we sit in the sunshine and muse about the campaign.

'Yeah, I get it,' she shrugs. 'Marriage equality is a short-sighted, resource-heavy fight benefitting only the privileged, corporate, picket-fenced gay not well-read enough on hate-capitalism to be a Real Queer. We don't need no state institutions validating our radical relating. The bubble will hold us, right?' Gala's not being sarcastic – she believes in the truth of these statements. She continues, just as earnestly. 'But the bubble doesn't exist in a bubble. And outside of the bubble?' She shakes her head. 'Sharp pointy things, ready to burst it.'

Gala is originally from the United States and has always been interested in politics, so she's intimately familiar with massive get-out-the-vote campaigns. 'You have to push so fervently to get each and every ballot in,' Gala affirms. 'I'm so acclimated to electoral politics in that context that I'm used to actually feeling like every vote counts.'

Feeling like every single vote genuinely counts was new for me, and I hated it. Mostly, Gala and I decide, because by extension it means every random person's opinion on my identity (and the quality of my professional work) is given value.

Like many LGBTIQ people, when the survey was called Gala felt a responsibility to do what she could to secure a Yes result. Gala wasn't at any campaign briefings or strategy development sessions where my colleagues and I isolated the 2s as our primary target. But she didn't need to be – Gala's grown up on get-out-the-vote campaigning. She knew what she needed to do.

'I thought "Who do I know who isn't queer and very much a Yes voter already?" I live in the queer bubble!' she laughed. 'And then I realised: the only access to people who aren't necessarily going to vote Yes that I have is my clientele.'

Gala is a prolific, lauded sex worker. Specifically, she works as a dominatrix specialising in kink, BDSM and fetishes. Her website reads: 'I fuck assholes (with permission, of course)' and she offers a range of services including corporal punishment, bondage, humiliation and piss play.

Her clients are almost exclusively straight, white men aged 30 to 60. 'That was my only demographic. The stakes were so high, I felt like it was my responsibility to talk to these dudes and see what I could do,' she told me.

Gala set up an ad on the website Backdoor: 'Marriage equality was never something I thought I'd be putting my body or my buck on the line for, but here we are. The people I love are suffering. Their children are being bullied and their families are being attacked. So here I fucking am, getting my tits out for your YES vote.'

The deal was this: clients were to bring their unsealed Yes ballot to their appointment with Gala, tick the Yes box, seal it and give it to her to post. In return, Gala would conduct her session topless (when normally she'd be clothed). The ad continued: 'If it were just about marriage, I can promise you, I wouldn't be throwing my tits around like this.' As an addendum, she added, 'I'm not even touching "No" voters this time – not even to beat them.'

Gala gave her campaign the brilliant title #YesMistress.

In very few places is sex work or kink considered a wholesome activity, though it absolutely can be. Gala's work is skilled, difficult, and, in my opinion, profoundly generous.

'I'm in a service profession; it's like going to get a massage, or see a lawyer or a counsellor,' Gala explains. 'My clients are agreeing to trust me with this aspect of themselves, for a fee, and I'm agreeing to try to create a space in which they feel safe and can get some pleasure or self-exploration out of that. If you're not familiar with kink, it can be difficult to wrap your head around that it can be nurturing and loving to give someone a spanking.'

My sense was that *The Australian* and the News Corp tabloids would have an absolute field day trying to link Gala's GOTV effort with the 'official Yes campaign', even if certain senior staff knew first-hand that it can be nurturing and loving to give someone a spanking. This is why I refrained from signal-boosting Gala's fabulous campaign on social media and why Gala didn't promote her work to the media, but her contribution to the success of the Yes vote was just as important and valid as mine or anyone else's.

When people think about the Yes campaign, maybe they think about a group of people wearing t-shirts with the same logo of a rainbow Australia on them. Maybe they think of some of the famous faces of the campaign, like Alex Greenwich and Rodney Croome. But actually, the Yes campaign was far bigger and far greater than what you might have seen on TV. The Yes campaign was bigger than you and I will ever know, because it wasn't just a campaign, it was a social movement made up of multitudes of different parts.

There are many different kinds of activism, but in a powerful social movement, all activism is connected, serving different purposes at different times. Activism can range from sending an email to your local MP about an issue to living in a tree for years to stop it from being cut down. Sometimes activism is marching in a protest with tens of thousands of people, sometimes activism is blowing the whistle on the dodgy operations of your employer.

I think we can broadly plot different kinds of activism in mass social movements, including the marriage equality campaign, along intersecting axes of centralised control and level of disruption. Imagine me standing at a whiteboard drawing this out for you; the two axes will cross over in the middle to look like a large plus symbol and make four quadrants.

The x axis is level of centralised control: at one end is when high-level strategy and objectives are controlled by a central body and satellite groups adhere to those instructions to work towards a common goal. At the opposite end is where every group and activist is determining their own strategy to their own objectives and executing tactics however which way serves their own goals.

The y axis looks at the level of disruption: just how much a decision-maker and/or your persuadable audience finds your activism pleasurable or comfortable. This spans from approval to disapproval from those in power, and whether your activism causes a stir in the press and raises eyebrows or voices.

So, a form of activism that's highly controlled and minimally disruptive would be something like a White Ribbon Day parliamentary morning tea, where high-profile men speak positively and inclusively to the powerful politicians in charge of the public purse, the contents of which are so desperately needed to keep women and children safe from men's violence.

Staying highly controlled but moving to the significantly disruptive end of the y axis you'll find, for example, the 2016 protest that saw local climate change activists join South Pacific climate campaigners in the largest anti-coal action the port of Newcastle has ever seen, forming a canoe flotilla of over 1500 people to block the passage of coal ships. The blockade took months of organisation and tens of thousands of dollars to pull off, and because of the high risk involved in blocking coal ships on water, it was highly controlled by climate justice organisation 350.org.

On the opposing end, something with decentralised, or minimal central control, that's not disruptive could be GetUp sending an email to its members encouraging them to call their MP to voice concerns about a specific piece of legislation. Yes, the idea has come from a central point, but with these kinds of scalable actions, where (hopefully!) tens of thousands of people take action, there is no control over what people actually say on the phone to their local MP. They could phone their MP and start singing 'Humpty Dumpty', if they wanted to.

And then, in the chaotic quadrant of our graph, you'll find activism that has no centralised control and is very disruptive. When I think of this quadrant, I remember when I was in London in 2011 and riots erupted in the streets in response to the police shooting an unarmed black man, Mark Duggan, through the window of his car. The city was alight. My office was evacuated because rioters were setting cars on fire and smashing shop windows. It was impossible to capture the precise reason each person was rioting, but people were angry at the overblown powers of the police, angry at being disenfranchised from the decisions made about their lives, angry at the injustices they experienced at the hands of the state, angry, angry, angry. The protesters showed up because they wanted to express that anger, not because they'd sent an RSVP two weeks earlier, attended a sign-making workshop and had been fully briefed on the riot's theory of change.

None of these approaches to change-making are more legitimate than the others, and no activism is inherently better than any other. Social movements are not only built on all different kinds of activism, they rely on that very foundation.

The campaign for marriage equality was so successful (aside from the part where we didn't win it for a few years there) because our activism could not be plotted in just one place along the axes of control and disruption: with a shared goal, we had a multitude of strategies. Our diversity was what made the campaign strong.

Different kinds of activism aren't inherently better than others but some forms of activism are far more effective, depending on the goal: Are you trying to get in the media? Are you trying to build a supporter base? Are you trying to make space for a politician to change their mind on something without being berated? For instance, a rally of 250 people in Taylor Square will be largely ineffective if the objective is for the prime minister to hold a free vote on marriage equality, but that doesn't mean it's bad activism. The objective of the event may be to energise the community, or communicate new campaign strategy to the 1s.

In my experience working on marriage equality – arguably the most powerful and significant social movement of a generation – I've come to believe that campaigns are most efficient and successful when strategy development is centralised, with a clear articulation of the goals and values, and the bulk of the work is decentralised, so that limitless people can apply their talent and time to work towards those goals and values to bring that strategy

How Powerful We Are

to life. Isolated cells of activists each doing their own thing with no shared goal likely won't bring about significant social change. Nor will a small, exclusive group of salaried campaigners who insist on militant control over interactions with decision-makers and the public.

Think of it like an orchestra. Up the front, you have the violinists, whose precise fingerwork carries a nuanced and delicate tune. And the strings play with the brass section, though they look and sound very different. The wind instruments complete the harmonies, at times leading the piece. Up the back you'll find the percussionists, bashing and clashing and keeping rhythm. But they need to be playing from the same score and be willing to look to the same conductor. This is how we turn noise into music.

Social change theorist and activist Bill Moyer clarifies the orchestra analogy in his Movement Action Plan model as the four roles of social activism: the citizen, the rebel, the reformer and the change agent. The citizens are the 'ordinary people' whose thoughts we refer to when we refer to public opinion or public narrative. The rebels are activists who engage in dramatic or disruptive actions to force issues onto the public agenda (which is viewed and considered by the citizens). Reformers work within established power structures and are sometimes considered the 'respectable face' of the social movement: they're the lobbyists in parliament, or policy advisors within peak bodies. Then there's the change makers, who Moyer says 'organise, enable and nurture others to become actively involved in the democratic process'. At different times I took the role of all these over the course of my work on marriage equality campaign, as Moyer says that a successful social movement actually requires all four roles, but during the survey I was a change maker.

I look back over the marriage equality campaign and LGBTIQ justice campaigns more broadly and see the work of these four roles at play, sometimes working together, sometimes spectacularly clashing, but all the while moving our fight forwards. Community Action Against Homophobia were fantastic at turning out the dedicated base to marriage equality rallies time and time again, their convenor Cat Rose would rev-up the crowd with chants of, 'we're here, we're queer, we're fabulous don't fuck with us!' through a student union megaphone. Cat is incredible at what she does but, for instance, she was not the right activist to work gently and closely with Liberal Senator Dean Smith on the intricate details of marriage equality legislation, which is why Lee Carnie and Anna Brown from the Human Rights Law Centre handled that.

Alex Greenwich, the Independent MP and co-chair of the Equality Campaign (via AME), was an expert in media communications who wrote and persuasively delivered the campaign messages to millions from television sets. Rodney Croome was a powerfully persuasive lobbyist who appealed to politicians of all stripes and inspired LGBTIQ people around the country to do the same. My work as a digital campaigner pressured MPs by showing them that their seats were in jeopardy if they didn't act.

Local groups around the country organised Town Hall meetings and stalls at Saturday markets, while beloved public figure Magda Szubanski used her profile to advocate for equal marriage from the media platforms she was given. People on Twitter organised boycotts or fundraised for the campaign, while high school students took on their parents and had difficult, ongoing conversations with just these one or two adults to try to shift their vote.

Musicians, comedians and creatives made videos and held events while wealthy individuals made direct donations. The way we made change differed, and that's why it worked.

It felt like moments after the High Court confirmed that Australia would hold a public vote on the lives of its LGBTIQ citizens that GetUp's Yes campaign burst to life. From the war room (love room) at GetUp, Ben Raue and Kajute O'Riordan made sure the Kooragang phonebanking software was calling the right people and reporting the right data, at scale across the country. Kirsty Albion and Kirsti Gorringe worked with smaller organisations who were running their own phonebanks, ensuring they had up-to-date scripts and recruiting an increasing number of volunteers. Anisha Humphreys led our digital advertising program. Paul Mackay, Patrick Morrow, Sarah Byrne and Niren Tuladhar made our social media content and videos. Zoe Edwards coordinated media. I was relieved of my normal duties to solely focus on writing campaign comms (emails, scripts, social media posts) and speaking to the press. Henny Smith managed the relationship with the Equality Campaign and she and Emily Mulligan oversaw the operation. For the years prior, most of the above had been in my job description but now that the campaign was exponentially bigger than ever before it needed a team at GetUp to take it on.

Over at the Equality Campaign, their national organisers were holding nightly phonebanks in capital cities. They were pumping out slick TV ads, speaking to media and continuing their powerful lobbying in parliament. In Melbourne, the Victorian Trades Hall Council and the ACTU mobilised hundreds of union members to knock on thousands of doors, and to have persuasive conversations with other union members in their workplace or industry. Equal Love and CAAH were bringing thousands to the streets to march for Yes. PFLAG, Rainbow Families, state-based Gay and Lesbian Rights Lobbies and just.equal were lobbying politicians on the final marriage bill, speaking to the media, running online campaigns and empowering their supporters to take localised actions in their communities.

People of colour–led organisations Democracy in Colour and Colour Code organised their volunteers to lead outreach programs into communities of colour, particularly focussing on supporting young people of colour to have conversations with their parents and grandparents about voting Yes. Equal Marriage Rights Australia, the largest social media channel solely dedicated to marriage equality campaigning, posted compelling and informative content every day.

Too many organisations to name went into campaign overdrive to push for a Yes victory. These groups who'd been working on the issue for years were playing like an orchestra, but we weren't alone.

The reason why the fight for marriage equality in Australia grew from a campaign to a social movement is because the activism was decentralised. People who wanted to support the Yes campaign could go online and find the tools that would allow them to not only be part of the campaign, but to help lead it. People who wanted to hold their own Yes event, whether it was a community picnic, a fun run, a phonebank or a door-knock could find everything they needed on the Yes campaign website, and they could register their event so like-minded people in their neighbourhoods could find them on a digital map and join them. People who were strong marriage equality supporters, the 1s, were empowered to step up in their own communities as Yes campaigners.

Australia's postal survey Yes campaign saw tens of thousands of ordinary people performing sophisticated work on centrally crafted plans on a scale that hasn't been seen before in this country. When I say this, I don't mean to belittle other extraordinary national campaign efforts. Far from it. The reason the Yes campaign was able to scale into the social movement it became was because of its unique imitation of a referendum, the overwhelming popularity of and familiarity with the issue, and because of the experience many organisations, such as the union movement, had with similar campaigns. We also took all the lessons learnt from mass movements past and ongoing like the anti-nuclear movement, the 1969 referendum, the campaign to save the Franklin River, and the republican movement.

Becky Bond and Zack Exley say in *Rules for Revolutionaries* that, if asked, people are ready to do big things to achieve big things. In fact, in their experience, people are more likely to do big things when they can see that they will achieve big things rather than doing something small when they know it will only achieve something small. Perhaps this is why so many people who'd never engaged in activism or campaigning before took responsibility for doing their bit to achieve the victory. They believed in the Yes campaign's theory of change: IF thousands of people use the power they have to reach the communities of people around them, THEN these people will post back a Yes vote. And they were ready to do big things.

Mary is 69 years old and with her gay son, Dale, she walked more than 60 kilometres in one weekend, putting leaflets in letterboxes in Northern Queensland, in George Christensen's electorate. 'There was a huge amount of walking over the three days including a lot of hills, but I didn't mind because of the overwhelming response from everyone we came across,' Mary told me.

Bruce Leighton, a 58-year-old straight man and proud father of a gay son, made flyers with the title 'Manly Voters Vote Yes!'

He stood out the front of former Prime Minister Tony Abbott's office to hand them out.

Denise Jepson and her friend Keith Jepson, who had been her husband before he came out as gay, placed a large advertisement in the *Midland Express*, their local paper in Central Victoria. The page-three ad cost $900 and, on a rainbow-flag background, read 'Support marriage equality. Post Yes!' Denise told me, 'Neither Keith nor I are associated with any advocacy group. We just decided on the ad as a piece of direct action.'

Big things don't have to be huge – everyone has different capacities. Eleven-year-old Edie was too young to vote, so she spent an afternoon making a rainbow sign that read 'Vote Yes!', which hung out the front of her house. My friends Amalie O'Hara and Cassie Daly crafted a novelty post box and put it in the reception of their workplace, collecting 40 votes. A straight woman I met who works at a major bank wore rainbow accessories to work every single day of the survey so that her LGBTIQ colleagues would feel her support.

People posted on social media why they supported marriage equality and encouraged their friends to join them in voting Yes. This is no small feat: making a political statement in writing, in front of your friends and acquaintances, particularly during such a polarised time, really shouldn't be underestimated. They argued their points in comments sections, often engaging in upsetting conflict on behalf of their friends and family members. That's activism. That's campaigning.

The Yes campaign didn't just happen in cities. Regional and rural towns across Australia turned their high streets rainbow and set up local Yes campaign hubs in community centres. More than 700 people organised themselves into a local Yes campaign in the regional Victoria town of Ballarat and organised a Walk for Equality, rainbow chalking around town and 'Honk 4 Yes' events on local roads.

People set up stalls at their local markets, and printed flyers to drop in the letterboxes of their neighbourhood. Yes posters hung from windows. People put stickers on their cars and changed their Facebook profiles. Thousands upon thousands used their spare time, their creativity and their determination to do what they could in their own communities.

Hand on heart, I think the postal survey brought out the best in most straight people. Don't get me wrong: I like laughing at dumb stuff that straight, cisgender people do as much as the next gay (I could watch 'gender reveal' announcement mishaps all day, every day). But I mean it when I say that straight and cisgender allies of LGBTIQ community were absolutely incredible during the campaign. When the survey was announced, many in the community were scared of how awful the public campaigns would be, of the increase in queerphobic violence on the streets and online, and of the existential assault on our lives as we're reduced to a tick box question in the mail. I begged the non-LGBTIQ people in my life to step up and help us out.

And they did. From my vantage point, I saw that across the country straight allies didn't just post their Yes the day they received it, they stepped up to put their power behind the campaign. The Yes vote wouldn't have won without them, because the LGBTIQ minority simply weren't big enough or strong enough to pull it off alone.

As well as powering campaign actions, many straight and cisgender allies stepped up as emotional supports for the LGBTIQ people in their lives. One story has stayed with me: Jenny Elson, a straight grandmother in Port Broughton, South Australia, saw that a gay man was defending himself and the queer community against homophobes in the comments under a Facebook article. Jenny didn't know the man, but she messaged him directly to let him know that he wasn't alone, and she supported him. He replied that he never thought the survey would be so hard and that he was facing threats of violence in his community. Jenny messaged him back and forth for hours, offering her ear and her kind words. She wrote to him that there were nannas like her all over the country who were ticking the Yes box for him.

Many of my straight and cisgender friends were incredible supports during the campaign. I was completely snowed-under with offers to help. My friends sent me messages of support and jumped into comment sections to fight trolls for me. They organised their own Yes phonebanks and offered to cook me food and wash my clothes. Friends and strangers on Twitter crowdfunded to buy me a day spa voucher. Meaningfully, they acknowledged the toil the process had on me and the community long after the Yes result came through. Friends, thank you.

The Yes campaign had power in numbers because of LGBTIQ allies and co-conspirators, but the heart of the campaign, of course, were millions – yes, I said millions – of LGBTIQ Australians, many of whom had been individually fighting for their acceptance, their inclusion and their respect from the people around them for their entire adult lives.

LGBTIQ people took the lessons they'd learnt from speaking to their family members about who they were and who they loved, and spread that message further. To their workplaces, their TAFE campuses, their churches and their sports clubs. LGBTIQ people used their humour, a defence mechanism many learnt in high school, and their creativity to write, draw, sing, perform and advocate for themselves to whatever audience they could find. LGBTIQ people drew from their deep, personal experiences of isolation and did what they could to prevent those feelings finding a home within other queer people in their lives. We did what we've always done in the face of loud vilification and mainstream exclusion: we fortified our community.

You'll notice I'm being very positive here. Even about gross straight people (kidding). There's no ulterior motive at play here; I do genuinely feel incredibly positive about the breadth, depth and vibrance of decentralised community campaigning for marriage equality. This isn't one of those instances where I have to fake a smile even though the interviewer is asking me why I don't think kids deserve a mum and dad. During the survey, though, even if I hadn't been feeling hunky-dory positive about thousands of people spending their spare time fighting for my community's rights I had to pretend that I was. Above all else, public-facing leaders of the campaign had to stay relentlessly, impenetrably positive.

This is the critical difference between campaign strategies for compulsory votes versus voluntary votes. For compulsory votes, like the elections we have in Australia, good campaigners know that candidates and their supporters must never say they're in the lead. They're the underdog, which is why they need every vote. 'It's going to be a close call and we won't know until every single vote is counted.' But when campaigners are trying to get out the vote, the message has to be positive and victorious. That's why you'll hear candidates from both Democratic and Republican parties introduced on the campaign trail as, 'the next president of the United States!' The idea is that if people can visualise the change they're voting for, they will feel compelled to join the winning team and motivated to show up.

As Anat Shenker-Osorio laments, 'One of our favourite things to do as advocates is say "We're the losing team! We're losers. We lose a lot so you should definitely join us!" But most people don't want to be on the losing team; that's not actually a thing that most people desire.'

I remember when Tiernan Brady arrived from Ireland just after he led the Yes side to victory in Ireland's referendum on same-sex marriage. Tiernan's first and most enduring message to all of us was that in the event of a public vote, the Yes campaign must always stay positive. Relentlessly, unshakably positive. The tone we set in any instance of a plebiscite campaign would be the tone that the LGBTIQ community would have to live with afterwards, specifically the most marginalised people in the community.

He warned that after a huge public debate and months of division, there would be LGBTIQ people in some parts of the country – particularly in areas and within intersecting communities who will predominantly vote No – who will feel even more marginalised than they did before the vote. The Yes campaign wouldn't be able to stop that entirely, this would be collateral damage of the process, but what the Yes campaign could control is the tone of their message, and a positive tone was absolutely vital for the wellbeing of LGBTIQ communities. If the Yes campaign was hostile or condescending, any resentment from No-voting communities could be directed at LGBTIQ people within those communities.

'Secondly,' Tiernan said, 'if you're trying to persuade people that a vote for your proposal will make society happier, more unified, more cohesive and more peaceful then you need to actually look like that. If you run around the country and say, "I promise you marriage equality is going to make you happy!" but you do it looking like you're chewing a bag of wasps, most people just aren't going to want to buy it.'

Tiernan's advice wasn't revolutionary, it was a warning for what was to come. As the survey campaign roared, it became extremely difficult to not look like I was chewing a bag of wasps, on account of all the wasps in my mouth. When I stood in front of a fraction of the 50,000 people who marched from the Sydney Town Hall to Sydney Harbour in support of the Yes vote and told them that the postal survey was an 'exciting opportunity' for us to show our support for LGBTIQ Australians, my mouth was full of wasps. When I debated Lyle Shelton on SBS, smiling through the indignity of being forced to engage with him and what he stood for and politely making the case for my own equality, my mouth was full of wasps. Each time I made campaign content that centred straight, cisgender people as the happy spokespeople for the Yes campaign, I felt like I was choking.

'Staying positive is really important to us because most people aren't gay,' Tiernan continued. 'They're not thinking about being gay, they don't plan to become gay, so their thought process about this is quite shallow . . . The tone is what gets absorbed.'

We had to look like the future we wezre fighting for: calm and happy. We had to keep things light and positive so that as many people as possible would support the winning team. We had to create a positive tone in the hope it would protect the vulnerable people in our community. We had to remember that the survey victory would be just one day, but it was part of the journey that started long before homosexuality was decriminalised and will continue long after marriage equality was achieved.

Because every adult in the country got a say on our rights, the survey period demanded from the public-facing Yes campaigners (like me) an even higher standard of good behaviour, lest our tweets or our raised voices be used by the media and the No campaign as fuel against us. Marriage equality has always been a 'respectable' campaign, but broader LGBTIQ activism in Australia certainly hasn't been. Much of the LGBTIQ uprising of the 1970s and the decades that followed were very firmly in the disruptive and decentralised quadrant of our tactics axes.

In the early days of the specific debate about marriage rights, back in 2004, Democrat protesters interrupted the National Coalition for Marriage's conference by unfurling a giant banner reading 'Hate is not a family value'. In 2016, students from Adelaide University trashed conservative Senator Cory Bernardi's electorate office, writing on the walls 'Ber-Nazi' and leaving signs saying, 'Go home, bigot'. This was in response to comments he'd made about the Safe Schools program but was also a response to his general, relentless homophobia and was lumped in with the marriage equality campaign in the public discourse.

Also in 2016, Simon Hunt, the man behind satirical activist character Pauline Pantsdown, disrupted the ACL conference by storming the stage dressed in striped pyjamas branded with a pink triangle – the uniform gay men were forced to wear in Nazi concentration camps – with fake blood on his hands, shouting to the crowd, 'This is the blood of the children you have attacked.'

Speaking at this conference were two men invited as esteemed guests from the United States. The first, Dr Jeff Ventrella, runs a legal organisation that sends lawyers to countries around the world to maintain their criminalisation of homosexuality and to make sure imprisoned gay and bisexual men remain in jail. The second, Eric Metaxas, is a high-profile commentator who advocates for dangerous LGBT conversion 'therapies' and is known for likening Christian acceptance for LGBTIQ rights to the church failing to stand up to the Nazi party in the 1930s. Sitting in the front row of the conference, eager to hear from Ventrella and Metaxas, was Australia's Federal Treasurer, who would soon become Australia's Prime Minister, Scott Morrison.

Hunt, who is bit of a scholar of the rise and rule of the Nazi party in Germany, explained to me that he was seeking to disrupt the passive consumption of the ideas the ACL were trying to normalise. 'With my act of protest, I had to directly skewer the difference between the mainstreaming of an organisation like the ACL in Australia and the reality of what their policies were saying and doing. What it meant for Scott Morrison to be in the same room as those two men from the United States.'

Activists who engage in disruption do so not because they think 'you have to break eggs to make an omelette', but because they believe that publicly smashing eggs, so to speak, will garner attention for their cause and polarise opinions on the issue. A disruptive action is meant to trigger heated public debate, polarising public opinions into support for the issue or opposition to the issue. Think about the First Nations activists who shut down cities by blocking major traffic arteries; this disruption is an attempt to force people to pick a side on an issue they had previously tried not to think about. Activists know it's going to make a lot of people angry – that's the idea. But, it's hard to get right.

Mark and Paul Engler write in *This is an Uprising*:

> For movements to benefit from a state of heightened conflict, its participants must make sure of two things: first, that they are drawing in more active supporters than their opponents and, second, that even if their methods are perceived as extreme or impatient, the tide of public opinion is pushing toward greater acceptance of their views.

But there are always exceptions to the rule, and with overly disruptive and 'distasteful' activism; the Englers give the example of the HIV/AIDS activist group ACT UP in the 1980s. ACT UP were extremely disruptive. One of their most famous actions was when they went to the house of US Senator Jesse Helms – who prevented any federal spending on HIV treatment or prevention and used his platform to demonise homosexual men – and covered it with a giant, yellow condom. That's right, they put a giant condom over the family home of a senator, and it read: 'Helms is deadlier than a virus'.

Putting a giant condom over the home of Senator Eric Abetz, for example, would have been extremely amusing but likely not helpful to the Yes campaign. But it worked for ACT UP.

Then in 1992, scores of protesters took the ashes of their loved ones who had died from AIDS complications and threw them onto the lawn of the White House. ACT UP's invitation read 'it is time to bring AIDS home to George Bush'. When the founder, Steve Michael, died in 1998 from AIDS complications at 42 years old, the activists marched his dead body in an open coffin to the White House, calling President Clinton a 'murdering liar'.

In ACT UP's disruptive activism, Mark and Paul Engler see the exception to their cautious rule that if tactics are too divisive and don't foster sympathy that deliberate polarisation fails:

> Unlike other AIDS campaigners, these activists were willing to make enemies and to polarize the issue of how the disease was being addressed . . . . Undertaking a notably confrontational strategy, the group stirred strong feelings and often confronted backlash. This strategy did not always make them popular. But it did allow them to stay in the public eye, to expose the injustice of official neglect and disregard, and finally to win broad support for their cause.

LGBTIQ rights activism has a long, proud history of disruption. A story that may surprise many who tut at young activists now is that Julie McCrossin, beloved broadcaster and proud Christian lesbian, was escorted from St Mary's Cathedral in 1975, dressed up in a nun costume, protesting for her friend Mike Clohesy who'd lost his job at a Catholic school after speaking on television about decriminalising homosexuality. As we touched on in Chapter One, Australia's first Mardi Gras in 1978 was a violent clash with the police after increasing tensions between the LGBTIQ community and the state over the years reached breaking point.

I love all activism, and as long as it's effective I think it's worth doing. Disruptive, conformist, whatever; if we're pushing power and we're making impact, then that's the right strategy. The thing is, during the survey I betrayed that belief. In the middle of the survey when the media had run out of meaningful things to say about the survey and so were eagle-eyed for any whiff of conflict a group of anarchist activists stormed the stage of a No event with signs that said 'burn churches not queers' while two women staged a kiss-in on stage. I freaked out. As you can imagine, it wasn't the women kissing that alarmed me.

I saw images and footage of the protest on Twitter and my stomach dropped. I knew how this would land in the press. I pictured the columns and the cartoons. I knew the press wouldn't miss a moment jumping on the story, and I wasn't wrong.

Within about fifteen minutes, I started receiving phone calls from journalists asking whether the Yes campaign endorsed the protest. In a panic of damage control, I tweeted the statement, 'Anarchists disrupting No events are not part of the Yes campaign, are not known to any of us and are not listening to the LGBTI community.'

Of course, I was called out. Friends told me my tweet was over the top. Strangers pointed out that, actually, the protesters were part of the LGBTIQ community and that protest and disruption had been at the heart of the queer rights movement for as long as it had been around. All their points were bang on.

I really regret that condemnation, and the way I shamed and policed those activists. Particularly, I'm deeply sorry for implying that the protesters were somehow not part of the LGBTIQ community (as if I am the arbiter of that, which of course I'm not). Those activists were and are just as much a part of the movement for LGBTIQ rights as me, and they didn't deserve my (forced) condemnation. I'm not the boss of marriage equality – nobody was. Nobody is.

But the most messed-up thing is, that if I found myself back in that exact same situation, I think I would still tweet out a condemnation. I would use much less offensive language (I hope), but the conditions that made the survey campaign so cruelly unique – the public opinion poll, a cashed-up No campaign, voluntary participation, a blood-thirsty media – meant that I compromised my own ethics in order to win. I'd venture other campaigners did too. The pressure of the vote was all encompassing. In that moment, I felt like I lost myself in it and became a function of the campaign, a public-facing cog in a PR machine.

•

When activists criticise other activists' work, it comes from a place of caring about an issue so deeply that we feel a need to be in control of how it's being treated. We care about activism because we want to win our campaigns, and we want to make sure other activists' actions are strategic. Criticising other activists' work comes from ego, and a desire to have our work viewed as being useful and important. And it's underpinned by a need to control the story that's told about our progress (the same need that leads me to write this book).

Many LGBTIQ activists will say that the modern queer rights movement was catalysed by the Stonewall Riots – an uprising of queer revellers against the New York police force, who were repeatedly raiding the Stonewall Inn bar and arresting patrons for 'dressing inappropriately for their gender' and 'solicitation of homosexual relations'. The story goes that Marsha P Johnson, a black, transgender sex worker and activist with the Gay Liberation front and Street Transvestite Action Revolutionaries, threw a brick at police who'd come to raid the bar. The throwing of this first brick started the riot that saw police retreat and the social movement for queer liberation (un)officially birthed.

The story of the Stonewall Riots is precious to me and my sense of community and identity, and inspires me to push back against oppression and act in defiance of power. It's a story we tell to remind ourselves and each other that the most marginalised within society and our own LGBTIQ community have always been at the forefront of our resistance. It's a story of fighting the state with fists and bricks, so we may remember to never get too close to the institutions of power that historically oppressed us.

But, of course, the story is complex. Even in 1969, there were tensions within the LGBTIQ activist community about how best to win our rights. On the third day of the riots, the wall of the Stonewall Hotel was painted with the message, 'We homosexuals plead with our people to please maintain peaceful and quiet conduct on the streets of the village – Mattachine'. The Mattachine was one of the earliest gay rights organisations in the United States, emerging in the 1950s. By 1969, however, their approach and painted message may have been considered conservative or assimilatory by the Stonewall rioters. The group met with the police and the city council to try to smooth over tensions and negotiate an end to the riot.

There's significant dialogue about whether Marsha P Johnson actually threw the first brick, or whether it was Sylvia Rivera – a Puerto Rican transgender activist. Others say that before the brick there was a punch thrown by Stormé DeLarverie, a black biracial butch lesbian and drag king, when police dragged her from the bar. People debate whether the brick was actually a high heel. Johnson, Rivera and DeLarvarie all denied that they were the ones to start the riot. DeLarvarie is reported to have said when asked about who started it, 'It was never anyone's business.'

Personally, and I'm aware that this opinion may initially smart, I find the idea that one person started the Stonewall Riots, and by extension the modern queer rights movement, a bit reductive. I think it minimises Johnson and Rivera's extraordinary contributions over the course of their lives to trans liberation and queer rights to a single brick. I think it erases the work of their peers in New York, around the country and around the world. It simplifies how social movements build and climax. The Stonewall Riots didn't come out of nowhere, and neither did that brick. We can honour the indisputable fact that transgender people and people of colour have always been at the forefront and the front line of queer activism without mythologising a disputed account of whether someone threw a brick. I say that as someone who's travelled to the Stonewall Inn to sit quietly and gratefully pay tribute to these women and their fellow activists. Vietnamese transgender poet Chrysanthemum Tran says that DeLarverie's own denial of being the person who started the uprising should challenge the LGBTIQ community's obsession with crediting protest movements to a singular person. Tran writes in *them.*:

> This focus on the 'first' punch/brick/molotov cocktail is intended to refute revisionist histories that undermine the labor of trans-gender women and lesbians of color (neither of which are mutually exclusive) within the LGBTQ+ community. But in our attempts to counter revisionism by uplifting the work and impact of LGBTQ+ women of color, we create and normalize false histories that fail

to accurately recognize their legacies and those of countless others who jeopardized their lives to resist the police.

I love that our LGBTIQ history is full of resistance and defiance, but I'm saddened that even the Stonewall Riot has an element of activists declaring who was the first, the most important, who was unhelpful and who wasn't even there. Some things never change.

Australia's marriage equality campaign is about as different as you can get to the trans and queer women of colour–led Stonewall Riot, but surrounding it I have noticed the same pre-occupation of LGBTIQ activists of who was the first, who did the most, who *really* won the campaign. While with the mythologising of the Stonewall Riot, the stories we tell are about rightfully celebrating trans and queer women of colour, in my time in the final years of the marriage equality campaign, I witnessed an obsession from some people not with changing the law, but with having their name in the imaginary history book. This manifested through self-promotion, but also in the criticism and undermining of other activists' contributions. Criticising other people's activism can be a useful evaluation of efficacy, but it became a constant stream of mean and personal attacks on other activists' work, designed to secure their own position in the history book.

When I announced that I was writing this book, people's reactions within the marriage equality activist scene included excitement that I would 'set the record straight' about who really contributed the most to the win, direct requests to write about people's own work and suspicion that I would make it look like I single-handedly won marriage equality. That would have been an impressive story!

When I interviewed Rodney Croome for this book, I asked him how he felt when he saw the Liberal party take credit for marriage equality. As part of his answer, he said, '[the] Liberals aren't the only ones who claim too much credit. After the Smith bill passed, quite a few people whose contribution came towards the end of the campaign, when reform seemed likely, took, or were allocated, much of the credit for winning marriage equality. Like the moderate Liberals, some of these people failed to acknowledge the everyday folk who had built the stage upon which they strode.'

Will the LGBTIQ activist community ever stop criticising each other and jostling for the spotlight? I'm not sure. I believe in justice and progress because I believe in abundance, not scarcity. I hope that one day we as a community will see that there is an abundance of praise and an abundance of credit, because we can make it ourselves and give it to each other. I hope we can see that there is an abundance of ways to win a campaign, and we need them all.

•

It's probably fair to say the campaign for marriage equality in Australia started in earnest in 2004. You might say that the specific campaign for marriage equality started on the streets, with the first rally organised by CAAH in response to John Howard changing the Marriage Act. You might say that Jac Tomlins and her wife, Sarah, along with Jason and Adrian Tuazon-McCheyne started the campaign when they took their Canadian marriages to the Australian judiciary to challenge our discriminatory law. You might say that, actually, the campaign started in earnest when Rodney Croome organised a teleconference, also in 2004, with LGBTIQ activists and decided to launch an organisation called Australian Marriage Equality. Maybe it officially started when the first marriage equality legislation was introduced to federal parliament by the Australian Democrats in 2006 but maybe it actually started in 1978 when Peter de Waal and his friends protested on Oxford Street in Australia's first Mardi Gras.

They all mark the moment where a collective idea began to take form, and pioneering people began to take action. It would be folly to attempt to pinpoint the singular moment the campaign was born, or the sole group of people who birthed it, because that's not how social movements work.

Some marriage equality activists may scour this book to see if they or their friends are named. Chances are they're not, but only because even if I had used every single word in this book to name people who've contributed to the historic victory of marriage equality, I still would have only captured a fraction. We will never have a written honour roll of all that we did. It's impossible to quantify and itemise what we did together and if we did – if we catalogued every conversation and every bumper sticker and every smile, every time we held hands with our partner, every dollar we donated or Facebook post we 'liked' – if we lay it all out in front of us as skin and bones and tissue, what would we achieve? We must find pride within ourselves. We've always created our own pride.

Each of us sit at different points of what is acceptable acquiescence to, proximity to and disruption of power. Critique is not lateral violence, though the campaign wasn't without it. Good critique comes from evaluation, and in order to make impact as effectively as possible activists need to constantly evaluate their work.

There will also always be disagreement on how to make change, but what I learnt from working on the marriage equality campaign is that in order to truly scale a campaign to mass-movement proportions, you need to embrace that disagreement. If you want to build a movement, activists must relinquish control and surrender aversion to risk. You've got to let the people who are the feet on the ground and the hands hard at work make mistakes because they will also make miracles. History-making campaigns are not going to be perfect; they will be messy, risky and fraught. People-powered movements are run by ordinary, flawed human people who are all just trying their best. But each of us has power, and when we organise ourselves in a way that's deliberate, strategic and measurable, then that power can be exponentially multiplied. We become more than a crowd of ordinary, flawed human people and become a force to be reckoned with.

The Yes campaign wasn't one organisation working out of a high-rise tower in Barangaroo. It wasn't a coalition of professional campaign groups like GetUp and just.equal. It wasn't a handful of us who you saw on TV, or who lobbied within parliament.

The Yes campaign was hundreds of thousands, if not millions of ordinary people realising that a postal survey on LGBTIQ people's lives was an exceptional circumstance and who felt called to do what they could to help. It was ordinary people who would never consider themselves activists putting up a sign in the kitchenette of their workplace, asking their colleagues to vote Yes. Or setting up a rainbow stall at AusKick with homemade Yes badges and maps of the neighbourhood letterboxes.

The Yes campaign for marriage equality was mass activism on a scale that has never been seen before in Australia. The scope of action, the willingness of so many people to do their bit was phenomenal. We weren't a homogeneous, synchronised, centrally controlled machine; we were a vibrant, noisy, messy rainbow. We weren't the Vienna Philharmonic, but if you listen to what we did together, we were a symphony.

By the end of the survey, my friend Gala the dominatrix had collected seven ballots from clients redeeming her #YesMistress deal. On top of the seven Yes votes she secured, she also received nine emails reporting Yes votes from previous clients and, in her words, '$2600 in whore money'. When the Yes result came through, Gala received several text messages from clients saying, 'Congratulations!'

Reflecting on her campaign, Gala said, 'My experience of social change and social movement is that it's always from the ground up, it's always multi-pronged and multi-faceted.'

Simon Hunt agrees with her: 'When you've got something as abstract as treating LGBTIQ equally, it has to come from all different angles. Different people have to speak to different people in order for the campaign to be won.'

He continues, 'During the campaign I would find myself sometimes annoyed with the Equality Campaign when I would see something that was very sanitised. At other times I would find myself personally annoyed with people who wanted to hold a conference about how marriage was a patriarchal construct and we're actually ruining the world by even trying to fight for marriage, you know? At the same time, I acknowledge the legitimacy of both those positions and both of those tactics. It's the multiplicity of styles of activism that actually achieve things in that way.'

Much like the Stonewall Riots, distilling the extraordinary scale of the campaign down to a single person, down to a single brick, will pave over the work of tens of thousands. Valuable, fascinating and conflicting work. Effective work and accidentally detrimental work. Work that in its culmination changed our country for the better.

11
Two Truths and a Lie

When I started out as an activist everything was black and white. The goodies were only good, and the baddies were only bad. There was a right way of doing things and every other way was both wrong and terrible. The goodies must not compromise, and any compromise from the baddies simply wasn't enough.

There was only one way to win a campaign and there was only one way to make change, particularly when it came to progress and justice for LGBTIQ people. The thought of right-wing political parties, corporations or the church being involved with the fight for my community's freedom – the freedom that those institutions had withheld for so long – was unthinkable. Why would we engage our oppressors in our liberation?

I wasn't interested in accepting how power works, how big decisions are made in our collective society and how the political landscape is rocky and swampy and hostile to those who refuse to get dirty.

During my time working on the marriage equality campaign I learnt that change-making isn't just bricks and barricades (physical and metaphorical), it's also breaking down barriers and building collectively with people you might ordinarily disagree with. And it's hard; compromise takes tenacity. It is far easier to stand still than it is to walk alongside people you fiercely disagree with on everything other than the common ground you're forging together. To change something as significant as the way our entire society understands what a family is, and then codify that vision into law, LGBTIQ people and those who love them had to rally everyone around us.

We couldn't stand alone; that's not how our systems of power work. And we weren't tearing down the system. Not this time.

I'm not religious, right-wing or corporate. Those institutions range from foreign to foul to me. I suppose some of my beliefs are a bit libertarian in that I support the full decriminalisation of drugs and think the state shouldn't have a say in who I can marry. That's a bit right-wing, but certainly not conservative. I worked as a temp for about six months when I was living in London and sat at the reception of dozens of corporations, answering phones and looking at Twitter. But that probably doesn't count as Big Business experience. I went to a Catholic high school as the token poor, atheist kid and went to a youth group for a bit because there were cool older girls I had crushes on. Reciting Hail Marys twice a day at school and dancing with girls to Christian pop-rock on Friday night probably doesn't count as being religious, though.

Once I realised I was gay, religion – Christianity in particular because that's what I had been most exposed to – felt like my enemy. I knew what the church thought about homosexuality. I had friends who had been kicked out of their religious family homes after coming out. Before I had even come out to myself, let alone anyone else, a young married couple from the youth group where I was flirting with girls orchestrated to give me a lift somewhere and used the car journey to tell me that being gay was wrong, and if I ever wanted to talk to anyone about it I could talk to them. I was fourteen, hadn't examined my desire to dance with the youth group girls and had no idea what they were talking about. When I figured it out, though, I thought Christian religions hated people like me.

As it turns out, it's more complicated than that.

I met Sam and Caitlin at a dinner party in Canberra. They met through work, as so many couples do. After moving in together they went in search of a new church, because Sam had been forced to leave her previous church when she started dating Caitlin. They found one they liked and, for the sake of being upfront, told the pastor there that they were a couple. The pastor repeated the official church position, that marriage was only between a man and a woman, but invited them to be part of the church anyway, telling them, 'You're welcome here.' They were the first committed same-sex couple in his congregation and often had dinner with their pastor to discuss the theology of sexuality, where he would try to convince them of his own views.

I imagine you'll be excited to hear that Sam and Caitlin, despite many conversations with their pastor, weren't convinced that they were living in sin. So, they got engaged. A win for love! Sam is originally from New Zealand and Caitlin from Scotland, so because they were both from countries that allowed same-sex marriages they were able to marry in Australia through their consulates, but their marriage wouldn't be legally recognised in Australia. A slight setback for love!

Sam and Caitlin had a lukewarm reception when they sent their wedding invites to their church. The pastor said he couldn't attend in good conscience. A small number came in support but were explicit in their opposition to the marriage.

'I can count on one hand the number who simply attended without judgement,' Sam told me.

Then, after the wedding, their pastor decided that having a married same-sex couple in the congregation would mean the church would be seen as endorsing same-sex marriage. He asked them to leave the church.

'He was as gracious as is possible when delivering a message like that, but it still felt like a deep betrayal of his first words when

I came out to him – that I was, and always would be, welcome there,' Sam told me.

Sam and Caitlin were heartbroken but left the church as the pastor had asked them to.

A couple of months later, the government decided to hold a survey on whether to acknowledge Sam and Caitlin's relationship and the ground beneath their feet became unsteady once again.

'While we didn't feel that our identities as queer and Christian were at war, the media seemed to decide otherwise. Then, almost every interaction became someone vilifying one aspect of my identity,' said Sam.

Caitlin and Sam's experience wasn't isolated. Not among Christians, and not among LGBTIQ people of other faiths.

During the survey, Sydney-based LGBTIQ activist and Muslim woman Cindy El Sayed found it incredibly difficult to be present in her faith community. She found it nightmarish to listen to what she describes as 'religious shaming' of LGBTIQ people, but at the same time felt pressure to defend her faith from Islamophobic stereotyping.

'As a Muslim, I wanted to protect my community from the white, colonial gaze that viewed homophobia as the norm among all Muslims,' Cindy explained to me.

'On the other side, speaking out against homophobia in my own community made me seem like I was embracing western culture and turning my back on my own. All in all, it was an awful time to have all these intersectional oppressions so distinctly present in my life.'

Australia, despite rising numbers of people identifying as atheist and agnostic, is still a fairly religious country. We organise around Christian traditions like Christmas and Easter, we have hundreds of Christian schools that receive public funding, and while Julia Gillard was a declared atheist, most of our prime ministers have been publicly Christian.

Religion has a funny place in the Australian parliament. Our constitution insists there be a separation of church and state, but each sitting day in parliament begins with the Lord's Prayer. There is also a far greater representation of hardcore Christians in parliament than in society, presumably because the kind of people who believe it's their duty to dictate how other people live their lives seek the power to do so. Folks who aren't overly bothered by other people's reproductive choices, health needs or sex lives tend to not dedicate their lives to controlling other people's reproductive choices, health needs or sex lives.

The existence of conscience votes or free votes in our parliaments – which was our campaign goal for marriage equality for so many years – also speaks to the level of religiosity in the chambers. These kinds of votes mean that MPs are given permission to each vote 'with their conscience' rather than party position on topics like abortion, assisted suicide and LGBTIQ issues. It's no coincidence that 'conscience votes' in parliament seem to frequently be wheeled out for issues controversial to the church.

As Labor Senator Doug Cameron put it during the Senate debate on the final marriage equality bill, 'Religious organisations are among the most powerful in the country. Among the richest in the country. They are not defenceless bystanders in Australian political life, or the economy. They are big players.' He should know, he was in parliament for more than a decade.

Yes, churches are very rich but for the large churches in Australia, their power and influence comes from their platform of moral authority with captive listeners. You can imagine how a political party might feel when threatened by the prospect of thousands of Catholic school principals sending a letter to hundreds of thousands of parents saying that, '[political party] plans to cut this school's funding', or indeed, '[political party] is threatening our religious freedom with same-sex marriage'. Keeping bishops happy mitigates negative public statements from the church authority to broader society. Consider the billions of taxpayer dollars that both the Labor party and the Liberal party keep committing to private, religious schools. Private, religious schools that in many states are legally allowed to expel a student if they are lesbian, gay, bisexual or transgender.

The leadership of Christian-faith churches powered the No campaign. As mentioned earlier, the Coalition for Marriage itself was run by the Catholic Archdiocese of Sydney, the Catholic Archdiocese of Melbourne and the two organisations, ACL and the Australian Marriage Alliance. And they didn't just work behind the scenes.

The executive of the Catholic Church used every platform they could to push their followers to vote No. Archbishop Anthony Fisher gave a letter to school principals for distribution to the parents of many thousand school children; it said: 'We will be voting NO and encourage you to do the same.'

Catholic parishes across NSW sent email bulletins with the message, 'A change in the marriage law has consequences for freedom of religion, including the ability of individuals to live out their faith in everyday life,' with a link to the Coalition for Marriage volunteer sign-up website. Thousands of flyers were sent to churches with a similar message and staff were asked to encourage worshippers to take stacks to deliver in their neighbourhoods and workplaces. The social media pages of churches from Parramatta to Clovelly were lit up with content advocating a No vote.

In an act of despicable intimidation, when the survey was confirmed, the Catholic church threatened its 180,000 employees – teachers, nurses, care workers and others – that should the law be changed they would face the sack if they were to marry a same-sex partner. Anti-discrimination laws in 2017 provide exemptions for churches and religious employers, granting them permission to hire and fire people based on their sexuality or gender, so it wasn't an empty threat.

Catholic Archbishop of Brisbane Mark Coleridge, one of the most senior religious figures in the country, compared same-sex marriage to incest, telling *ABC News*, 'Parents can't marry their children, children can't marry their parents. Sibling marrying sibling has always been ruled out. People underage have been disqualified from marrying and so too people of the same sex.'

The Anglican church was the largest donor to the No campaign on the public record, contributing $1 million. The Archbishop of Sydney, Glenn Davies, wrote in a letter to Anglican churches, 'Some have questioned whether the money would have been better spent on social justice issues – feeding the poor, Sydney's homeless, refugees etcetera. The reality is, however, that our participation in the Coalition for Marriage is not at the expense of our commitment to social justice, but because of it.'

Comments like these from religious leadership don't just evaporate from people's consciousness. They're not scrubbed from the record by the result of a survey or the passage of legislation.

'It would be a mistake to think the postal survey happened and now it's over,' Sam says. 'I see a recurring theme in many accounts of queer people who have had to leave their church or their faith because of who they are. The people who were told, over and over throughout this debate, that their identities as Christian and queer cannot exist in the same person. They're angry and hurt – not just because of the rejection from the church, but because something precious was ripped from their lives. They miss their faith. They miss their community. My faith will never be as innocent as it was, and I mourn that greatly.'

The leadership of other religions joined Christian churches in their opposition. The Rabbinical Council of Victoria, a peak body for Jewish leaders, issued a statement encouraging a No vote, 'Our Torah clearly upholds traditional heterosexual marriage as the ideal family unit'. The Victorian Board of Imams, Muslim religious leaders, ran a social media campaign urging a No vote, and said, 'Like Catholic and Jewish people, we have always maintained marriage is between a man and a woman and that's widely known to people. This is a democracy, we are being asked to vote, and we've had a say on that matter.'

But it was Christian leaders who were exponentially more vocal in their opposition and who hold enormous power in this country. Christian religions also know a thing or two about persuading masses of people to believe something, and they were smart enough to figure that going full fire-and-brimstone wouldn't help their case. They weren't quoting Leviticus or shouting about Sodom and Gomorrah by arguing in a biblical frame.

It must be said, though, that even though Christian religious leaders aren't in the public domain reciting bible passages, it is that scripture and the interpretations of those words by their institutions that underpins their opposition to homosexuality. It all comes back to powerful figures in organised religions interpreting words written thousands of years ago and deciding that it means that God doesn't like anal sex. Between men, of course. Heterosexual couples doing anal to preserve their real virginity until marriage is canon.

Opting to not bang on about their weird obsession with Butt Stuff, the church spoke to their congregations using the frame that worked best in their favour: 'religious freedoms'. Churches warned that if the legal definition of marriage changed to include LGBTIQ people's relationships then religious schools would have to explain to children that marriage included LGBTIQ people's relationships. Religious charities and companies might have to recognise their employees same-sex spouses in parental leave. Religious care organisations like hospitals and nursing homes would have to recognise same-sex couples and give them the same rights as everyone – heavens!

In a statement to *The Australian*, Sydney's Archbishop Anthony Fisher asked, 'Will Catholic welfare agencies be required to provide marriage preparation or marriage counselling for same-sex couples on pain of being dragged before anti-discrimination tribunals?'

Forget the children, won't somebody think of the Catholic charities forced to provide counselling support to same-sex couples experiencing marriage breakdown!

Even though the Yes campaign assured voters this reform wasn't about religious freedom, because it wasn't, it certainly brought the tension between anti-discrimination policies and religious enforcement of discrimination to the fore of public debate.

LGBTIQ people don't choose to have our lives and freedoms exist in opposition to religious doctrines. Religion insists our existence is a sin, not us. It's not the fault of LGBTIQ people that religion has a problem with our equality as human beings, if the church is forced to back out of public policy because we are demanding our rights then so be it.

We never know, maybe the major religions of the world will one day embrace LGBTIQ people, deciding that we are indeed made in God's own image.

Here's the thing: people in senior positions in organised religions just *make things up*, based on their interpretation of their holy text or, in some cases, a new directive they claim to be given. People make church rules.

You might remember Pope Benedict declaring in 2007 that babies who die before being baptised would no longer be trapped in limbo but would instead be allowed to go to heaven. How generous of him! Blessed be 2007. One must wonder if the rule was retrospective, with 800 years of dead babies suddenly joining heaven all at once, or whether the rule was grandfathered and only applied to the babies who died thereafter. Perhaps instead, the Catholic church had been wrong the entire time and every unbaptised baby who died went to heaven all along. If that was the case, I wonder what the cut-off age was? Would it be like catching a plane: if the baby is over two it needs a full adult fare? Are unbaptised three-year-olds still stuck in limbo?

The Church of Jesus Christ of Latter Day Saints, commonly known as Mormons, used to teach that black people weren't allowed in the church because they were cursed and if they only repented for their 'sins' then they'd turn white. Then in the 1970s, the church's membership began declining, particularly in comparison to other Christian religions who'd got to work sending missionaries to African, Central and South American countries. So in 1979, the church leadership changed the rules and decided black people were totally fine to be in their religion and now there are Latter Day Saint temples across Africa. Convenient!

What about religious leaders who accept the theory of evolution, thus rejecting their sacred text's story of creation (or deciding it was actually a metaphor)? The reality is that religions change to adapt to the societies they live in. Churches must keep up with the rest of society, lest they damn themselves to irrelevance.

There's huge, real-world disadvantage and discrimination that LGBTIQ people face because Australian society is built around these religious rules and the powerful influence of the church. And the real kicker is that the leadership of Christian religions in Australia is completely out of step with their congregation.

It's just not true to say that religious people don't support LGBTIQ rights. The data shows it's a big lie. A Newgate poll commissioned just before survey ballots reached people's homes found that 66 per cent of Catholics and 59 per cent of Anglican and Uniting Church members said they planned to vote Yes in the survey. Of people with a non-Christian faith (comprising an incredibly diverse list including Judaism, Islam, Sikh and Buddhist faiths) 67 per cent said that they would vote Yes.

It's also not true to say that all religious leaders oppose marriage equality. Let's talk about Christians again. Within an hour of the High Court confirming the survey would go ahead, the Anglican Parish of Ormond in Victoria changed the sign at the front of their church to read, 'Jesus loves the LGBTIQ community. We know this because he died to save them too.' Don't get this sign confused with the famous signs of the Gosford Anglican Church under the stewardship of Father Rod Bower. Father Bower immediately changed his church's sign to: 'Dear Christians, some people are gay, get over it. Love God' and continued to campaign for a Yes vote to his church and from his public platform. Father Bower said, 'When faith leaders actually come out and say to their communities, "It's okay to vote Yes", it's quite a strong thing for people to hear, and it gives them that little extra bit of encouragement.'

For the same reason, Christians for Marriage Equality was formed, who were a group of priests, pastors and laypeople who practised what they preached by working to end discrimination against the marginalised.

When I posted on my personal Facebook account that I'd been receiving torrents of horrible messages from people who subscribe to the Marriage Alliance's email list, (who had sent a newsletter to their supporters with my name and photo in it saying that I wanted to destroy marriage), telling me I was perverted and going to hell, Justin Whelan and Anglican Minister Margaret Mayman visited my office with flowers and a card that read, 'Dear Sally, we heard some people claiming to be Christians have been sending you abuse. We are so sorry this is happening and want you to know you have our love, support and appreciation for all that you're doing for marriage equality and for all LGBTIQ people. Blessings, Australian Christians for Marriage Equality.'

When the Rabbinical Council of Victoria put out the statement encouraging Jewish people to vote No, Rabbi Ralph Genende resigned in protest. Two days later, the president, Rabbi Daniel Rabin, apologised. When *Australian Jewish News*, Australia's largest Jewish publication, ran an ad opposing 'transgender marriage' (reminder: many transgender people are already married), hundreds of Jewish people crowdfunded to put their own ad in the paper in response, and ended up with an extra $10,000 to donate to the Yes campaign.

Fahad Ali, a gay Muslim man from Sydney, started the organisation Muslims for Marriage Equality which supported Muslim LGBTIQ people during the vote and advocated for a Yes vote within Muslim communities. Imam Nur Warsame, who runs the Marhaba ('welcome') LGBTIQ Muslim congregation in Melbourne, told Muslims across Australia, 'Marriage equality will give hope to a lot of youth.'

It's true that religion – and in Australia, Christianity in particular – is overwhelmingly responsible for the discrimination against LGBTIQ people, through homophobic interpretations of ancient scriptures that have significant influence over our country's social fabric and law-making processes. That is indisputable. It's also true that the leadership of Christian religions in Australia, who wield this discriminatory power, do not represent the majority of Christians' acceptance of, love for and identification within the LGBTIQ community. Both things can be true, and it's a lie to say they aren't.

●

Mixing big business with politics is, in my opinion, usually unfair and potentially dangerous.

My experience engaging in corporate campaigning while at GetUp was largely limited to boycotts or complicated divest-ment campaigns (where ordinary people coordinate to all pull their investments, stocks or bonds out of financial institutions) including those that saw the four major Australian banks pulling out of funding the Adani coal mine, and multinational corpor-ation Broadspectrum, formerly Transfield Services, walk away from running the Manus Island refugee detention camp. Both approaches, boycotts and their more sophisticated sibling, divest-ments, are very different to a third option: working with giant corporations to use their power to push a cause.

I didn't realise just how present corporations were in parlia-ment until I was right in the thick of it. Parliament sits for, on average, about 60 days a year and big business groups host dinners or functions most nights to wine and dine our policy-makers. Staff from these corporations walk the corridors of parliament as lobbyists, all-access passes hanging around their necks as they move between closed-door meetings. These corporations make massive donations to political parties.

In theory, people donate to increase the party's likelihood of winning an election, which means the donation is to support the chances of a preferred policy or set of policies becoming law.

But when it comes to big corporations, they're far more likely to make equal donations to both the Labor party *and* the Liberal party. For example, ANZ Banking Group Limited – one of the four major banks in Australia – gave an identical $100,000 in registered political donations to the Labor and Liberal parties in the 2017–2018 financial year. I'm no mathematician but that doesn't seem to give one party a leg up on the other, does it? Surely equal donations would cancel each other out, rendering them as useless as my credit-sapping text messages from my Nokia 3310 to support both Casey Donovan and Anthony Callea in the 2004 *Australian Idol* finale?

It seems counter-intuitive but, as you'd expect with a high-stakes collision of money and power, it's not as simple as that. These donations aren't given in the spirit of supporting a campaign, though that's what they're likely spent on. These donations are primarily for access and influence over specific policy decisions.

The Minerals Council of Australia (MCA), who represent the interests of the mining industry, admitted to a Senate select committee on the influence of political donations that they make political contributions 'because they provide additional opportunities for the MCA to meet with members of parliament' to lobby politicians on the 'policy priorities of the MCA'. Nine Entertainment Co. told the committee that their donations gave them access to the business forums of both major parties, to 'provide informative policy briefings', while Crown Resorts – Australia's largest gambling group worth billions of dollars – say that they 'rely heavily on donations in order to communicate their messages and policies to the Australian public'.

Of course, not all groups make political donations to both parties. For example, in the same year the Labor party received just over $1 million from the Victorian branch of the Electrical

Trades Union – money which was amassed from tens of thousands of small contributions from their union members – the Liberal party received $2.3 million from Vapold Pty Ltd, a mysterious associated entity group run by Rupert Murdoch's brother-in-law.

There are rules that apply to explicit political donations, but they're a pretty tokenistic attempt to regulate who can donate to political parties and how much they can give. The Australian Electoral Commission monitors political donations and requires disclosure of domestic donations over $13,800 (at time of writing, indexed to CPI). Foreign donations are capped at $1000. Donation disclosure happens during the forced annual campaign finance disclosure, and it makes for some interesting, if depressing, reading. This is how it became public many months after the Liberal–National Coalition won government in 2016 that then-Prime Minister Malcolm Turnbull tipped in $1.75 million of his own money in order to return his government to power. Imagine if we all had a spare million bucks lying around to help our preferred political party win power!

These disclosure laws allow us to see that, for instance, Coopers Brewery is among the largest donors to the Liberals in recent years. This is the same Coopers that co-sponsored a parliamentary event with the Bible Society that encouraged a 'light debate' on whether people should vote Yes or No in the survey. I can only imagine the conservative corporation's confusion at the free market's response to that decision, as pubs and bars across the country pulled Coopers from their taps until the brand clarified their (I assume new) support for marriage equality.

Money also doesn't just land in political parties' purses in the form of donations. Special interest groups and big business lobbies are able to funnel vast amounts of money to political parties through memberships to business forums or tickets to fancy dinners that cost thousands of dollars. Access to these corporate functions and events allows lobbyists to strategically build relationships with politicians, often over a period of decades. And unlike official donations, this can be private – events held by, for example, the Business Council of Australia don't have to declare who paid thousands of dollars for an event that ministers are attending. Furthermore, no one is checking the guest list to see whether someone who paid thousands of dollars to attend actually went.

The complex, covert money-funnelling between trusts, associated entities, in-kind contributions and off-the-shelf shell companies into the coffers of political parties would require pages and pages that we don't have to spare. But what I want to impress upon you is that these highly complicated donation systems are created, and remain untouched, because they are mutually beneficial for political parties and rich people. Rich people want to use their money to buy power, and the evidence suggests that political parties are more than happy to sell it to them.

Corporations love power. Corporations *are* power, and they're insatiably hungry for more. They gobble up everything that's weaker than them – smaller corporations, workers, natural resources – and grow bigger, stronger and more powerful. Corporations aren't built to care for people, let alone those pushed to the fringes of society. They're built to make money.

Back when being LGBTIQ wasn't seen as cool and profitable, corporate advertising frequently lent into homophobic and transphobic 'jokes' to sell their wares. In 2008, Snickers was forced to pull a global TV ad where Mr T appeared to mock the way a gay man was walking along the footpath. As recently as 2014, Meat and Livestock Australia came under fire for making a joke in their lamb ad about how lesbians look like men. This social backlash wouldn't have happened in the 90s.

Nowadays, Troye Sivan poses for Valentino and American Eagle. Transgender goddess Indya Moore models Calvin Klein underwear. Makeup brands like Fenty Beauty feature gay men in their ads, while Sephora heavily advertises free makeup classes for trans women, which is both a lovely gesture and also a deliberately crafted marketing move. Queer pride now sells.

Here in Australia, lesbians kiss on television ads for Kellogg's and Magnum ice creams. My friends Antony and Ron recreate their wedding for iPhone. Jordan Raskopoulos, Australia's most famous (and beloved) transgender woman, is in high demand, partnering with brands Audible, Junkee and, seemingly working with a different agency than they were in 2014, Meat and Livestock Australia. The Sydney Gay and Lesbian Mardi Gras parade is chock full of companies wanting to align their brand with LGBTIQ pride, including major Australian brands like Holden, Telstra and Qantas.

Is this progress? I don't know. If queer liberation is inextricably tied to freedom from capitalism, corporations are not our friend. There's nothing liberating about our identities being packaged up into something shiny and marketable, sold back to us and used for private profit. There's certainly nothing freeing about our history of protest and resistance being appropriated by major banks, who are responsible for widespread financial corruption – we aren't fooled just because you put a rainbow on your ATM.

Then again, seeing our identities, relationships and families reflected back to us in the media is vitally important for young LGBTIQ people. We know that representation and inclusion in mainstream advertising is profoundly meaningful to people from minority groups; and it models acceptance and celebration of marginalised communities to the broader population.

The truth is, whether we like it or not, big business played a powerful role in Australia achieving marriage equality, and they didn't all come on board at the last minute.

'Corporate Australia showed early leadership in the campaign, at a time when still no one in the Labor party was showing support for marriage equality, in a way,' Alex Greenwich told me. Before being elected to state parliament, Greenwich worked in recruiting and had close relationships with the business community. One of his earliest projects with AME was to secure public support of several large corporations, including Westpac, Seek and Qantas.

'People didn't necessarily see corporations as our friend. Because I had worked with so many, I knew that they actually were,' he explained to me.

In 2008 Greenwich and AME placed a story in the *Sydney Morning Herald* about corporate Australia's backing of equal marriage, to impress upon parliament that it was becoming a mainstream issue. From there, the business community flocked to put their weight behind marriage equality.

In the years leading up to the survey more and more of corporate Australia publicly signed up to support the reform. Business leaders like AGL Energy CEO Andy Vesey and Visy CEO Anthony Pratt all put their names, as well as their business empires, to the cause.

Some companies went even further. Ben and Jerry's, who sold ice creams with names like 'I Dough', ran an in-store effort to encourage customers to record voice messages that would be sent to members of parliament. In 2016 and 2017, Lush Cosmetics, the company responsible for many shopping centres smelling like bath bombs, transformed their stores into Yes campaign hubs, training their staff to have persuasive conversations with customers and decking out their shopfronts in marriage equality collateral.

Coca-Cola issued a company statement supporting a Yes vote and lit their iconic sign in Kings Cross in rainbow colours with the message, 'We say yes to love'. If there's anything more emblematic of the commercialisation queer liberation, it's a gay Coca-Cola sign. Qantas CEO Alan Joyce donated a million dollars of his own money, saying: 'We are vocal on gender equality issues, Indigenous issues and on LGBTI issues. That's what good businesses do. They're part of society. They help promote societal changes. They help promote what's good for our people.'

Imagine for a moment, if that was true. Imagine if all business dedicated the power that they wield to supporting First Nations Australians in their fight for sovereignty and self-determination. Imagine if corporations donated to political parties and used that financial leverage to call for an overhaul of how the justice system treats survivors of rape, or people addicted to drugs. Imagine if, instead of turning a logo rainbow coloured for a pride parade, companies made public statements calling for lifesaving gender affirmation surgery to be covered by Medicare.

Alex Greenwich isn't lying when he says that corporate Australia showed early leadership in the campaign – that's true. But I'm not lying when I say that capitalism isn't concerned with 'social good' unless it's profitable for them. Both are true.

These contributions made by some in big business were a glimpse into what could be possible from the business sector for future social movements. But big business has got nothing on LGBTIQ campaigning and solidarity compared to the Australian union movement, who have been on the front lines of our community's fight for liberation since it began.

In the 1970s when gay men, bisexuals, lesbians and trans people began the political process of coming out, often the first arena of discrimination they faced was in the workplace. When gay, bisexual and lesbian teachers across Australia were sacked when their schools found out their sexuality, the Teachers Union were at the forefront of the fight to protect their jobs. In 1976 at the women's conference of what is now called the Australian Council of Trade Unions (ACTU), the conference passed a resolution that unions would fight against discrimination on the basis of race, sex and sexual orientation. From then, unions across the movement adopted that same commitment.

Wil Stracke, my friend and colleague from Victorian Trades Hall Council (VTHC), explained to me with a chuckle, 'The plumbers union was one of the first to adopt that 1976 resolution. Not the most obvious union to pick it up, I must say, but they went with it!'

In the 1980s and 1990s during Australia's HIV/AIDS crisis, gay men faced profound stigma and discrimination. They struggled to get work, housing, and safe and compassionate medical care. The nurses' union took action and, working with the ACTU and VTHC, ran education programs for the rest of the union movement to destigmatise HIV/AIDS.

In the 1990s, Australian unions pushed for a redefinition of the word 'spouse' in employment contracts so that LGBTIQ couples would have the same workplace rights as married couples. They fought test cases in regard to taking carer's leave, but the tribunal wouldn't grant the entitlement to same-sex couples. They managed to secure a middle ground, which was that workers could take carer's leave for someone they lived with. This reminds me of how my late grandma used to describe my first girlfriend – who I lived with in a one-bedroom apartment for four years and, you know, kissed on the mouth and stuff – as my 'friend'. Still, it was the 90s.

It wasn't until about 2008 that the unions got stuck in with campaigning for marriage equality (they were quite busy fighting

Work Choices under John Howard's government), but when they joined the campaign, progressive unions were there at every turn. When the postal survey hit, the union movement were there. They provided communications and social media guides for different unions to speak to their members about voting Yes. The ACTU and UTHC developed a proud visibility strategy, printing posters and banners that were distributed to workplaces across the country. Unions organised door-knocks and phonebanks, and ran massive enrolment drives in TAFEs and workplaces with young apprentices.

Some parts of the union movement have been standing in solidarity with LGBTIQ people for decades. Others, like the SDA, who are said to have held Julia Gillard's leadership ransom to their demand that she uphold marriage discrimination à la Malcolm Turnbull circa 2016, took far longer to come to the (gay) party. Still, they came on board long before the conservative Liberal party. It's time to talk about the Liberal party, and what they *actually* did to achieve equal marriage.

But first, it must be said that the Greens have supported marriage equality since their inception and have been a strong, consistent voice for marriage equality within state and federal parliaments long before either of the major parties. The first federal leader of the Australian Greens was Bob Brown, who, in 1996, was the first openly gay person elected to federal parliament, as well as the first openly gay person to lead a political party.

'We're a party that obviously has a very strong activist base, and this has always been a core Greens issue for as long as I can remember,' Greens leader Richard Di Natale told me when I met with him a few months after the victory.

Di Natale takes pride in the efforts the Greens went to over the years. 'We're a really good campaigning organisation,' he told me enthusiastically. 'We organise and mobilise in a way that I think other parties can't.' I suspect the Labor-aligned union movement may disagree with him here.

The Greens were among the first political parties to push for marriage equality, second only to the Australian Democrats, but by the time the change became law, the issue didn't run so neatly along party lines. We have also discussed the Labor party's journey to supporting, and then helping to lead on, marriage equality, including the party taking it to the 2016 election as their number one priority. But again, it's not as simple as left versus right. Not only did the final legislation pass under a conservative Liberal government, but more Liberal-held electorates delivered a majority of Yes votes than Labor electorates (there was only one electorate held by the Greens, the seat of Melbourne, which obviously returned a Yes vote).

The truth is, marriage is inherently conservative. Traditionally, marriage is about commitment. Marriage is a promise to try everything possible at any time to make a partnership work, and through that promise marriage supposedly manifests stability. Marriage is, usually, about monogamy and financial interdependence. Conservative societies organise themselves around the marriage of their citizens, so that society repopulates itself, which provides economic growth and the human resources to defend itself from war. Marriage is about people caring for each other in a buddy system, rather than relying on the government. Marriage is about the state keeping tabs on who and how we're fucking, to make sure it's only the missionary position while thinking of the Queen.

Elizabeth, not Beyoncé.

This is why I didn't want to campaign for marriage equality when it was first given to me in my early days at GetUp: marriage was a conservative, traditionalist institution that belonged with all the other heterosexual nonsense I'd decided to liberate myself from. Over time my view of marriage as solely conservative changed, but it was this view of marriage as a conservative ideal that motivated most within the Liberal government to eventually support equality when the legislation came to its final vote.

The truth is, Australia would not have achieved marriage equality when it did without Liberal Senator Dean Smith. Senator Smith is a constitutional monarchist, an Anglican, a conservative and joined the Liberal party when he was just seventeen years old. He was also the first openly gay parliamentarian with the Liberal party. It was his legislation that made marriage equality law. Speaking to the Senate as he introduced the bill, he declared, 'One of the reasons this bill is so vital is that it reflects the deepest of liberal and conservative ideals. Liberal because it advances the sum of freedoms, and conservative because it nurtures our families, affirms a vital institution, and strengthens the social fabric which is but the sum of all of our human relationships.'

Before Senator Smith arrived in parliament, marriage equality had another conservative champion; a former crocodile farmer from far north Queensland, the Liberal member for Leichhardt, Warren Entsch. Entsch championed equality because of his deeply held belief that LGBTIQ Australians deserved the same rights as everyone else. Not exactly rocket-science, is it?

Prime Minister Malcolm Turnbull, who would like you to believe he was responsible for delivering marriage equality, told the crowd at the launch of the Coalition's Yes campaign vehicle Libs & Nats for Yes, 'Many people will vote "yes" – as I will – because they believe the right to marry is a conservative ideal as much as any other conservative principle.'

The Liberal party should take no pride in their government's complete mishandling of same-sex marriage, because it delayed a simple law change, derailed their own policy agenda for about three years and spilled two prime ministers. It should also be ashamed of forcing LGBTIQ Australians to suffer a process completely alien to our democracy, entirely unnecessary to legislative requirements and deeply traumatising.

It's true that the most conservative members of the Liberal party, like Senator Eric Abetz, Minister Kevin Andrews and Tony Abbott, were responsible for forcing the country to uphold discrimination against LGBTIQ people for as long as they possibly could. It's true that the conservative faction of the Liberal party tried to stymie the passage of marriage equality legislation right up until its final hours and that the party remains overwhelmingly oppressive to the LGBTIQ community. It's also true that the reason the overwhelming majority of Liberal politicians voted Yes in parliament on marriage equality legislation isn't because they decided to have a progressive moment, it's because they embraced marriage as part of their conservatism. We cannot deny that the government who passed the legislation was conservative even if they did it to save their own arse.

The campaign for marriage equality was built on contradiction, and that was its power. I don't stand here on the other side of the campaign to advocate blithe centralism, diminutive compromise or that political differences need shelving in order for there to be legislative progress. I stand with the reflection that in large-scale social movements many things can be true, all at the same time.

Religion and its associated ideologies and institutions have been the ultimate perpetrator of violence, oppression, vilification, mass death and direct murder of LGBTIQ people than anything else in the world. Dogmatic, powerful religion has caused so many LGBTIQ people to die alone and afraid. There is no question of this truth. What is also true is that some religious leaders and people of faith led some of the most gallant, persistent advocacy for LGBTIQ's people's right to marry, and for their acceptance into society. The marriage equality campaign taught me that it's a lie to say that religion and the LGBTIQ community must be at odds with each other. Historically, this has certainly been the case (and not because queer people were persecuting the church), but it *doesn't have to be*. It's on religious institutions to fix this.

It's true that corporations are shamelessly co-opting queer bodies and identities in order to turn a profit. It's true that corporations are not our friends. It is also true that the business sector's involvement in the marriage equality campaign was incredibly influential, and profoundly meaningful to the workers for those companies. So, tentatively, I now believe that corporations and companies can get involved with activist struggles. It's true – I do. But there needs to be new compulsory terms of service. It's not good enough to join the fight when the fight looks good for your brand. From here on in, if you want to use LGBTIQ imagery in your marketing, if you want to march in our parades, if you want to claim to be an ally, you'll need to first take the following steps:

1. Make your workplace safe for LGBTIQ staff: hire a consultant to deliver diversity and inclusion training for your team; think about your company's language around gendered ideas and policies; provide at least one bathroom that's gender neutral; celebrate days like Wear it Purple and the International Day Against Homophobia, Biphobia & Transphobia in your office. Be proud of your LGBTIQ staff. Ask them how their partner is doing.

2. Explicitly encourage LGBTIQ people to apply for your roles and then practise affirmative action in your hiring, particularly for trans and gender non-conforming people. Transgender people face excruciatingly high levels of unemployment. Hire them.

3. If your transgender staff need time off for gender confirmation procedures, give it to them as extra leave. Don't ask any questions. Send them a gift basket.

4. Put your money where your mouth is: donate to causes that don't have the same exposure as marriage equality, and then tell your customers and supporters why this cause is important to you as a business. Be the leaders that Alex says you are.

It's true that when we found it, marriage was a conservative institution. It's true that for some, it will remain a conservative institution. What's also true is that it doesn't have to stay conservative; now we can make it our own. We can be walked down the aisle by our logical family, our marriage certificate witnessed by the kids' sperm donor. We can gender-bend our outfits, all suits or both dresses or a mixture of everything. We can walk down the aisle to 'True Colours'. Our foster child can read a poem at the altar we made out of flowers and know that he can stay with us as part of our family. We can hold the reception on Oxford Street to be close to the ghosts who made it all possible. Instead of rice we'll throw glitter, and we'll count ourselves as the luckiest because we made it to that day.

12

A Respectful Debate

The Australian Marriage Law Postal Survey ran for 56 days, cost more than a hundred million dollars and was absolutely, monumentally, catastrophically cooked.

The entire country was forced to suffer this ridiculous exercise as the vote consumed our airwaves, our timelines and our conversations at the watercooler. I hope we never do anything like it ever again, but to impress upon you just how distressingly absurd this absolute pantomime was for the nation to endure, I hereby submit a highlights reel of the postal survey. Here we go.

As the postal survey is born, Liberal Senator Eric Abetz warns on national television that allowing marriage equality could see people trying to marry the Sydney Harbour Bridge.

Tennis legend and miserable ghost Margaret Court reminds everyone that she is boycotting Qantas flights because of the CEO's support of marriage equality. She joins the No campaign, believing that homosexual people are 'after our young ones' and that transgender kids are 'the work of the devil'. She declares that widespread condemnation of her horrible comments is 'bullying'.

Flyers appear in Western Sydney letterboxes saying 'homosexuality is the curse of death' and that women are being raped in change rooms of countries where same-sex marriage had passed. Posters featuring seatbelt buckles as some sort of weird metaphor for sexual anatomy pop up across Queensland, and we are cross about it but joke that the poster-maker should learn about anal sex. Posters saying 'Stop the Fags' and '92% of children raised by gay and lesbian parents are abused, appear in

Sydney and Prime Minister Turnbull suggests that we 'put our arms around LGBTIQ people' distressed by the awful advertising materials being produced, as if he wasn't responsible for creating the setting for that distress. He tells young LGBTIQ people to 'believe in yourself'.

Poster-truthers immediately emerge, questioning whether marriage equality campaigners faked the posters in order to portray themselves as victims. Multiple investigations are launched that see reporters examining scraps of sticky tape and torn shreds of paper as if they were on *CSI*. They conclude the posters were, in fact, real. By then people have forgotten the substance of the posters but have spent a decent amount of time being told that Yes supporters are probably shifty.

The ACL push for a suspension of Australia's anti-discrimination laws during the survey so they'd be able to argue their discriminatory case. The Equality Campaign sends a press release announcing that Olympic Swimmer Ian Thorpe calls on Australians to enjoy their long weekend.

The AEC reports that tens of thousands of young people have enrolled to vote for the first time. The penny finally drops within the Liberal party that a national vote on marriage equality that made young people enrol to vote might have been a bad idea.

The official Yes campaign launches and though I have somehow managed to stay alive for the first week of the ordeal my best friend Rebecca Shaw announces on Twitter, 'The "Yes" campaign's site just launched! Check it out because getting it done killed Sally Rugg. Honour her memory.'

Dr Stephen Chavura, an academic from Macquarie University, suggests in what reads like a coded threat in *The Spectator* that 'the LGBTIQ liberation movement needs to be humbled', and the best way to do that is to vote No. GetUp tries to explain that they don't support a third-party petition calling for a doctor's medical licence to be revoked because she believes in conversion therapy, and we don't, but also I secretly hope that the doctor never comes into contact with any queer kids.

The No campaign puts a mother in a TV ad who says that her child's school told her son he could wear a dress and this was somehow connected to a change in marriage law that hadn't yet happened. Within days, the school's principal flatly denies that this incident ever happened. In an attempt to prove the No campaign's claim, Lyle Shelton tweets a photo of a Minus18 poster that schools can order, if they want to, showing a smiling transgender girl wearing a school dress.

Tim Minchin released a song to the tune of an iconic national song, but changed the words to 'I Still Call Australia Hom-ophobic'.

Mark Latham gets on TV and genuinely argues with his full conviction that transgender and intersex people shouldn't be allowed to marry, ever. Full stop. Despite the fact that many heterosexual transgender and intersex people could already marry under the current law.

The Telethon Institute publishes the most comprehensive study of trans young people in Australia, finding that 79 per cent of these kids have self-harmed and 48 per cent have attempted suicide.

The 7.30 Report profiles a gay couple, Ben Rogers and Mark Poidevin, who don't want to get married themselves and so have decided to vote No. Mark tells of how he proposed to Ben, who told him that 'it wasn't really his cup of tea' and Gay Twitter explodes with supportive calls for Mark to dump Ben's crusty arse and find a man who loves him back.

I debate Lyle Shelton on TV and he taunts me, asking if a No vote is returned whether I'll accept the result. Though my knuckles are white, I beam a smile and tell him that I'll never stop fighting for marriage equality.

When ballots start arriving, Shelton suggests that conversion therapy for gay children is appropriate, forcing the Australian Medical Association to swiftly remind everyone in a public statement the medical community's unequivocal condemnation of conversion therapy.

Telstra announces very loudly they will take a neutral position on the postal survey. There is significant backlash, and they change their mind and say they support the Yes case. There is more backlash, so they quietly retreat and think about their PR choices.

Margaret Court pops up again, this time saying that LGBTIQ people only want marriage to destroy it, and also there will be no more Christmas. A man crowdfunds $2500 to skywrite 'Vote No' above Sydney, and then complains to the media he is being silenced.

Roger Corbett, the former CEO of Woolworths, announces that well, actually, current marriage laws aren't discriminatory against LGBTIQ people. We consider packing everything in and cancelling the campaign in light of this revelation but decide against it.

ReachOut, Beyondblue and Headspace report that they are struggling to keep up with the demand for mental health services since the survey started. Senator Matt Canavan calls LGBTIQ young people 'delicate little flowers' and tells them to 'grow a spine'.

A young businesswoman publicly sacks a party-planner who posted on social media she was voting No, and *The Australian* have an absolute field day.

Some people receive a text message from the Equality Campaign encouraging them to vote Yes and it's a national catastrophe. An unsolicited text message is deemed completely unacceptable, despite the fact that some of us quite literally have the entire country voting on our lives and our rights. The LGBTIQ officer of the National Union of Students Chris di Pasquale is sent a message from a No voter saying, 'You pack of Nazi scum have stooped low enough to actually send SMS messages to people actually demanding they vote yes! Fuck you dirty Nazi cowards I wasn't going to vote but after your Nazi acts I'm voting NO NO FUCKING NO'. Everyone is having a totally normal time.

It becomes apparent that the No campaign think I shouldn't marry a woman because we can't have children, but also that I shouldn't marry a woman in case we have children.

Lyle Shelton apologises at the National Press Club for the awful things that anti-LGBTIQ campaigners said during the AIDS crisis, before prosecuting the exact same arguments. During his speech he scoffs, 'homophobia – whatever that is!" to a spattering of awkward laughter.

The ABC holds their 900th *Q&A* special on marriage equality and decides to invite only one LGBTIQ panellist. Fortunately, it's national treasure Magda Szubanski and she brings the house down.

A 16-year-old transgender girl is assaulted in Hobart, her attacker screaming hate speech. More and more homes are vandalised with eggs, spray paint and rocks. Cory Bernardi announces that he'll target one million homes with a robocall encouraging people to vote No.

American popstar Macklemore is booked to sing his marriage equality song at the NRL grand final. Tony Abbott announces that people who just want to go watch the footy shouldn't be exposed to the campaign because, as it turns out, the man who announced the protracted public debate doesn't actually like the protracted public debate.

Peter Dutton declares that Macklemore should also sing a song for the No campaign otherwise it's not free speech. Eric Abetz asks if FreeTV will add the authorisation needed for all campaign materials to Macklemore's concert (they do not). Macklemore laughs that he's made a lot of 'old white dudes really angry'. Comedian James Colley observes that the culture wars have caused some awful things, but 'force the left to endorse Macklemore' might be the worst among them.

Tony Abbott announces that his favourite band is Savage Garden. Darren Hayes, the lead singer of Savage Garden and a married gay man, retorts that he doesn't like Tony Abbott.

In the end, 79.5% of Australians vote in the survey, which doesn't include Senator Malcolm Roberts, who has managed to accidentally send his No-voting ballot to the ABC instead of the ABS. Every day was a decision whether to laugh or cry, or scream that the government had made the entire country endure this pointless, ridiculous survey.

•

On the afternoon of Tuesday, 25 October 2017, GetUp's chief of staff announced that we were all to go home immediately because there was a good chance the police were about to raid our office.

Moments earlier, the news had broken that the police were raiding the Australian Workers' Union (AWU). A body called the Registered Organisations Commission (ROC), set up by the Liberal government and tasked with investigating unions, had decided that in 2017 the AWU might be suddenly destroying documents pertaining to a completely above-board donation they made to GetUp from 2006 and had asked the federal police to raid them.

This was questionable in terms of political motivation, but there was nothing illegal or untoward about the donation, which had been on the public record for more than a decade. The bit that was particularly outrageous was that when the police arrived at the AWU office, they found a crowd of TV cameras and journalists who were all waiting to capture the action.

See, the media aren't supposed to know about the secret operations that police have planned. Firstly, because it could compromise investigations. Apparently union workers asked why the journalists were gathered. They responded, 'We're here for the raid!'

Secondly, because the media aren't meant to work as an arm of the state. The media are meant to hold power to account, not be tipped off by the government that it's organised a raid on its political opponents in time for the footage to hit the nightly news.

We had nothing to hide, and the idea of police storming in to GetUp, overturning our filing cabinets and going through our computers was outrageous and kind of exhilarating. It was like we were preparing for a showdown. In the years prior, the Liberal government had launched attack after attack on GetUp's ability to operate, whether it be an AEC investigation (which GetUp passed, three times), trying to pass laws that would make it near-impossible for GetUp to fundraise from the community or running a relentless smear campaign against us. Being unnecessarily raided by the federal police would be the cherry on top. I almost wanted the police to raid us, for the sheer excitement of it all, except for one big reason: about 85 Yes volunteers were due to arrive at the office for a phonebank.

It's not the most ideal volunteer experience, is it? Arriving to make phone calls for the Yes campaign only to be greeted with a hostile police operation. It just wasn't the optics we were going for, you know?

My team and I went into crisis mode: we had to find a new space for the phonebank, and fast. We called Patrick Gartrell from the Equality Campaign to see if they could help out, but their office wasn't available. There was another office that the Equality Campaign had been using for phonebanks, but nobody could meet us with the keys. It was 5.45pm, the phonebank was set to start in fifteen minutes, and we were still expecting the police at any moment. Cancelling the phonebank felt almost as bad as having the volunteers be greeted by police. There was only one thing left to do. We went to the pub.

Around the corner from GetUp's Sydney office is one of the weirdest pubs you'll ever find. It's huge, has no natural lighting and some sort of fancy fish tank arrangement. There are pool tables, raised platforms with couches and on Tuesday nights they move all the furniture to do a salsa dancing class. Obviously, it was the perfect solution.

My colleague Kirsti greeted the volunteers at the front door of GetUp HQ, directing them to the pub. Once there were about 60 people in the bar, I stood up on a stool and apologised for the change in the venue.

'Is this because police are raiding GetUp?' someone called over the crowd. Several volunteers gasped.

'Ah, well, no. But we thought they might, so decided to come here instead,' I replied, keen not to worry anyone.

'Why are the police raiding GetUp?' another volunteer called out. The crowd seemed agitated, whispering to each other.

'I don't think they will in the end, actually,' I started, which turned out to be true.

'Is this why we're at this ridiculous pub, because the police would try to search us?' came a shout.

'No, no one is getting searched,' I replied, 'so if everyone wants to take a call script and pass them back, we're aiming to do 10,000 calls over the next few hours!'

'I would have taken the police on, no worries!' offered an older woman, and the crowd laughed. It turns out none of them were particularly bothered that they were almost part of a police operation. The volunteers spaced themselves along the long tables and funny pleather couches and started making calls.

About 90 minutes after we began, a staff member from the bizarre pub approached me. 'A gentleman who's a regular realised what you were doing and has left five hundred dollars behind the bar for you all to have a drink afterwards,' he told me. 'He doesn't want me to tell you who he is, but he said to say thank you.'

It was such a touching, generous gesture from a stranger. When we finished making calls, more than half of the volunteers stayed for a drink. We shared stories from the evening, the funny conversations we'd had, the occasional swearer, the guy who we'd called as he was on his way to another Yes phonebank.

We talked about why we were volunteering, and the stories ranged immensely. One man had travelled from the Blue Mountains to attend and had enjoyed the session so much he decided he'd lead phonebanks back in his community, now he'd got the hang of the Kooragong tool. There was a woman who worked for a major news outlet and couldn't use her voice in her official role, so was phonebanking each week to use her voice privately. One of the younger volunteers spoke English as his second language and apologised a few times about people perhaps not understanding him, but said that he got hold of someone who spoke Cantonese and so they were able to have a good conversation.

The evening was wild. It was chaotic, imperfect and defined by many kinds of generosity. It remains one of my favourite memories of the campaign.

Months later, thanks to the dogged reporting of journalist Alice Workman, it was revealed that Liberal Senator Michaelia

Cash's staff had alerted the media about the police raids on the
AWU, because they saw it as an opportunity to smear Bill Shorten
in the press. It was all a set-up.

•

I thought very long and hard about including in this book the
bullying and harassment I experienced at the hands of people I
worked with on the marriage equality campaign. People on the Yes
side, not working at GetUp. It could fill pages and pages. It was
humiliating, cruel and perverse. Several times, it almost broke me.

Maybe you're surprised reading that, because I always seemed
so happy and positive? I hope so. I tried very hard to not let it show.

When I announced I would be writing this book, several
people hastily apologised to me. A few people struck up renewed
friendships with me as if nothing had ever happened. I wonder if
they see that I haven't outed their horrible behaviour towards me
that they'll relax, and go back to being nasty again?

I decided a story of bullying and infighting was not the story
I want to tell about the incredible marriage equality victory that
so many people pulled off by working together. But there's one
point I want to make.

Bullying and harassment thrives in industries that are small,
specialised and whose hierarchies are built on social cliques.
It thrives when the people who are put in leadership positions
are allowed bad behaviour because they're doing 'good work'.
It thrives in sectors where young women in particular are so
committed to the work that they'll take the shit that's thrown
at them every day in the desperate hope of contributing as an
activist. It thrives in organisations that hire people from marginalised backgrounds but keep those staff members at junior levels,
prioritising 'diversity' but replicating patterns of discrimination
and exclusion.

Outside of working in campaigning organisations, I've worked in an intensely busy juice franchise, in huge corporate offices in the banking district of London and a brief stint in the engineering department at Qantas. I spent six months as an office temp, bouncing around the receptions of big companies where no one would bother to learn my name. I've worked on film sets, as a youth leader for kids with behavioural problems and in a specialised boxing gym. I've worked in male-dominated industries, and I can take a lot of shit from people.

But I have never, ever been spoken to the way male marriage equality campaigners spoke to me in my years working with them. From the moment I started the campaign right through to the day the law changed. I've ended phone calls gobsmacked and shaken, gritted my teeth in meetings to hold my nerve, forwarded emails to colleagues to attempt to explain why I'm crying at my desk.

There's a theory that says kids who grew up being bullied can go on to be bullies themselves. I think this is true when it comes to some of the men I worked alongside during the campaign; it's as if they grew up disempowered and excluded because of their sexuality, and so, as adults, enjoy being at the top of the social food-chain, exerting their power over women, trans people, and people of colour. These are men who come to activism because of discrimination they have faced but, in my observation, cannot extend their imagination to think about the experiences of fear or discrimination of other people who aren't also white gay men, or their fiancés. But this isn't about sexuality, it's about male dominance and patriarchy, something men aren't automatically immune from just because they're gay. And it's about women and non-binary people suffering it for the greater good of the cause.

For years, in the face of rudeness, exclusion and hostility, I hugged hello and gave unnecessary praise, extended invites and bit my tongue. I was a young woman, and I had to put up with it.

One very senior male marriage equality campaigner once tutted to me with a frustrated eye roll that Magda Szubanski was difficult to work with, lamenting that she 'wants to know every single detail of what's happening'. As if Magda wasn't actually part of the campaign. As if Magda's only contribution was her profile and not her expertise in communicating to broad audiences, her decades of experience working with the media and her brilliant, canny mind. Bestselling author, Magda Szubanski. Award-winning producer, Magda Szubanski. To me, the comment sounded like, 'she doesn't know her place' and I only repeat it to demonstrate that in the eyes of many of the men at the helm of the campaign, even a woman of power, experience and expertise like *Magda Szubanski* should know her place.

Of course #NotAllMaleMarriageEqualityCampaigners are unkind to women, but there were more unkind men than I can count on one hand. In my experience, it was a broad problem, not limited to two or three people. And it was a problem for the many women I spoke to. Almost none wanted their stories published, even anonymously. One woman told me of a close work colleague, 'It was gross having to provide the emotional labour for the protection of his reputation, in order to not fuck up the organisations' reputation, by pretending to be happy families.' Another admitted, 'I really developed my expertise in gay male ego management during the campaign, because there were a lot of egos and, generally, they weren't the women that had their egos.'

In preparation of this book, I told Rodney Croome of my experience being treated unkindly and disrespectfully over the years by men in the equality campaign. His response was, 'For thirty years I have worked with other people to make change. If I was a consistently difficult person to work with, others would not wish to work with me in the way they have, and I would not have been able to make change.'

The dominance of gay men at the expense of women in the campaign was interpersonal but it was also structural.

In *Yes Yes Yes*, Equality Campaign co-chair Alex Greenwich reflects on feedback he received from people within his own organisation that the work of women on the campaign was overwhelmingly administrative, interpersonal, operational and 'completely unseen'. He offers, 'perhaps capacity was lost because of barriers experienced by women in the campaign'.

What curious phrasing, written as if the capacity lost itself. Capacity was lost, people were hurt, mistakes were made. But capacity wasn't lost by a mysterious, unknown force; women's capacity to contribute to the campaign was hindered and obstructed by men who chose to build a male-dominated environment that recognised and rewarded gay men over women and non-binary people. Alex writes the 'critical role women both LGBTIQ and straight played was never publicly celebrated or acknowledged as it should have been' and I wonder why it's a concession made after the campaign is long won.

To be clear, I don't include myself as someone whose work was obscured from the limelight, and I've been honoured with public celebrations of my work many times. And to be double-clear – when I speak of being treated poorly, I'm not speaking about a select few individuals whose names feature in this book, I'm referring to what I saw as widespread sexism throughout the marriage equality campaign.

There is no suggestion that the men I have listed in this section, Rodney Croome and Alex Greenwich, were sexist or unkind. And again, I am not referring to anyone at GetUp.

It's likely that every gay man over 40 loved someone who died from HIV/AIDS complications. It's certain that these men experienced homophobia that I will never know, and the reason I'll never know it is in part because of their work. I'm not here to say that all gay men are sexist – absolutely not – I write of my experience with some men on the marriage equality campaign because I don't want white gay men to take their equality in isolation from everyone else's. I don't want men to stop thinking about patriarchy.

I can't name the people in the marriage equality sector who bullied me during the campaign. I might need to work with them one day. I work with some of them still. I can't even properly tell you what happened.

It doesn't matter who these people are, but I can tell you that I still can't make sense of how someone can treat another person with such cruelty, and how so many people can just stand by and let it happen.

I could tell you the way I was spoken to during the survey, day in and day out, for months and months – you would be absolutely stunned, but I'm too embarrassed that I was treated with such disdain. I can tell you how this experience of bullying at the hands of people I was working with and people I thought were my friends, at the climax of five years of passionate work, was the second most traumatising experience of my life. I've already told you about the first. But I won't name them, because it's not worth risking my career, or worth being written off as emotional or difficult to work with.

The presence of sexism and bullying in the marriage campaign may surprise some, because it's a movement based on equality, but it isn't unique. As much as progressives would like to think they're super feminist and passionate about equality, male seniority and dominance, and the poor treatment of younger women and non-binary people is a feature across the left. I don't know if we'll ever see a #MeToo-adjacent movement within progressive, activist sectors though. Women working in social justice don't speak up not just because of the fear of losing work or opportunities, but for fear of damaging the cause they're so passionate about. I fight feelings of guilt as I write this – will I cause damage to the LGBTIQ activist community? Will my writing my truth be viewed as selfish and damaging if someone writes it up in the paper? Will I be accused of simply airing dirty laundry? This is why sexism, racism and transphobia thrives in some progressive movements, because we don't call it out.

Again, this is not about sexuality; this is about male dominance and sexism.

In 2016, *The Age* reported of a mass exodus of nearly two dozen staff from the Asylum Seeker Resource Centre, including six out of its seven directors, over claims of bullying and a toxic work environment. A co-signed statement from staff said that they were greatly concerned about the safety and wellbeing of staff due to 'an increasingly volatile CEO'. Former staff at Amnesty International Australia came forward in early 2019 to blow the whistle on allegations of systemic workplace bullying and harassment, saying 'The impact of stress right now is extremely serious and has the real potential of leading to suicide and self-harm attempts'.

Both of these public disclosures were incredibly brave, but anonymous. The stories disappeared quickly and every person watching on who experiences bullying themselves takes note: it's not worth it.

Instead, we resign from NGOs in our silent masses. We stop coming to meetings or volunteer shifts. We settle with non-disclosure agreements outside of court. We protect the reputation of our movement, for the greater good. I've now said something small, but I wonder if I'll regret it.

•

Four nights after the postal vote was announced, the woman I'd spent a year loving from her arms' length broke up with me. I'd just flown in from Canberra after spending the week in parliament, the plan for five Liberal MPs to cross the floor in the House of Representatives and bring on a free vote was now in tatters. I was shattered. We sat on her couch, dinner settling and wine glasses half full when she looked me in the eye and told me she wasn't in love with me. She didn't want to be my girlfriend. She didn't love me.

Her words seared through my chest and into my guts. Within minutes I'd left her house, distraught and confused and embarrassed. I've been dumped before, and had relationships far more meaningful than this one, but this unexpected break-up shook me deeply. She gave flimsy reasons that rang hollow, but I knew it was because I was a woman. I knew that she couldn't yet accept herself as bisexual, and the homophobia she'd grown up with had taken root within her. I don't envy her coming to terms with her sexuality on the brink of a national, public vote about whether that sexuality is equal or not.

The shock turned to bitterness, and then an anger at my entire life. It felt perversely cruel that I had to publicly market the love I longed to give to another woman as perfect, wonderful and deserving of national celebration when, to me, that love felt fragile, hurt and frightened. I didn't want to campaign on something so intimate to who I was and what I yearned for when it was that very love that caused the prejudice we were fighting against.

Love that's criminal. Love that's stigmatised. Love that isn't wanted.

What does this have to do with the campaign? Nothing, really. I could tell you about how I cried in front of my GetUp teammates in the war room (love room) before a radio interview, and the team joked that it was fortunate I didn't have to go on TV. Or that I was ashamed to tell anyone at first, because I'd been warned by smug friends that I shouldn't date someone who wasn't out yet because I'd get burnt. There's nothing really to be learnt about the Yes campaign in my tales of post break-up woe, but perhaps there's some relevance to marriage equality. And when I say marriage equality, I of course mean marriage inequality.

Late at night as I would struggle to ease my whirring mind to sleep, my mind would go around in circles stitching this woman's feelings into my work. I would wonder if anything would have been different if this woman had grown up in a world where loving me wasn't taboo. Would she have told her mother about me? Would she have allowed me to post photos of us online? Would she have seen a potential future with me, because that future was visible, accepted and codified into law? Or, just as importantly, would she have ended it with me far earlier and spared my dumb heart because she would have given an unwanted relationship with me the same weight as she would an unwanted relationship with a man, instead of stringing me along as if I was just a friend. It felt like I was never real to her. In the dark hours of the night, cradling my bruised heart, this was what I wished for. Legitimacy.

I felt humiliated, rejected, inadequate; all the things you feel when you're told you're not loved, but this time those feelings were strong-armed with the crushing homophobia of a postal survey.

Love is love, and break-ups are break-ups. Except for this exhausted, increasingly frantic marriage equality campaigner this break-up felt like a personal blow from the No campaign.

The sadness of being dumped only lasted a few days. It was soon displaced by the stress of trying to win a Yes vote in the face of a malicious No campaign. I didn't have time to think about an individual person not loving me when it felt like half the country felt the same way. A break-up paled in comparison.

During the survey campaign, my wellbeing suffered immensely. I woke up every day with my heart racing and my chest painfully tight. Some days it felt like I could cry at any minute. I didn't want to see anyone or talk to people, but I also didn't want to be alone. I felt like I'd been locked in a pressure cooker as the weight of a nation's expectations grew harder to bear. The envelope with my name on it bore down on me from where it was stuck on my bedroom wall, like a horcrux.

I kept notes on my phone during the survey campaign. Reading them now is really difficult. It's like they were written by a stranger. One note reads: 'Numbers from ABS now confirm we'll have won the postal survey. I don't feel anything. It's meaningless.'

I remember washing my face before bed one evening, my hands shaking with exhaustion after weeks of work without respite. As the hot water ran off my skin, I stared at my flushed, makeup-smudged face in the mirror. I didn't know my reflection, and all I could think was, 'Cut-throat. You've become cut-throat.'

I couldn't sleep at night, thinking of the decisions the campaign had made to focus solely on turning out existing supporters of marriage, our 2s, and to not try to persuade anyone else. I thought about how we'd centred cisgendered, white voices in order to win even though I knew the damage and hurt it would cause to LGBTIQ people who were neither. I thought about how I made that decision thinking of the greater good – of winning the survey – and wondered how I'd got to the place where I would compromise my black-and-white activist ethics in order to become a fierce campaigner. I still couldn't believe we were forced to win a public vote. I felt overwhelmed and empty.

I thought about my public criticisms of disruptive activists, my avoidance of talking about Safe Schools or gender diversity or how great LGBTIQ parents really are because the data said that those topics lost votes; how looking at photos of people voting Yes made me angry, not heartened, because I hated everything about this vote. I looked at my reflection and thought, 'You've become cut-throat.'

Then I tell myself that I don't have the luxury of being pure and uncompromising in the face of such a powerful, sophisticated opposition. I tell myself that if I am a leader, I have to accept making hard decisions.

I was desperately, desperately lonely. I was receiving so much kindness, generosity and admiration from strangers, but I felt like nobody understood what it felt like to be fighting this campaign from where I stood. Most of the people who did understand this – those of us working on the campaign – were horrible to me and couldn't stop fighting among themselves.

People I'd considered friends and colleagues suddenly seemed to blame me for the survey and resent me for the work I was doing to try to win it. I became fair game for people to write horrible things about me in message threads and Facebook groups, and it hurt because I could have written their words about myself. I was criticised for gaining the smallest of profiles as I spoke publicly for the cause we were all fighting for, as if I took pleasure in having to defend my community from attack because it meant that I was sometimes on television.

Strangers were sending me messages every day, telling me that I was a pervert. That I was going to hell. That I should get my throat slit. That I was a lesbian because my dad didn't love me.

My world turned into a rainbow, splattered colours across shop windows, taking every inch of my news feeds, bellowing at me from the airwaves and following me into every conversation. While I'm sure most other people felt buoyed by the visual displays of support, I felt absolutely suffocated. The survey followed me, haunted me. I couldn't escape it.

As the public debate wore me down, I fought deep feelings of nihilism. In dark, shameful times when my face was wet with tears under the blankets in my bed, I couldn't see the point of trying to prevent a loss in the survey because the damage had already been done. The lives of the people I cared about the most had already been profoundly damaged by the process. How could it get worse than what it already was?

I was desperate to fuck. I wanted to get out of my mind and into my body. While my sexuality was on trial and my identity unpicked in the public arena, fucking felt like a protest. I didn't want to smile at cameras or brief my team or write another speech, I wanted someone to push me up against a wall before I pushed them down onto my bed. I wanted to block everything out in a breathless, dripping reclamation of my queerness. My sex was taboo again. It was subversive, it was defensive, it was preserving. And I wanted to be held, tightly, and loved.

I felt like nothing was in my control. I changed dinner plans with a friend and instead made her come with me to get both my nipples pierced. I wanted to feel like I was making the decisions about my pain and my body. I gasped in agony as the needle pushed through me, distracting me from everything for just a few seconds.

I never posted my survey. I couldn't even open it. On the final day to vote, I pulled it down from my bedroom wall and stuffed it into my bag, giving it to my best friend Sam at GetUp to tick the box and post it for me. He promises me he did.

It wasn't just me who was crumbling under the pressure. It felt like everywhere I turned my friends and people in my community were falling apart.

Benjamin Law was surprised how personally angry he was for the months of the survey. 'It's that dehumanising feeling when powerful people who don't share your lived experience debate your life and rights as if it's an abstract concept,' he told me. 'I felt angry for my friends who wanted to get married; I felt angry for myself that my life was just another political issue up for community debate.'

He went on, 'Along with the rage, I just felt this bone-weariness that this was even a debate at all, when poll after poll showed us what the survey eventually confirmed. I loathed how the media elevated pathological liars and bigots into suddenly respectable figures who apparently warranted a national platform. Seeing journalists I respect tangle themselves into knots for the sake of "balance" – and giving unchallenged airtime to blatant lies about same-sex parents, Safe Schools and rainbow families – was galling.'

Jace, a trans teenager who grew up in a small country town, told me that, 'Everyone wanted to know how I felt about it, I would be asked a million questions almost constantly. The No campaign just seemed to make it so much worse. I remember watching TV one night when an ad came on and I just started crying because I was so sick of it all, I just wanted it to be over.'

Ryan Skinner, a 28-year-old Christian from Wollongong, told me that he'd only come out a few months before the postal survey and he thought his conservative family had been supportive, but the vote forced them to pick a side that they otherwise wouldn't have. 'They voted No, and it's really damaged our relationship. I can't help wonder if they had more time to process me they would have voted a different way a few years later. But now they'll always have voted No, with their ideas of marriage equality significantly influenced by the No campaign. It's hard to get past.'

Peter Gassner told me that where he lived seemed to be over-whelmingly 'No'. He told me that 'As an intersex person I was disturbed that there was still a rampant belief that marriage was not to be enjoyed by intersex people.'

My friend Clementine Ford told me that she felt disconnected from the process. 'I felt much the way I do as a bisexual person all the time, that when I'm partnered with a man, I'm not "allowed" to claim space in the queer community.'

Jac Tomlins told me about the effect the survey had on her kids. 'They were listening to the most awful things being said about them and their parents every day; the judgement, the mis-information, the naked hostility. It was ugly and it was gruelling.' Jac told me about two families she knew; one child came home from school and asked his dads, 'If we lose the vote, will they take you away from me?' Another child from a different family asked her parents whether they would have to go to prison if the No side won.

Jordan Raskopoulos didn't feel safe in her own home. A queer family with kids in her apartment complex stuck a 'vote Yes' sign on their door, and someone else tore it down. In response, the family sent a letter to everyone in the building saying that they didn't feel safe knowing that one of their neighbours wanted to demonstrate that they're not welcome or accepted. In a frenzied escalation, many of the occupants of the complex posted 'vote Yes' and 'vote No' signs on their doors. The elevator began filling up with nasty graffiti about LGBTIQ people, and Yes signs kept being ripped from doors.

'It was just this silent battle that was just happening within my own space where I lived. Even now, I look at the people in my apartment block and think, "Are you one of the people that tore down the Yes posters? Are you one of the people who is against the families living here?"'

For many of us, the survey intruded into nearly every aspect of our lives. A state-sanctioned 'debate' over the rights of our relationships, our families and our kinship ties, and our communities roared; every day we braced for what would be thrown at us from our television sets or passing cars. Public scrutiny stormed uninvited into the spaces we built for ourselves to keep each other safe. We clung to each other, trying our best to protect ourselves and our loved ones. Every conversation between friends began with 'Are you coping okay?' And we were the lucky ones. Many people were alone, without community around them to soften the blows of the No campaign. And for what?

I think Magda Szubanski captured it perfectly when she told the National Press Club, 'The LGBTIQ community were used as unwilling human guinea pigs in a political experiment. We may never know the human cost of this experiment, causality may be hard to prove, but anecdotally we know that the truth is some of us did not survive this process.'

And then, 56 days after it began, the survey ended.

In those 56 days, 4296 volunteers in towns and cities across the country picked up the phone and made 782,961 calls to total strangers, asking them to vote Yes. The scale of this volunteer effort is unprecedented, both in sheer numbers and in the short amount of time the campaign had to organise so many people to use complex technology to take a high-barrier action. Our target was 500,000 calls.

On 13 September, the day after the first ballots appeared in letterboxes, 275 call recipients told Yes volunteers that they'd already posted back their Yes vote that day. A week later, on 21 September, the majority of people who received one of tens of thousands of calls that week from a Yes volunteer told us they'd sent back their ballot, on the day they received it.

Within the first twenty days of the survey campaign, 622 community events were registered on the Yes campaign website, from picnics, parades and market stalls, to town hall meetings and door-knocks. These events were organised and hosted by ordinary people, stepping up as leaders in their communities. In registering the event, it became discoverable on the campaign website so that others could enter their postcode on the website to find local events for the campaign. We can never know how many events weren't officially registered, but my guess would be that they numbered in their thousands.

Over the 56 days, Yes campaign volunteers using the GetUp map tool knocked on 102,620 doors to have conversations with people about posting back their ballots. This astonishing figure doesn't even include the enormous door-knocks run by the union movement.

Can you just imagine for a moment, the power we would have if ordinary Australians organised on this scale regularly? Could we demand, deafeningly, that no person living in this country should be without a home? Could we save our Great Barrier Reef and the Great Australian Bight from mining and drilling? Could we create a tidal wave of support for a treaty with the Indigenous people of the land we call Australia? We have the power to achieve all of this, and more. We've shown what we are capable of, and it's extraordinary.

By the end of the survey, 12.7 million people cast a vote on whether LGBTIQ people should be allowed to marry. That's 79.5 per cent of the voting population participating in a non-compulsory vote. To put that in perspective, the average voter turnout in the United States to elect their president is 60 per cent. Around 67 per cent of citizens turn up to vote in the United Kingdom's general elections. The Yes campaign's primary goal for the survey was to get the highest Yes vote possible by getting out the vote – to rally people to post back their ballots, rather than persuade them to change their minds – so a voter turnout of 79.5 per cent was truly incredible.

Of those 12.7 million people, 7.8 million people voted for equality, delivering a victory for the Yes campaign at 61.6 per cent. We won!

61.6 per cent. If you round it to its nearest whole number, 62, you'll find it throughout this book. Public support for marriage equality in Australia had been settled at 62 per cent of the population for years, confirmed in poll after poll. The results of the survey didn't provide new information with which the government could make its decision. It produced the same exact figure as every other poll for years.

Public votes take the temperature and social movements turn up the heat, but we mustn't think that because the survey returned the same result as all the other polls that we didn't turn up the heat. In fact, it's the exact opposite.

When Wil Stracke, Tim Gartrell, Patrick Batchelor, Kajute O'Riordan, Ben Raue, Henny Smith and I crunched the numbers that we would build the Yes campaign strategy around, we believed that if we used all the power available, in the face of a massive No campaign and all the aspects of the survey that disadvantaged the Yes vote, we could get a turnout of 65 per cent, with 5.5 million people voting Yes and that we'd pull off a result of 55 per cent.

To sandbag the Yes vote *so strongly* against No campaign advertising and Murdoch-press fear mongering that it delivered the same result as it had done in the polls over the years is truly remarkable. Sixty-one-point-six per cent represents difficult, sophisticated work from thousands and thousands of Australians who rose to the challenge of delivering equality for their friends and neighbours. It represents ingenuity and initiative, and dogged persistence. That number exists because of the creativity and courage of volunteers and supporters around the country, and the willingness of millions of Australians to go out of their way to tick a box and post a letter for something that will likely never affect them. When that number came through, through the sickening relief of avoiding a No victory, I also felt enormous pride. We will have that forever.

In the wake of the results, many people were shocked and devastated that so many people voted No. It was 38.4 per cent of Australians who voted against allowing LGBTIQ people to marry, and seeing that number in its hard, empirical form came as a blow. I understand why people would feel hurt and afraid. The only reason I don't feel that way is because I have a unique insight into how that number was produced. If you feel this way, I would like to try to alleviate some of that pain and worry.

Thirty-eight-point-four per cent of people cast a No vote, but hard opposition to same-sex marriage (the 5s) has been settled at about 12 per cent of the population for as many years as 62 per cent have supported it. Our campaign research suggests that roughly 18 per cent of 4s who voted No don't hate LGBTIQ people, they've voted No because of another reason: they're scared about gay sex ed in schools or they've accepted what some leaders of their religion say about marriage. I still don't think it was okay to vote No, but I hope to diminish the anti-LGBTIQ sentiment that the overall No result might indicate. I think as time goes on and LGBTIQ people continue to push for equality and inclusion those 4s will become 2s (or even 1s).

According to Tony Abbott, the No campaign raised $6 million in funds. That's an extraordinary amount of money, about three times as much as the Yes campaign had to work with (including the $1 million personal donation from Alan Joyce). That money paid for the same tactics that the Yes campaign used – TV and radio advertising, online ads, community events, posters and flyers – but instead of making the case for the biggest social change in a generation, it warned people that the change was dangerous. The No campaign had a sophisticated strategy to tap into the community's latent, irrational cultural fear about LGBTIQ people.

It's far, far easier to threaten 'unknown consequences' to frighten people into sticking to the status quo then it is to convince them to be brave and support a reform. If someone is scared, they are not going to take a risk. Not all No voters are against LGBTIQ people. Some definitely are, but not all of them. They were targeted by a campaign willing to lie, misdirect and manipulate people's fears.

The Yes campaign, and the marriage equality campaign over the years prior, worked as hard as it could to alleviate any hint of moral panic about LGBTIQ rights within citizens. We worked hard to be the reassuring hand on the shoulder, telling people that it was okay, we weren't going to hurt anyone.

The strides that the marriage equality campaign had made over the decade leading up to the survey were possible because we mainstreamed our identities and we mainstreamed our relationships. The imagery and narratives that were pushed by organised campaign outfits, including GetUp and Australian Marriage Equality, were primarily white gay and lesbian couples showing how their relationships were just the same as non-LGBTIQ relationships. Speaking very broadly, with exceptions, the marriage equality campaign made LGBTIQ people look and sound and live like the ideal 'Aussie bloke' and 'girl next door'. I want to try to capture the main criticisms of the marriage equality campaign from the LGBTIQ community; that the campaign didn't adequately include and look after transgender and gender non-conforming people, or LGBTIQ people of colour.

I am white and cisgender, so have relied on other people to help paint this full picture. I want to air some criticisms and offer some thoughts, because this accountability is how activism improves and our communities become stronger, but at no point do I aim to sound either defensive or self-flagellating.

Non-binary activist and writer Nevo Zisin told me they saw marriage equality like a David Jones catalogue. All upper-middle class, white men smiling as if to say, don't be afraid, we're just like you. We want a picket fence and 2.5 kids and we will not threaten your way of life.

'This representation is cool for people like that but we're not all "just like you",' Nevo explained. 'We're queer and gender bending and polyamorous and we don't want to assimilate into the status quo. Some of us want to change the world, and if people feel threatened by that then it's probably because they're part of the problem.'

This was magnified intensely during the survey, and it meant that the people in the LGBTIQ community who didn't look like these cereal-box archetypes were marginalised once more, this time from the campaign that was supposedly there for their liberation.

For years, transgender people spoke up about feeling deliberately excluded from elements of the marriage equality campaign. A criticism from trans activists was that larger organisations acted as gatekeepers to the campaign and deemed anything that wasn't squeaky clean and assimilatory to be detrimental to the cause. Trans and 'queer-looking' people felt like they weren't invited to speak at events, represented in advertising or campaign videos or represented fairly as part of the organisation's staff.

Trans activists tell me that they felt like they were always told to 'just wait', that there would be a time and a place to talk about transgender rights and how transgender people were impacted by marriage discrimination too, but their visibility would spook conservatives.

'When marriage as the most conservative institution was so difficult for us to gain, even with so many assimilationist politics at play, it made us feel like the true radical politics many of us hold will never ever be given time or space,' Nevo said.

I think Nevo's criticism is valid and earned. And, as someone who worked at the forefront of the campaign and who continues to work on LGBTIQ rights, I take responsibility for that, even the bits that didn't involve me.

Jordan Raskopoulos explained the way she saw it to me over a coffee in Marrickville. 'You use different tactics in time of peace and in times of war, and there's a part of me that understands that we needed to get a particular result. In a three-month period, if you were trying to get people to vote in a particular way, if you're trying to reach the way that their pen's gonna hit that paper, you are not going to be able to take them through a full journey of accepting every letter in the alphabet. That work is ongoing.'

'And it sucks,' she continued. 'It sucks that the only way men will listen to criticisms about their behaviour is if it comes from a man, or the only way that straight people will change their mind [is] if it's said by a straight person. I think, so long as you are aware and critical about the tactics that you are using in a time of stress and in a time where you need to get a result, and you make the effort to repair afterwards and you continue the work, I find that acceptable. I don't find it okay. It's not okay, but I understand.'

The No campaign were right about one thing: the campaign for equality did not end with marriage rights. Sure, some of us can get married now, but trans people who want to medically transition are still forced to find tens of thousands of dollars for their affirmation surgery because Medicare won't help cover it. Yes, John Howard's awful line in the Marriage Act is gone, but non-binary people still face bureaucratic torture if they want to book a holiday, take out a loan or rent a house. Or they have to lie about their gender.

Weddings are heaps of fun for everyone now, but Australian surgeons are castrating and sterilising babies and infants born with intersex variations in the name of making their perfectly natural bodies 'normal.' None of these urgent issues were solved during the marriage equality campaign, and the campaign sucked the oxygen from them. Temporarily. Now, each of us who voted Yes has a responsibility to plug in our power behind transgender and intersex activists and organisations who are fighting for progress, as they have been for years.

Many trans people felt left behind by the campaign, but what is also true is that transgender activists were among the leaders of the marriage equality campaign – people like Martine Delaney,

Norrie, Brenda Appleton, Sally Goldner, April Holcombe, Kirrily Hayward, Ted Cook and so many more. In acknowledging that the Yes campaign of the postal survey cis-washed much of the campaign, I don't want to imply that trans people weren't part of the marriage equality campaign from its inception to its victory. Trans and gender diverse people were part of the heart of the campaign.

Another criticism of the campaign was that some LGBTIQ people of colour felt left out by parts of the Yes campaign.

'LGBTIQ activism tends to be incredibly white (middle class and urban based),' bisexual Chinese-Australian anti-racist activist Carrie Xin Hou explains. 'The people being platformed, the stories being told, the language being used and the people being reached out to are white.'

'The Yes campaign's messaging was incredibly white. Saying "love is love" does not work on migrant communities: it's confusing and it's not translatable,' said Carrie. 'From overseas data and surveys, messaging that does work in culturally and linguistically diverse (CALD) communities is emphasising a narrative of equality and anti-discrimination to these migrant communities – which actually makes much more sense to their experiences. The Yes campaign didn't use that as effectively.'

'I think this is the reason we saw the high No vote occurring in Western Sydney,' Cindy El Sayed told me.

Cindy refers to the collection of federal electorates in Western Sydney who all returned majority No votes, forming a geographical outlier in NSW (and in the entire country). Only 26 per cent of people living in the Labor-held seat of Blaxland voted Yes, despite it being just a half-hour drive from Anthony Albanese's seat of Grayndler which, at 80 per cent, returned the fourth-highest Yes vote in the country. Eight of the ten seats with the lowest Yes vote in the survey were in Western Sydney.

Cindy believes that Australia has deeply entrenched racism, which is why it's more difficult for communities marginalised by racism to properly engage with civil issues. 'There is such a failure to even attempt to engage with communities that are seen as Ethnic,' Cindy continues. 'There needs to be active efforts for all campaigning on such important issues to be intersectional and to include all communities.'

Carrie suggested that 'a lot of migrants disengaged from the issue as the media tends to position this as a "white issue" when there isn't more diversity platformed.'

Fahad Ali, who founded the organisation Muslims for Marriage Equality, agrees that the Yes campaign didn't have the same penetration in migrant communities, but says, 'the Yes campaign had to make a strategic decision to focus on voter turn-out rather than persuasion, given the abrupt announcement of the postal survey and the criminally short campaign period. The Yes campaign was able to respond appropriately well in advance of the survey, and there were prominent examples of people from culturally and religiously diverse backgrounds represented in the campaign.'

Some analysis from well-meaning academics and commentators suggested that the lack of support for marriage equality in the concreted No-voting electorates was due to higher migrant communities and people from non-English speaking backgrounds. Less well-meaning commentators put their own spin on events, with conservative commentator Caleb Bond declaring, 'Many of the seventeen electorates that returned a majority No vote were areas with a high Muslim population in south-west Sydney. Surprise surprise', and outrage-columnist Andrew Bolt writing, 'Let me spell it out. All those seats had lots of Muslim voters.' Even Prime Minister Malcolm Turnbull jumped on the radio to announce, 'The numbers speak for themselves, and you can see the biggest No votes were in electorates with a large migrant population, and in particular with a large Muslim population.'

Let's get one thing very clear: the 2016 Census records 604,200 Muslim people in Australia. There are roughly 435,000 Muslim people over eighteen. Even if, by some sort of get out the vote miracle, every single Muslim person voted No in the postal survey (or even if they all voted Yes in the survey!) it wouldn't have come close to changing the outcome of the vote. This commentary is bare-faced racism. 'The places we lived, the places we had grown up had all come up with "No",' Neha Madhok, the co-National Director of Democracy in Colour told me. 'My heart sank as my social media feed went from YES to "build a wall!", "never going west of Parramatta ever again". And I knew, while the white queers wouldn't say it openly, we all knew what they meant; "those brown people, they aren't like us".'

Do you know who wants you to think that Muslim people and people from non-English speaking backgrounds voted No? Right-wing politicians and right-wing publications. Please don't think that in condemning Muslims and immigrants for their supposed homophobia, anti-LGBTIQ conservatives are now on our side; their selective defence of queer people is purely to try to show that these communities can't assimilate and don't share 'Australian values'. It is in the interest of the Liberal party and the Murdoch press to stoke division between marginalised communities: right-wing political parties are notorious for trading in fear and demonising minority groups to score votes, and one need only flick through the *Daily Telegraph* to see that the paper relishes in conflict and division.

It's not a coincidence that the No campaign sunk millions of dollars into the electorates in Western Sydney, with larger concentrations of new Australians and communities of colour, rather than focussing on the areas that already had the lowest support for marriage equality. These electorates are considered, 'bellwether seats', which means whichever political party can win them in an election is likely to be able to win government. At the 2019 election, all these Western Sydney seats had swings against Labor.

Plus, the No campaign would have viewed these communities as easy targets to prey upon with their scare campaigns.

'The language barrier is a huge advantage when it comes to effective fear mongering,' Carrie Hou explains. 'The deceptive bilingual material pumped out of the No campaign into these specific communities was old school shit like "gay marriage = aids", "gay marriage = rape of your children/wives", "gay marriage = removing your son's penis".'

'Many people I engaged with in Mandarin had these weird fears until I explained to them what this survey actually meant, and they said, "Oh shit, I would have voted yes" and "This survey is incredibly confusing".'

Data from before and after the Coalition for Marriage launched their No campaign is illustrative. In 2016, before the No campaign spent millions of dollars on a targeted scare, the ten electorates who were least supportive of marriage equality were in order of least supportive to slightly more supportive: Maranoa (Qld), Groom (Qld), Flynn (Qld), Hinkler (Qld), New England (NSW), Kennedy (Qld), Grey (SA), Barker (SA), Parkes (NSW) and Braddon (Tas).

Compare those seats with the seats that delivered the lowest support for marriage equality just twelve months later in the postal survey, after the No campaign unleashed onto the community, again in order of least supportive to more supportive: Blaxland (NSW), Watson (NSW), McMahon (NSW), Werriwa (NSW),

Fowler (NSW), Parramatta (NSW), Chifley (NSW), Calwell (Vic), Barton (NSW), Maranoa (Qld). Maranoa is the only electorate that makes the bottom ten in both lists, and only scrapes through into the bottom ten after the survey. Every NSW seat listed after the survey campaign is in Western Sydney.

The massive difference between the ten least supportive seats before and after the survey shows that there is nothing inherent about Western Sydney or migrant communities that make them opposed to marriage equality – this is cold, hard proof of the terrifying efficacy of well-funded anti-LGBTIQ fear campaigns.

The Yes campaign could have done more for a higher Yes vote in Western Sydney, but instead we chose the goal of the highest Yes vote possible, which meant not using all our resources where the No campaign were using theirs. It was a hard, horrible decision that I want to be honest and accountable for. To the LGBTIQ people in Western Sydney – I'm sorry. I want to hold space in this book for this criticism of the marriage equality campaign, and I also want to ensure that the huge amount of people of colour–led campaigning and community organising, and to a lesser extent the genuine (albeit smaller) efforts from big organisations to engage communities of colour during the survey, isn't erased. This is some of the extraordinary activism led by and working with communities of colour.

Muslims for Marriage Equality mobilised LGBTIQ Muslims and their friends to run phone outreach to their community, ran social media campaigns and provided postal addresses to people who could not, for safety reasons, have their ballot sent to their home.

'Muslims for Marriage Equality and countless other CALD and religious organisations were on the front lines of the campaign,' Fahad explained to me. 'It's not that we didn't do the work, it's just that the work we have cut out for us is so much harder.'

Edie Shepherd and Tarsha Jago founded Blackfullas for Marriage Equality, a grassroots organisation that focussed on community outreach to Aboriginal and Torres Strait Islander people. Blackfullas for Marriage Equality organised young people to talk to their families about voting Yes and encouraged regional communities to organise collection points for survey ballots. They were also a powerful presence online, providing visibility and representation for Aboriginal and Torres Strait Islander people who are also LGBTIQ.

Democracy in Colour – a racial and economic justice organisation led by people of colour – ran phonebanks, handed out campaign materials at train stations, created powerful social media content to tell the stories of queer people of colour during the survey and worked with the Equality Campaign to resource efforts in Western Sydney. Neha Madhok says, 'With no budget, and no staff, we decided to run our own Yes campaign. We launched a crowdfunder and a video that went viral. We used messages of family, togetherness and community. While we didn't have resources to stem the tide of a multi-million dollar No campaign, we were still able to have an impact.'

Racial justice organisation Colour Code ran targeted social media campaigns and created video content encouraging people of colour to have conversations with their parents about supporting the vote.

The Equality Campaign brought in a Multicultural Outreach Coordinator and a Multifaith Coordinator as two of their first hires, who focussed solely on working with people and organisations from those communities to get out the Yes vote and support LGBTIQ people from those backgrounds.

GetUp ran complex micro-targeting on Facebook, advertising tailored messages supporting marriage equality to people from migrant backgrounds in their native tongue and held phonebanks specifically for people from migrant backgrounds to call other people from migrant backgrounds.

Yes campaign material was translated into five different languages, and one of the seven high-production videos made by the Equality Campaign was in Vietnamese. Anna Brown told me that the Equality Campaign had interviewed and prepared hundreds of stories of people of colour along the way, but 'many, sadly, didn't make it online because when you doubly face oppression based on your sexuality and race . . . it is tough to put your story and face out there.'

She adds an important reminder, 'There is a privilege that is required to be able to do that. Obviously, we can always do better. But we actually did a lot of stuff that I think is important and not noticed (often online).

I list this activism not to avoid criticism, but because it was just as much a part of the Yes campaign as my work, as Gala the dominatrix's work, as your work.

The reality is that the postal survey was not an exercise in movement building. It was not a new opportunity to reach out and begin new conversations about LGBTIQ justice. For the professional campaign bodies that were responsible for the outcome of the vote, the survey was a high-stakes race to get as many marriage equality supporters as humanly possible to tick a box and post a letter. That, and to minimise the damage of public debate and the loudly platformed No campaign messages by blasting out positive, mainstream messages like, 'vote Yes for fairness'.

But, we're not in a postal survey anymore. There's nothing stopping this work from happening now. As our society becomes increasingly polarised by politicians who try to divide us and a dying traditional media trying to enrage us, this work is more important than ever.

I can list facts and figures here, electoral analysis and budget ledgers, but the truth is that many LGBTIQ people from Western Sydney, LGBTIQ people who are Muslim and LGBTIQ people from migrant or non-white backgrounds did feel abandoned and excluded by the Yes campaign. That's what matters.

The late Candy Royalle, an award-winning poet and performance artist whose spirit is both missed and felt closely by Sydney's LGBTIQ community every day, wrote in *Going Postal* (a powerful anthology of stories of the postal survey from the LGBTIQ community), 'Personally, it felt like the Yes campaign didn't even know there were queers of colour; that we have families; that our lived experiences may be different to many white queers, and that doesn't mean our communities should be excluded.'

This is the impact of the decisions the Yes campaign made to triage resources in order to win the vote, laid bare. The people on the ground who experienced the real world consequences of those decisions probably don't care if the overall plan was strategic. In writing this book, I want to take responsibility for my part in that. I want to condemn a national vote on the rights of a marginalised community once more as harmful and dangerous. In reading this book, I hope you will join me in continuing to fight for inclusion, representation and celebration of LGBTIQ people of colour.

As Fahad Ali puts it, 'Our next step should be to work to eliminate homophobia from society wherever it may linger. Scapegoating the Muslim community, although a favourite pastime of the conservative press, only makes it more difficult to convince an already embattled community to open up. It is immensely counter-constructive, particularly when coming from marriage equality advocates.'

Carrie says, 'We need to ask ourselves how we can reach out to these communities long term and take care of the queer (often people of colour) affected. We need to think, what intersectional ways can we make LGBTIQ activism more understandable to working class and migrants in these areas?'

•

I never understood the lyrics of Christina Aguilera's hit song, 'Fighter', until I survived the postal survey. In the raunchy, electric guitar-riffing banger, Xtina thanks those who've treated her terribly, because they have made her that much stronger, made her work that little bit harder and so much wiser. This is how I feel about the people who were horrible to me during the marriage equality campaign – other campaigners, abusive strangers and the No campaign. It almost broke me at the time, but now my skin is thick, my hand is steady and I'm strong enough to dismiss personal insults or projected insecurities, to make space to hear criticism that matters.

Similarly, the postal survey bruised and dislocated the LGBTIQ community. When forced to fight for our lives, we weren't able to do so without the dominant members and values of our community hurting those of us who live with intersecting marginalised experiences. I'm not sure that we as a community have come out the other end stronger, or with thicker skin. That work still needs to be done.

After 56 days and 12.7 million pieces of paper, it was over. And we, the lucky ones, survived.

13

Remember

I have told you why the postal survey was unnecessary, expensive and harmful. Now, I want us to take what we can from it. I want you to remember the feeling of a Yes victory in the Australian Marriage Law Postal Survey forever.

Do you remember where you were? Were you gathered in a park or city square with thousands of people dressed in rainbows? Were you at work, at a morning tea someone had organised? Were you at school, with a teacher telling you what had happened? Were you alone, too afraid to look?

The Yes result was so much more than a majority in a survey. It was so much more than winning a campaign. It was even more than finally clearing a path forwards for marriage equality.

I want you to remember that in towns, suburbs and cities across Australia, shoulder to shoulder, we stood up for the country we want to create together.

We nailed our colours to the mast – in our front windows, in our workplaces in our timelines – to proudly proclaim our support for LGBTIQ Australians.

I want you to remember how we had conversation after conversation after conversation with the people around us and with total strangers about why marriage equality matters.

When you're feeling alone, when you're feeling insignificant, when you're feeling like you don't have the power to change your country and your society for the better, I want you to remember this fire in your belly. Remember what we did together and the history we have made.

I want you to remember the elders of the LGBTIQ community who aren't here today – who were criminalised, hospitalised, stigmatised, ostracised – imagine the pride they would feel. The entire country owes this victory to them.

I want you to think of the LGBTIQ teenagers across the country who hopefully believe a little bit more that they have every opportunity in life that they dreamed of, no matter who they are or who they love.

I want every single person who voted Yes to know that because of them, LGBTIQ Australians walk a little safer, hold hands a little tighter and live knowing that the majority of the country has their back.

At the beginning of this survey, the LGBTIQ community pleaded with our allies to step up and fight with us. We couldn't win the vote alone. And they did.

Thank you, so much. All seven million of you.

When the Yes result was announced, even though I already knew we'd scraped a Yes win, I buckled in half and burst into tears, on camera. The wind completely knocked out of me. 'We won,' I repeated.

We cheered, and we embraced each other. Social media burst into rainbows. #EatShitLyle trended for the rest of the day.

Tens of thousands of us marched down Oxford Street in the footsteps of our ancestors, and I lay down on the road with my friends. But later that night, I peeled off from the party.

The Yes result was a glorious relief, but we weren't any closer to getting a bill passed. We were back where we started; back in August 2015, before any of the plebiscite and postal survey delay tactics were forced on us.

We had a government bill. We had a slim-but-dependable majority in both houses of parliament. We also had a hostile minority of the Liberal National MPs who would still do anything to thwart the passage of the legislation in parliament. It was not a done deal.

So the party continued on Oxford Street, and I went home, had a shower and a couple of hours sleep before boarding a 5am plane to Canberra. To Parliament House.

14

Yes, Marriage

It was 9am on the morning after the Yes victory and I felt like I was going to throw up. Oh god. It was finally going to happen.

I was sitting in the shoebox-sized Sky News studio in the Parliament House press gallery, about to go live on air. I'd been up since 4am. As the news package played on the screen, I wondered if I'd have to unhook my microphone and earpiece and run to the bathroom. The lights were beating down on me and there was no air in the tiny studio.

The last 24 hours had felt like an absolute blur; was I really in Canberra right now? I started to wonder if I'd had more drinks than I'd realised yesterday . . . there was that longneck the police tried to confiscate on Oxford Street, and I did have those glasses of champagne at lunch . . . I did get off air at SBS that afternoon thinking, 'Oh dear, I think that champagne went to my head,' and giggling to myself that I'd just done live television a bit tipsy.

My intense vomit phobia saved the day and I did not throw up (never!) so I managed to plough through the interview, telling host Samantha Maiden that I was a relentless optimist and so I was almost certain that now the nation had voted Yes, parliament had a mandate to pass Dean Smith's marriage equality legislation before Christmas.

The majority of people who'd voted in the survey probably believed that a resounding Yes victory meant that parliament would have to make marriage equality law as soon as possible, but this was far from guaranteed. The passage of the bill faced several obstacles, including more than 100 amendments brought by Liberal Senator James Paterson in an attempt to delay a vote on the bill by weighing it down with dozens of fifteen-minute second reading statements, where every single senator is invited to give a speech about the amendment. This could not only run down the clock before parliament wrapped for the year but could also extend the process for months into the following year.

Another rather significant obstacle was that Prime Minister Turnbull was fearful of facing a 'vote of no confidence' in the House of Representatives, which is basically a vote to show that he no longer has the majority of votes in that chamber (which means he isn't in control of the House of Representatives and therefore shouldn't be the prime minister – it's a big deal!). The hard right faction of his party (Tony Abbott, George Christensen, Kevin 'cycling buddies' Andrews) were furious that the survey had produced a Yes result and that Prime Minister Turnbull was finally going to allow the Liberal party a free vote. These guys weren't having a bar of it, and threats to Turnbull's leadership started anew.

As established, it was not in Malcolm Turnbull's nature to stand up to the hard right faction of the Liberal party, or their coalition partner, the Nationals. I would suggest that he's also fairly comfortable with completely fucking with traditional parliamentary process. As such, instead of sticking up for himself and the rest of the country by getting his own party under control, he just cancelled parliament for a week. A very dramatic move? Yes. Unprecedented? Sure. Did it work? Can't face a vote of no confidence in parliament if you cancel parliament!

With the House of Representatives now off for a week, the marriage equality legislation was introduced into the Senate. It's uncommon for bills to begin in the Senate, which is designed to be the house that reviews the laws that the House of Representatives pass, but as long as legislation passes both houses of parliament it becomes law. Plus, the bill was Dean's.

Senator Dean Smith introduced the cross-party marriage equality bill the day after the Yes vote was announced, on 16 November. A Thursday. The Senate then rose for a week, meaning that the legislation hung in the air, waiting to be praised and pummelled and eventually passed.

In that November week, the LGBTIQ community marked Transgender Day of Remembrance, an annual day to honour the memories of transgender people who died from violence or suicide in the previous year. I lit a candle at a vigil on Taylor Square by Oxford Street and mourned those we'd lost in the survey. Some who we know, some who we never will. Two days later, it was the one-year anniversary of Tyrone Unsworth's suicide. I wished that he had lived to see the day his country showed him that he was equal. I wished he knew how much we wanted him to be here.

In another attempt at being strategic, Malcolm Turnbull tried to appease the hard right of his party once more, who were throwing toys out of the pram about the Yes vote signalling the end of days, and he announced that following the passage of marriage equality, the government would hold an inquiry into 'religious freedoms'. Former Liberal minister Philip Ruddock was appointed to conduct the review, to double-check whether marriage equality would take away religious freedoms. (Spoiler alert: it doesn't.) It didn't matter that the government had literally just concluded an inquiry into religious freedoms in the country, Turnbull announced another one, hoping that it would soothe Abbott and his ilk. (Spoiler alert: it didn't.)

Then, in a final curtain call to the absurdity of the postal survey debacle, Bob Katter, infamous for his Christmas party hors d'oeuvre and rampant homophobia, gave one of the most bizarre press conferences in living memory.

'I mean, y'know, people are entitled to their sexual proclivities,' Katter said. 'Let there be a thousand blossoms bloom, as far as I'm concerned,' he said with a giant smile across his face, chuckling away, before his face contorted in fury and he began to shout. 'But I AIN'T spendin' any time on it,' he bellowed, 'because in the meantime, every three months, a person is torn to pieces by a crocodile in North Queensland!'

The interview went viral, and I was pleased that it may have given the people of the world an insight into what we were dealing with when it came to marriage equality in Australia.

The week passed and the senators resumed their places in the chamber, ready to make a new law. So, let's talk about the law. The change to the Marriage Act was that instead of stating that marriage was between, 'one man and one woman' it would read that marriage was between, 'two people'. Simple, right? No problemo. A small change of wording that MPs would vote to support, because we'd just done a stupid national survey for them, and then Bob's your gay uncle. All done by Christmas.

Except it was never that easy with marriage equality, and anti-LGBTIQ politicians weren't going to go down without trying to sink the reform with them. I won't delve into every amendment levelled against the marriage equality bill, but I submit the following corkers from the Senate.

First, some Liberal senators argued that instead of making the Marriage Act inclusive of LGBTIQ couples, Australia should instead make a new kind of marriage – but not called marriage – to run alongside actual marriage, which was still just for heterosexuals. 'Those who voted Yes haven't voted to obliterate the idea of there being a union between a man and a woman,' Liberal Zed Seselja told the Senate.

Then there was a lively discussion about whether passing marriage equality would actually be undemocratic because, even though the Yes vote won the survey, some people voted No. Liberal Senator Concetta Fierravanti-Wells gave the Senate a very interesting maths lesson, saying, 'Sixteen million voters were eligible to participate and of those just 7.8 million returned a "yes" on this survey form. This represents 48 per cent of the voting population. This is not the enormous majority that the elites are spinning. Indeed, it is not a majority at all. In fact, 52 per cent of the voting population either voted No or did not vote at all.'

Liberal Senator Eric Abetz also forgot the way votes work, declaring, 'To assert that, because the "No" vote lost, its voice should be obliterated from the public discourse is a display of ugly hubris.'

Then, anti-LGBTIQ senators seemed to cede ground. They accepted that gay men and lesbian women could get married, but nobody else! Liberal Senator Eric Abetz carried the torch on this one:

'[Australians] were asked: "Should the law be changed to allow same-sex couples to marry?" The legislation before us is not restricted to same-sex couples; it goes a lot further. For example, this would include an intersex person and a gender diverse person who is legally recognised as having a non-specific gender.'

It was a very peculiar thing to say. I wondered to myself if Senator Abetz would be able to grasp the idea of a heterosexual transgender person? Probably not. That afternoon as he was pressed on his ridiculous statements to the Senate on *Sky News*, the senator admitted, maybe for the first time, the existence of intersex people. Sadly, it was to confirm that he really did believe that people with intersex variations shouldn't be allowed to get married, much to the confusion of many happily married intersex people.

Once it became clear that the definition of marriage was almost certain to change, conservatives tried to introduce completely new ways to discriminate against LGBTIQ people in what I assume was an attempt at tit-for-tat.

Senator James Paterson pushed for a 'no detriment' clause that would literally mean, in his own words, 'ensuring there are no negative consequences for anyone else from allowing gay Australians to marry.' This no-detriment clause would mean that LGBTIQ could face new discrimination at work, in hospital, in the justice system and at the shop counter, so long as those discriminating could prove that treating LGBTIQ equally would be 'detrimental' to them.

Thankfully, when the moment came for each of these amendments, the Senate voted them down.

Conservatives weren't the only ones who introduced amendments to the bill – the Greens did too. Had the Greens amendment been voted for in the Senate, thereby attaching itself to the original bill, marriage equality wouldn't have been legalised. There's no way it would have passed the Liberal-majority House of Representatives. The Greens knew this, but saw their amendment as strategic.

'It was a dance of putting things on the record,' Richard Di Natale told me, 'but also, we knew that amendments were going to be coming from people like [Senator] Paterson and it was really important to demonstrate, "Well hang on, the Greens have actually made some concessions and we'd like this bill to go in the opposite direction. And if you guys are going to threaten and potentially play around with that, then remember this is also on the table – and we lose everything."'

Greens Senator Janet Rice said to me, 'The strategy was knowing that the right were putting up outrageous amendments, and so we wanted to be putting ours up as a counter-balance to the amendments of the right so that if it did need to, it could be seen that Dean's bill was the middle road.'

Normally, these sorts of parliamentary tactics aren't something that different political parties work on together. Legislating marriage equality saw something completely different. When it finally came time to pass the bill, many politicians were working together across party lines, for the greater good of the country. It's worth noting that Greens Leader Richard Di Natale and Senator Janet Rice were co-sponsors on Liberal Senator Dean Smith's bill in the Senate, along with Liberals Linda Reynolds and Jane Hume, Labor's Penny Wong and Louise Pratt as well as cross-benchers Skye Kakoschke-Moore and Derryn Hinch.

Labor Senator Louise Pratt, a lesbian from Western Australia whose years of work were crucial in achieving marriage equality, explained the way she and other senators worked in collaboration, rather than in combat, to pass the bill. She gave me an example of a time that the Greens were using legislative tactics to further their goals just after the Yes vote had come through.

'You know, they put up some motions to try to get the government to be a bit accountable on some stuff,' Senator Pratt told me, 'but essentially Dean counselled [Senator Rice] and said, "Look, that's going to be really unhelpful to [the Liberal party]. Can you please withdraw it? I know you would like that visibility on it, but can you please withdraw it?" And she did. That's a really high level of trust to do those kinds of things. To create that space so we could get it done.' Senator Pratt smiled.

Senator Rice, who is bisexual and whose wife Penny is transgender, agreed: 'Essentially we knew we could talk with each other and trust each other to have the issue itself at the foremost of our focus. We weren't going to betray each other because we knew that was going to betray the issue, and we knew we wanted to achieve this outcome.'

Senator Pratt told me that the reason so many different political parties came together on marriage equality was because in 2017 there were lesbian and gay people across parliament, and that the LGBTIQ public were there to hold them all to account.

When Senator Smith introduced his marriage equality legislation to parliament, he spoke of the thousands of conversations he'd had with LGBTIQ people over the years, which revealed what holds our community together:

> There is a commonality in all these conversations and in all of our lives: it is that of rejection and acceptance, isolation and inclusion – but, acutely, of shame and pride. It is the silent chord that runs through all of our lives, but acutely through the lives of LGBTI Australians. All too often the biggest hurdle for so many is that of self-acceptance and finding that path where we can honestly reconcile who we are with the hopes and dreams we have for our own lives and what we think are the expectations of others.

I believe there is something crucial to be learnt from how lesbian, gay and bisexual politicians, and their sworn allies, handled the passage of marriage equality legislation. They worked to pass this bill with accountability, diligence and with trust in their colleagues because they knew that the most important thing was delivering the reform. They were part of something that was bigger than politics. The marriage equality campaign saw some of the very worst from politicians and from parliament, but also some of the very best. The best bits came from shared experiences and shared goals across party lines, and it came from lesbian, gay and bisexual people being in positions of power.

When marriage equality became law, there were openly LGB politicians sitting in parliament for the Liberal party, the Labor party and the Greens. Whether you like their politics or not, or think political reform is valid or not, we had members of the queer community sitting at the most powerful table in the country, pushing for our rights. This is why representation in politics matters. Parliament accurately representing the demographics of the population isn't some sort of token of fairness – it's absolutely vital if we want policy-makers to write laws with the experiences of people other than rich, old white men in mind.

If we want to create a society of fairness and justice for everyone in Australia, we need to elect more women to parliament. We need to elect people with disabilities. We need to elect poor people, newly arrived immigrants and young people. We need to elect transgender and intersex people, not just LGBs. We need to elect nurses, school teachers, accountants, engineers and artists, and not just career politicians who joined the student branch of their party in university, going straight into a job as a political staffer before getting preselected into a safe seat.

Many First Nations people don't vote or want to engage in colonial power structures, and I understand that. For those who believe a theory of change that works within systems, we need to elect more Aboriginal and Torres Strait Islander people into our parliaments. More important than electing more First Nations people into our settler parliament is negotiating a treaty with them as sovereign peoples whose land we're occupying.

If you are reading this and want to make change by going into politics let me tell you this: you are not going to be tapped on the shoulder. If you want to go into politics you've got to make it happen yourself. Working from within the system isn't for everyone, but we can't just let white men run the place forever. So, run.

•

When the marriage equality bill passed the Senate, Rodney Croome, Peter Furness and I were sitting on the floor of the chamber in special advisor's seats. The bells rang announcing the vote, and I wanted to savour every detail of the moment. The Senate carpet beamed red under the chamber's bright lights. I noticed from my up-close seat that Attorney-General George Brandis, who worked within the Liberal party to achieve marriage equality, wore a tie with small pink triangles on it. The pink triangle was the symbol put on the shirts of gay men by the Nazis at Auschwitz and has been reclaimed as a symbol of survival and pride. The press gallery was filled with journalists, many coming to just witness the moment, and the public gallery heaved with excited onlookers.

I closed my eyes, as if that would slow down time, and waited. I knew the bill would pass, but when you've dreamt of something every single day for so long there's almost a fear of it actually happening. I wanted to just hold on to that moment of hope and anticipation.

Then, with 43 Ayes and twelve Noes, the bill passed the Senate. The chamber erupted into cheers, and – not for the first time in this campaign – I burst into tears, too. All that was left to do was for the bill to go to the House of Representatives, and if it passed there the same way it passed the Senate, the law would change.

That night I joined dozens of marriage equality support-ers at the Canberra bar everyone always ends up at when it's time for a drink. It was packed with a jubilant hubbub of more than 100 activists, politicians, journalists and staffers. Liberal Senator George Brandis leant against the wall chatting to Labor Senator Penny Wong. Ties were loosened, lanyards removed, cigarettes bummed. Some of the unionists got shots. I sat at a table with Magda Szubanski and my friend Nadine, who worked for the Greens, and we talked about what our dreams for the future might look like, now that we might be afforded the right to marry. Already, things felt different.

November ticked over to December and, in parliament, love was truly in the air. On the Monday of the final week of parliament for the year, LGBTIQ people from all over began descending on Parliament House to witness history be made. People travelled from the farthest points of the country, from Cairns in far north Queensland and Esperance in far south West Australia. The Equality Campaign, I suspect in an arrangement with their generous sponsor Qantas, flew about 40 of their staff in from around the country.

Walking through the corridors of parliament, there was only one thing on the agenda and nearly every MP walked with a spring in their step and a smile on their face. They knew they were about to be part of history too.

The marriage equality bill was introduced to the House of Representatives on 4 December, by the straight man who pushed for marriage equality long before most in the chamber with him, the former crocodile farmer from northern Queensland, Warren Entsch.

'In 2004, when the parliament changed the definition of "marriage" to exclude LGBTI Australians, I stood in the Liberal party room and questioned the decision,' he told the MPs in the chamber. 'I didn't understand why we needed to do this. Hadn't LGBTI Australians been through enough? Why did we have to kick them on the way out the door? To me, it didn't make any sense. Denying any Australian equal status and the same level of dignity is in my mind completely un-Australian.'

'For me it was really quite simple,' he continued. 'I don't understand how one section of our community should be treated any differently to any other. Life is tough enough and sometimes very hard, and if you're lucky enough to find someone to join you in the good and the bad, well, in my mind it's fantastic.'

That was first thing on Monday morning. The House of Representatives dealt with almost nothing else that week, as they had to go through all the amendments that the Senate had already rejected, thrown at the marriage legislation once more from Liberal MP Andrew Hastie. And so, we watched politicians debate the law from the galleries for days and days. For many of us it felt like so much of our lives were in these people's hands.

We heard Linda Burney's voice wobble and crack as she honoured her late son, Binni, a gay man who took his own life during the survey. 'I have seen first-hand the confusion, anxiety and pain that many young people experience in dealing with their sexuality,' she said, saying how much marriage equality would have meant to him.

Labor frontbencher Terri Butler, who over the years working on the marriage campaign became a dear friend of mine, thanked me for my work on the campaign, saying, 'Sally has worked incredibly hard over a very long period of time.' I knew that she meant it, because she was there for so much of it, and it meant the world to me.

Independent MP Cathy McGowan used her speech to the House to educate her parliamentary colleagues and put on the parliamentary record a lesson about gender diversity. 'The little bit of learning I'd like to share with my colleagues today is about pronouns,' she announced from her bench. She told of how young people in her electorate had explained to her that while some people feel like a 'he' or a 'she', others simply don't.

'Now I'm much more tactful, I hope,' she smiled to the House, 'and say to people who are gender non-defined, "Tell me your preferred pronoun. How would you like me to refer to you?" as opposed to making the assumption that they are male or female. When they share with me their preferred pronoun, letting me know that they might be transgender, genderqueer or gender fluid, they are giving me an opportunity of trust.'

For me, sitting in the gallery and looking down on the members of parliament making their statements, mostly in support of marriage equality, was extraordinary in and of itself. The majority of people in those seats each opposed the reform at some point. Each time someone spoke on the bill, I remembered when it was that they'd publicly affirmed their support for marriage equality: Christopher Pyne, 2014; Tony Burke, 2015; Andrew Laming, just a few months prior.

Most of the MPs below signified months or years of work from hundreds of people just to get them to change their minds. The majority of MPs elected in the 2013 and 2016 elections were already supportive, but each time a longer-serving MP stood to speak, they told a story of why their mind had changed. It was fascinating. They spoke of meeting with constituents and listening to their communities, who emailed and called and rallied, and many of them also spoke about having a family member, a neighbour or a staff member in their parliamentary office who was LGBTIQ.

The House of Representatives stayed back late, missed breaks and bumped all non-urgent matters from the agenda so they could power through the marriage equality debate. Three days passed, I had an argument at a Christmas 'party' and then the final parliamentary sitting day of the year was upon us. If the law didn't pass on this last day, and it spilled over to the next year, there would be absolute mutiny from the general public. Prime Minister Turnbull and the majority of his government knew this but a group of wreckers within the Liberal and National party were still trying to stop it.

I got to parliament house at 8am on 7 December. The House of Representatives wouldn't sit until about 9.45am, but there were limited seats in the public gallery and there was no way that I would miss watching marriage equality become law. I was the first person in the queue. Over the next 90 minutes, hundreds of people arrived, creating a line that twisted around the curved wall of parliament like teenagers outside a rock concert. I felt like a teenager waiting at a rock concert. My early arrival paid off, and I managed to get a seat in the prime position to watch the vote. Next to me were my friends Kerryn Phelps and her wife, Jackie, with their daughter Gabi; Christine Forster and her wife, Virginia; Magda Szubanski; Ian Thorpe and his partner, Ryan; Tom Snow and his husband, Brooke Horne. I was there with my one true love and longest relationship to date, albeit unrequited: a Liberal free vote.

You're not allowed to take anything into the public gallery with you, at all. No water bottle, no snacks, no mobile phone, no pen and paper. Nothing. Normally, you can come and go from the gallery with the same ease as coming in and out of airport security: it's a small line, you get scanned, bit of a walk, no fuss. You can do it easily in order to pop out for a glass of water or to eat some lunch. But because it was the day that marriage equality was going to become law, hundreds of people remained queued outside the House of Representatives throughout the day. If I or anyone from in the gallery left, someone would take our seat and we'd be sent to the back of the line where there'd be absolutely no chance of getting back in again. When we took our seats at 9.45am, we knew that we'd be sitting there all day.

Four hours later, I checked the time and it was only 11am. How could only 60 minutes have passed? Our stomachs were rumbling and our backs already ached. I was desperate to wee but would sooner piss my pants in parliament than miss the final vote.

Midday came and we were in a bad way. Poor Jackie's back had seized up and she was trying to stretch it out lying across the gallery bench, Kerryn and I leant in towards each other so that security wouldn't notice there was someone vertically missing from their seat. I brought out a packet of Butter-Menthols I'd smuggled in my bra, telling the security guards 'It must be my underwire?' when the metal scanner kept beeping, picking up the packet's metal foil. Slowly, as quietly and secretly as I could under the eagle-eyes of the security team, I opened the pack and plopped out a lozenge. The row beside me passed the Butter-Menthols down in a covert smuggling operation, putting our hands to our mouths in mock-concern to disguise slipping a lolly in.

At some point in the early afternoon, the security team must have realised that we weren't planning on leaving our seats. They finally relented and told us that there was, in fact, a single toilet that we could use, just this once. I like to think that this was part of a risk management strategy to prevent us from soiling the parliamentary gallery.

I don't like to use hyperbole but granting us access to the toilet was probably the second-best thing that happened to the group of gathered activists that day, potentially even that week. Being able to relieve ourselves was an absolute lifesaver, and each time I went to use the bathroom there would be another activist bent over the sink, lapping hot, aerated water from the tap out of desperate dehydration.

The hours ticked by and we slowly but surely began to go mad. Each time an MP got up to speak about their feelings about the legislation we groaned and whispered, 'Just get on with it!' before being shushed by security. As the endless speeches below bore on, we transformed from polite and silent supporters of the Yes campaign to an audience worthy of a Jerry Springer show. The Speaker of the House kept ordering us to be quiet, but we'd lost control.

At one point, Bob Katter made a rare appearance and started complaining that the word 'gay' was used to describe homosexuals when it shouldn't be, because the word 'gay' was meant to mean happy, beautiful, ethereal. The rabble in the gallery, a few hundred of us, all began hooting and applauding.

'These people – all these people up here who are clapping – they go around calling themselves beautiful, happy, light, attractive and ethereal, and they're proud of it!' Katter exclaimed. 'You know, I would be embarrassed if I went around calling myself all these great adjectives, thinking I'm a really wonderful person. They take the most beautiful word in the English language and take it for themselves. I think you've got a damned hide to be perfectly honest with you!'

We did not care that the speaker was shouting at us from the chair to be quiet, we'd lost the plot. We booed and hissed and cheered like the House of Representatives was a panto-mime, and it was.

It seemed that the Labor party had decided to go into damage control, because for the following hour, one by one, Bill Shorten, Anthony Albanese, Tanya Plibersek and many more took turns to come up to the gallery and give us a bit of attention and tell us firmly that we really needed to be quiet. Labor MP Emma Husar heard we all hadn't eaten anything and smuggled up a muesli bar for an older woman who was struggling with low blood sugar. Greens Senator Sarah Hanson-Young popped up from the Senate to say hello and *her* excitement got *us* all excited again!

It got to about 4pm and we knew that the bill would have to pass soon. It had to happen in the next few hours, or it would be bumped to the new year and in our parched, ravenous delirium we just couldn't see that happening. Suddenly one of us asked, 'Hold on, what song are we going to sing? We must sing from the gallery!'

When New Zealand passed marriage equality into law, the public gallery burst into a beautiful Maori song and the video went viral. From across the ditch, marriage equality activists watched that footage and longed to have a moment just like that for our own.

I had thought that thirteen years of campaigning for marriage equality was intense. I had thought that the interpersonal conflicts and factional fights of the LGBTIQ activist community over the course of a highly personal, highly political fight for our rights on the nation's main stage was fraught. I was wrong. Nothing compared to the battle that ensued over the song we should sing from the gallery.

Christine Forster proposed we sing the national anthem, saying it was a proud and patriotic day for Australia and the anthem would mark that appropriately. I pushed back, saying the anthem would completely alienate First Nations LGBTIQ people who hated that song.

'Who cares!' hissed someone in my row. 'It's our day!'

'We absolutely cannot sing the anthem!' I whispered back.

'SHHHH!' a security guard pointed at our row, gesturing at us to sit back in our seats instead of leaning over in a huddle.

We weren't really allowed out of our seats and so activists across the three galleries at the left, right and front of the chamber devised a complex system of secret communication.

Then word came via a whisper chain that the Sydney Gay and Lesbian Choir had prepared 'Love is in the Air' by John Paul Young. Someone from three rows back whispered to me as I walked past, pretending I needed the bathroom again despite being completely dehydrated, 'The choir's dotted themselves across the galleries to lead the song!'

I fed the news back to my row and the message spread from there. Ten minutes later, Felicity Marlowe leant forwards and told me there was no way that Rainbow Families would sing that song.

'We've all travelled here with our kids – they don't know that old song!' she pointed out. And she was right – at 29 years old I barely knew that song. And those poor kiddos, who'd been rolling around in a *Lord of the Flies*-style madness with the rest of us since the morning deserved to at least be able to sing the song with us. Several people had started to write out the lyrics to 'Love is in the Air' on the backs of the MP seat maps provided to us upon entry to the gallery, with what must have been contraband pens, smuggled in like my Butter-Menthols. The message was passed along with our muggle imitations of sign language, waving our arms about in 'no' and 'cancel' gestures while the helpful scribes looked confused.

'What about "I am Australian"?' suggested Magda Szubanski.

The negotiations were on. Backers of the song made more excuses to use the tiny bathroom, walking slowly up the stairs whispering out of the sides of our mouths 'We're doing "I am Australian" – pass it on!'

'"I Still Call Australia Home"?' asked an activist who'd travelled from Adelaide.

'No, the other one!' I shook my head, subtly, the security guard peering over at me, well aware we were all up to mischief but trying to make a judgement call on how disruptive it would be to intervene.

Once again, slowly but surely, we got the numbers. We would sing 'I Am Australian'.

One after another, the conservative amendments levelled at our marriage equality legislation were voted down by the majority of the House. And then at quarter-past six, after hours, months, years . . . it was time for the final vote.

The bells that echo through parliament house rung, alerting everyone inside that there would be a vote. This was the moment, we were about to change the law. A minute passed, bells ringing, and I could barely breathe. On the floor of the House of Representatives, 131 MPs moved to the right-hand side of the speaker's chair including Rowan Ramsey, the MP who I'd argued with two nights prior at the Christmas party.

The official transcript of the House of Representatives that day reads:

> The SPEAKER: As there are fewer than five members on the side for the noes in this division, I declare the question resolved in the affirmative in accordance with standing order 127.

What the transcript didn't record is the small smile that spread across the speaker's face as he nodded to the chamber and said, 'It's done.'

We jumped to our feet, whooping, clapping, sobbing – activists and politicians alike. People in the galleries and people on the House floor had smuggled in rainbow flags and they were pulled from inside jackets and waved into the air. We hugged and held each other, and we burst into song. We were many, but we were one.

My mum told me afterwards that she could hear my voice singing in the crowd when she saw us on the news that night. I didn't have the heart to tell her that I could barely squeeze a note out, because I was crying so much.

Just like that, the lives of so many people were changed. In marriage we were no longer second-class citizens in our own country. Our families, relationships and identities were finally legally equal. We'd done it.

When the bill passed and we sang from the gallery, embracing each other with tear-stained faces, Peter de Waal was at home. Alone.

'It was a very lonely day,' my 80-year-old friend told me, as I smoked his late partner's cigarette. 'I had so many mixed feelings that day. It was so bittersweet. It seemed so simple for them to fulfil that wish, or dream, and we missed out.'

•

The National Library of Australia first finds the phrase 'marriage equality' used in 1997. Ten years later, in 2007, public support for marriage rights for LGBTIQ people ticked over the 50 per cent mark, becoming the majority opinion. Ten years again, in 2017, we not only changed the law, but we did it together, as a nation.

The final years felt excruciatingly long and the time it took was brutally unfair to every LGBTIQ person who wasn't able to marry the person they loved while successive governments insisted on upholding discrimination. And yet, when I look at those dates lined up, I see a breathtaking, history-making social movement. Within two decades we forced the state to recognise our love and formally redefine who gets the privilege of being recognised as a family. Even if you anchor the campaign for marriage equality in the LGBTIQ activism of the 1970s, as I do, that's revolutionary.

'In my lifetime you can measure decriminalisation, anti-discrimination, relationship recognition, marriage, transgender recognition; the progress is extraordinary. Fucking extraordinary,' Wil Stracke told me after the vote.

'I think about what marriage equality would have meant to the gay men who died of AIDS in this country, whose partners weren't allowed a say in their care, or funeral arrangements,' HIV activist Nic Holas reflected. 'Men who were referred to as their dead lover's "friend" during religious funerals. Marriage, and better anti-discrimination laws, would have changed a lot of that.'

'It's worth remembering now that it's all done how often we were told by many politicians, mostly opponents, that this was not a thing that people cared about, this was not something people were talking about on the street in their electorates. We all know this was bullshit, and an excuse for inaction,' journalist Michael Koziol told me. 'And it's been shown up twice: it's shown up by the fact that the politicians themselves were arguing about it so passionately for so long that obviously it was a big deal to them, and then it was shown up again by the fact that you had people breaking out into song in the gallery when it's passed. No one, no one else in parliament could think of a time when they've seen that happen before.'

When I started writing this book, I wanted the title to be: 'Love Wins?' and it would have been pretty different to the one you're almost finished reading.

'Love wins' or 'love will win' was a longstanding catchcry of the marriage equality campaign. It was defiant, and perhaps a little smug. It declared that we would achieve marriage equality because it was good and right, and a bit magic. I liked the slogan a lot. But even with the joy of the win, I was left unable to shake the fact that it had taken the Australian government so long. That they had played politics with so many people's lives.

Love wins? If love was some sort of indestructible force, unable to be twisted out of shape by fear or poisoned by suspicion, there wouldn't be prejudice. If love was the ultimate power, there wouldn't be systematic discrimination, exclusion and violence. If love was enough, a man who spent 50 years of his life loving his partner wouldn't leave this life still being told by the Australian government that he's not worthy of equal rights under the law. Peter and Bon's love for each other wasn't enough for successive Liberal, National and Labor governments, who let countless Australians go to their graves as second-class citizens, denied the right to marry the person they loved with all their heart.

I conceded that love, the noun, did win, in the sense that in achieving marriage equality our campaign was successful. If we consider love conceptually as an entity unto itself that should be free, multi-faceted expansive and unlimited then, absolutely. Love was the winner.

But love as a verb? No, I thought to myself. Love did not achieve marriage equality. We didn't force power to bend and relent because we loved it. We didn't change the minds of the politicians because we showed them love. We didn't remind seven million people to post a letter in a timely manner because we told them we loved them. We didn't force the hand of a government built on a Coalition agreement to not legislate same-sex marriage because we loved our partners very, very hard.

Expertise achieved marriage equality. Persistence achieved marriage equality. Fundraising and community organising achieved marriage equality. Discipline, hard decisions, and complex, highly informed strategy achieved marriage equality. It wasn't pleasant, it wasn't cuddly; it was a gloves-off political struggle for survival. We did not win by loving, we won by fighting.

But then, in the eighteen exhausting months it's taken me to write this book, I've found a new birds-eye view of the campaign, spanning peaks and troughs to far horizons. And I now believe that, along with the execution of highly sophisticated, multi-dimensional campaign strategies, love, as a verb, did win.

To love is to be truthful and vulnerable, and each time someone came out to their family and friends, that was an act of love. To love is to teach without judgement, and every time an LGBTIQ person shared their personal story for the campaign, that was an act of love. To love is to speak up for the people you care about, even if you've never met them. When thousands of 1s called hundreds of thousands of 2s, that was love. To love is to show up. When 50,000 people marched in the streets of Sydney to rally for equality, or just a few dozen back in 2004, that was love. To love is to protect your family at all costs, and when the LGBTIQ community fought tooth and nail to stop a public vote on our lives, this was burning, desperate love. When Peter and Bon fought to stop the plebiscite to protect children of same-sex parents who they'd never even met, knowing that it might cost them their dream to marry, that was the ultimate act of courageous, selfless love.

Even though the process was cruel and had questionable legality, 7.8 million people had my community's back and voted Yes. When I first heard that news, it felt like sickening relief. Now, it feels like love.

I don't want the road to marriage equality paved over with falsehoods. There is too much at stake in our future for us to not know where we've come from and I wrote this book so that activists may learn from our tactics, and from our mistakes. I want people to understand this fight, because there will be many more to come. But more than anything, I hope that as time rolls on, we remember the love that powered us through. Because in the years to come, the memory of the campaign will fade. We won't be able to remember how many rallies we went to, how many times we emailed our MP, the Facebook posts we shared. We'll forget the names of different organisations and politicians. None of that will matter. Not really. It's the change that we made from the work that we've done that will be here forever.

I feel it everywhere. It's there in a father's tears of pride as he walks his daughter down the aisle. It's there in the trembling hand of a young man about to get down on one knee. In the moment a teenager realises she's gay and knows she doesn't need to feel afraid.

It's there on Christmas mornings, at the gates of school pick-ups, and on the documents that preserve traces of our lives for generations to come.

It's there at every wedding you'll go to, in the words read aloud: 'Marriage is the union of two people'. It's there when someone looks into the eyes of the person they love and says, 'Yes, I do.'

Marriage equality was never inevitable. We made it happen because we fought for it. In the face of factional fuckery, vested influences and an enemy who spent millions of dollars trying to stop us, we changed the law, and we did it with love. We made history, and now we're getting married.

That's how powerful we are.

Epilogue

So where are they now?

Lyle Shelton resigned from the ACL to run for the Senate with Cory Bernardi's political group, Australian Conservatives. He secured just 1 per cent of the vote and wasn't elected. It would seem he is currently unemployed.

Nationals MP Andrew Broad, who threatened to blow up the government if it passed marriage equality, was caught using a 'sugar baby' website in Hong Kong to solicit extramarital sex from young women. Text messages emerged, revealing his attempt at dirty talk: 'I pull you close, run my strong hands down your back, softly kiss your neck and whisper, "G'day mate."'

Barnaby Joyce's marriage broke down after his affair with a young staff member was spectacularly exposed in the media. Following national outrage at the hypocrisy of how he treated LGBTIQ people during the postal survey, he was forced to resign as leader of the Nationals and as deputy prime minister. He asked for privacy for his relationship and family.

George Christensen revealed himself to be the subject of police inquiries into his regular travels to the Philippines and allegations that he transferred money to 'seedy' areas in the region.

In an eleventh-hour attempt to save his leadership, again, Malcolm Turnbull ditched the Liberal party's climate change policy to try to stop the far-right faction rolling him. Days later, they disposed of him as leader anyway.

Tony Abbott put on a brave face attending his sister Christine's wedding before trying to take credit for marriage equality himself.

Some guessed it was to try to smooth things over with his furious electorate in the lead up to the 2019 federal election. It didn't work. He was voted out of parliament.

•

The first LGBTIQ couple to marry, just a week after the law passed, was Jill Kindt and Jo Grant. The law wouldn't take effect until weeks later, but the couple was granted an expedited marriage licence because Jo was dying of terminal cancer. The couple wed in their garden on 15 December 2017, and were married for 48 days before Jo passed away.

After marriage equality legislation passed, staff at the Department of Births, Deaths and Marriages worked over weekends to help same-sex couples get their marriage licences in time for the moment the law came into effect. The Department also set up a stall at the Sydney Mardi Gras Fair Day.

My friends Antony and Ron married on 9 January 2018, the first day the law came into effect. I wore pink and cried off my makeup.

Wil Stracke married her partner, Lisa. I wore blue and cried off my makeup.

Karen and Treen, who I met in Tasmania in 2015, got married in the wildlife sanctuary. They sent me photos over Facebook, wondering if I would remember them. Of course I did.

In the first twelve months of equal marriage rights, 2490 LGBTIQ couples tied the knot. The sky didn't fall in.

•

When parliament passed marriage equality legislation, then-Treasurer Scott Morrison took the opportunity to warn that the passage of marriage equality would lead to a new national debate, on religious freedoms. 'Our own nation was founded, built, and undeniably shaped by Christian values, morals and traditions that helped to unite a fledgling country – a nation blessed by and formed on Christian conviction,' he told the chamber. He abstained from the vote. In 2019, he was re-elected as Australia's prime minister, promising to introduce anti-LGBTIQ 'religious protections'.

Peter de Waal's advice to me, and to you, is that as activists, we must remain vigilant:

> If you look at Berlin, before the Second World War, it was an extraordinary place of liberation. And then there comes Mr Hitler and he's able to drag the whole country with him, and change the whole attitude of the country. We then get to the stage where homosexual men are put into concentration camps and were to wear the pink triangle.
>
> It can happen again. Look at what President Trump's done, banning transgender people in the military. Bermuda; they had marriage equality and overnight a new government came and it was reversed. We don't want to go backwards. We must remain vigilant.

A Note on Terminology

LGBTIQ stands for lesbian, gay, bisexual, transgender, intersex and queer. Lesbian, gay and bisexual are identities that describe a person's sexuality. Lesbians are women solely attracted to women; gay men are only attracted to men. Bisexual people are attracted to all genders and are not straight, even when they're in an opposite-sex relationship.

Transgender describes not sexuality, but gender identity and means that the person identifies with a gender different to the one they were assigned at birth after a stranger looked between their legs. Transgender people have the same range of sexualities as any other person, so you can be transgender and heterosexual, or transgender and bisexual, and so on. The opposite of transgender is cisgender, which means that a person identifies with the gender they were assigned at birth.

Intersex describes people born with biological variants of sex characteristics, it's different to being transgender. Sex characteristics in humans exist on a spectrum, with most people fitting in one of two (very broad) categories, but intersex people have variations that exist outside what is conceptually agreed to be 'male' or 'female'. Many intersex people identify as straight and cisgender, many do not.

Queer is an identity in and of itself, fluid and political, and can be used as an umbrella term for other orientations and gender identities that are not heterosexual and cisgender, such as non-binary, genderfluid or pansexual. Queer is a reclaimed slur, and some LGBTIQ people don't like to use it. I identify as queer and

333

a lesbian, and as it's a word I use for myself and my community, I also use it throughout this book.

Over the years, we have chosen to use the phrase 'marriage equality' over 'same-sex marriage'. Firstly, because how we name things matters in a campaign. Secondly, because the discriminatory marriage laws didn't just preclude lesbian and gay Australians from getting married, they also meant that some bisexual people, some transgender people, some queer people and some intersex people also couldn't get married, depending on what sex was recorded on their legal documents and the legal documents of their partner.

I use the terms 'LGBTIQ people' and 'LGBTIQ couples' opting to include all of the people that the law, and the change in the law, could affect.

There is discussion within intersex communities about whether the 'I' belongs grouped in the LGBTIQ acronym when talking about issues faced primarily by people with diverse sexualities and genders (LGBTQ), particularly when there are very different, very urgent issues affecting the intersex community. Some intersex people would prefer not to be lumped in with the LGBTQ community at all, and some feel the community is their home, even if they're also straight and cisgender. I have chosen to include the I in the acronym I use, unless referring to specific law that exempts intersex people or quoting from the United States, for the same reasoning as above.

Labels are very important to some people because they give a name and a community to their marginalised experience. Other people don't like being put into boxes, particularly after they've liberated themselves from the expectations of heterosexuality and assigned gender. Everyone is different, and that's kind of the point.

Acknowledgements

I am so grateful to the team at Hachette who helped bring this book to life, in particular my wonderful Publisher Robert Watkins and kind, careful Editor Sophie Mayfield. Thanks also to Hachette Group Publishing Director Fiona Hazard, Production Manager Isabel Staas, Publicist Jemma Rowe and to Ngaio Parr for designing the cover.

Thank you to the team at GetUp, in particular National Director Paul Oosting and former Impact Director Kelsey Cooke, who hired me and worked with me for much of the marriage equality campaign, particularly when I was a goofy kid who sent politicians packages of glitter.

Since campaigning my way out of a job and leaving GetUp, I am now the Executive Director at Change.org Australia and I would like to thank the global executive and my team here in Australia for their support while I wrote this book in my free time, especially when I brought some writing stress into work with me.

Thank you to Jessica Craig-Piper, Mel Gardiner, Tammy Piper, Alice Rugg and Luka Phillios who collectively transcribed more than 100 hours of interviews that I conducted for this book. The interviews featured as direct quotes and also as background research.

The people I interviewed include Alex Greenwich, Anna Brown, Anne Aly, Ben Raue, Benjamin Law, Bill Shorten, Carrie Xin Hou, Cat Rose, Cindy El Sayed, Dylan Caporn, Fahad Ali, Gala Vanting, Jac Tomlins, Jace Reh, Janet Rice, Jenny Joy, Jo Hirst, jonny seymour, Jordan Raskopoulos, Kylar Loussikian,

Lane Sainty, Louise Pratt, Michael Barnett, Michael Koziol, Miriam, Neha Madhok, Nevo Zisin, Nic Holas, Paul Karp, Peter de Waal, Peter Gassner, Phil Coorey, Richard Di Natale, Rodney Croome, Sage Amethyst, Sam and Caitlin Launt, Samantha Maiden, Simon Hunt, Terri Butler, Tiernan Brady, Wilhelmina Stracke.

There were many more people who told me about their experiences of the campaign who I haven't listed above. To everyone who so generously gave me their time, their story and their insight in interviews, thank you. It's an honour to have been able to listen to and publish your words.

Thank you to Rebecca Unsworth for allowing me to write about her nephew's life and death, and to the Unsworth family.

Thank you to Teela Reid, Nayuka Gorrie, Nick Henderson and Paige Burton who each gave me advice on different sections of this book that I needed a pair of expert eyes on. Lane Sainty's coverage of the marriage equality campaign and postal survey for BuzzFeed news was an invaluable resource for facts and figures that I needed to refer back to and is a meticulous, canny and heart-filled archive of the campaign. For this book and for the LGBTIQ community, thank you for all your work, Lane.

To my friends who have relentlessly encouraged me and made me feel so loved. Thank you so much. You are too many to mention, but I need to name a few.

Amelia Lush and her giant heart believed in me and introduced me to Robert Watkins at Hachette and seems to spend her free time hyping me (and everyone else she loves) up to the people she thought should be part of this process. Dr Viv McGregor helped me with my first edit of chapters 1–5, bounced broader ideas around with me and cheered me on while writing for months. I received very practical advice, generous guidance and relentless encouragement from my book-writing friends Jamila Rizvi, Bridie Jabour, Clementine Ford and Benjamin Law. This book may not have materialised from a dream to a draft without all of you.

Rebecca Wilson read my draft and gave me flags, feedback and the belief in myself that I could and should do this, like she always does. I'm so grateful for you. Terri Butler, thank you for your support, collaboration and friendship over the years and for your work, so often behind the scenes, to make this law a reality. Thank you to Samantha Maiden, who is a living encyclopedia for niche political details of the last 20 years, for being an invaluable soundboard, my emotional rock and for being like family.

Thanks to my best friend Rebecca Shaw who put up with me being stressed, obsessive and exhausted by marriage equality for years and then emotionally supported me while I wrote this book. She also read through a draft of mine to check I didn't embarrass myself too much.

Kate McCartney, thank you for impressing on me you can make anything interesting if you explain it well and you're passionate about it. Thank you for your endless care and support, emotional and practical. I love you so much. Let's never get married.

Thank you to my precious sisters, Bessie and Alice Rugg, for allowing me to write about the death of our dad, and for constantly believing in me as I wrote this book. To my mum, Susie Buckee, who took me to protests as a child and instilled in me that we each have the power to make a difference. I love you all.

To my Twitter followers, who helped me on many occasions to track down information and people to interview, for cheering me on when I was dead-set certain that writing a book was the worst decision of my life and for filling my inboxes with beautiful messages of love and support throughout the campaign. Your support means the world to me.

To the 1s, this book is dedicated to you. Thank you for creating the social movement that I have written about. Thank you for the marriage rights.

And finally, to the LGBTIQ community. In you, I have found my history; uprising, resistance, solidarity and community. I've met so many of you across this land, and you've embraced me as your own. You have held me and taught me what it means to be proud. You are my family. I am yours.